Thanks so much for
all you've done for me.
With Love,
Peggy Lins

A Cruel Legacy

A Novel

Peggy Lins

ISBN: 1499709307
ISBN 13: 9781499709308

To Bobbsey

A Cruel Legacy is a work of fiction. Any resemblance of characters to any person living or dead is coincidental.

Acknowledgements

For believing in me, my husband, Del. Mary Ber, for her editing, guidance and direction. Cathey Langione, for her cover design. Jon Langione for his guidance and expertise. And to Terry Ahern, Harry LaMoine Greene, M.D., and Ava Young for their help and encouragement.

Cast of Characters

Tom Foster	Family patriarch
Molly	His wife
Clint	Their son
Pearl	Their daughter
Nancy Foster	Tom's sister
Ben	Nancy's son
John Foster	Tom's brother
Doctor Davis	Family doctor
Lillian Miller	Molly's sister
Lilly and Faye	Lillian's daughters
Alvin	Lillian's husband
Ira White	Town's leading citizen
Edna	Ira White's wife
Alice Benton	Town gossip
Warren Benton	Alice's husband and town banker
Marvin Benton	Alice's son
Emma Teeter	Alice Benton's friend
The Berkeys	George, Dorothy and Bill. The town's lowest class citizens
Red Donavon	Clint's best friend
Emily Peters	Clint's teacher
Frank Peters	Emily's brother and Ben Foster's best friend
Brian Cunningham	Clint's army buddy
Monique La Blanc	Clint's French lover
Nell Cunningham	Brian's sister and Clint's wife
Jack Foster	Clint and Nell's son
Mona	Their daughter
Kate	Their daughter
Bridey Richardson	Kate's best friend
Lance Edwards	Jack's friend and benefactor
Mary Pauley	Mona's supervisor

Chapter 1

August lays heavy on Missouri, spreading her steaming blanket on man, woman and beast. But in the summer of 1904, folks in Lowell say she took pity on them, and dumped it instead, squarely on the shoulders of young Tom Foster.

Not that he couldn't handle a good-sized load. Broad, muscled, and six foot three; he was the most powerful man in Hamilton County, no doubt about it. "But there's times," he muttered "when a man's strength don't amount to a tinker's damn." As he stepped off his porch into the thick heat of the morning, his huge body sagged, weakened by a force like nothing he'd ever imagined.

If it hadn't been for two year old Pearl, he would have set himself down somewhere and cried his eyes out. But she had to go the out-house and it was up to him to take her.

"Where's Momma? I want Momma," she whimpered.

"Momma's sick. Dad kin take care of ye. No need to cry." His calloused hands dropped her coarse cotton drawers and lifted her to the bench. When she finished, he reached into a rusty bucket next to the door and pulled out a fresh corn cob to clean her with.

Her tiny hand engulfed in his, Tom ushered her to the house. "This ain't no job for yer Dad," he muttered. "Tendin' our girl's your Ma's job. But she's upstairs, suffering awful. I gotta tend her too. Don't reckon I'll be able to do much else without some help."

There was so much to do he swore he didn't know where to begin. In the garden, vines sprawled, pulled to the earth by the weight of ripe, bursting fruit. Along the fence, fat cucumbers lay ready for the pickling barrel, as the big yellow squashes grew by the hour. Next to the gate, limbs of an apple tree bowed to the ground with this year's ready yield.

Clint reached for a sample as he sauntered through the gate. Tall and thin, he wore a faded blue shirt and dungarees long grown out of, the frayed hems reaching halfway between knees and ankles.

Tom eyed his boy with pride and was grateful he'd had been helping, much as an eight year old was capable. "You fetch the eggs?" Tom asked.

"Yessir." Clint scratched a pattern into the dirt with a big toe. "Few of 'ems broke, Dad. Straw's gone outta the nests."

"I ain't worried about a few eggs son. You did the best you could."

God knows there were a lot of other things a man ought to worry over, Tom thought. He looked past the boy to his cattle, lazily feeding on the pasture beyond the barn. There were fences to mend or they'd be out again. And time was running out on getting the hay mown and up in the barn. A good rainstorm could come along anytime and ruin the crop.

"Thank the Lord, I'm done cultivating. At least the corn can wait awhile. I reckon what won't wait is your Ma and you young'uns." Reaching out, he pulled Clint to his side. "Think you could stay with Ma while Pearl and me go for Nancy?"

Clint stiffened and pulled back, his eyes wide. "No! Don't get Auntie. Ma hates her, Dad. It'll just make her worse. She might bring Ben, Dad. Please."

"Son, I gotta have help. My sister's the only one ain't gonna talk about what's going on here. She can bring her boy if she wants, but at his age, I think he'll stay in town. While I'm in there, think I'll go see Doc Davis. See if he's got some medicine to help your Ma."

Pushing back dark hair, Clint looked up at Tom, his blue eyes spilling tears. "Think he can do anything?"

2

"I don't know. But I sure ought to ask." Tom reached into a pocket of his sweat drenched overalls for a stained kerchief and wiped his brow, then lifted Pearl and headed for the kitchen. "We gotta get going a'fore the heat of the day, little girl. It's gonna be a real scorcher."

"Corcher," echoed little Pearl.

Tom looked around the dim room. The only light a bright shaft of sunbeam that peeked between drawn curtains and onto the cluttered table. Last night's dishes had been pushed to one side, leaving room to set breakfast. As the kids ate, he buttered a couple slices of bread and spread them with blackberry jam to take upstairs to Molly. He knew she wanted oatmeal, but he wasn't going to heat the kitchen by firing up the stove. He poured a glass of milk, cool from the cellar, thinking, hot as it was, she'd be appreciative enough to forget the hot cereal

Palms sweating, he climbed the stairs, took a deep breath, opened the bedroom door and looked in. The room was dark, shutters closed tightly against an unopened window. Hot, acrid air stank of sweat and an unemptied chamber pot.

She was on her side, turned from the door, her long dark braid spread on the pillow behind her. She'd taken her heaviest quilt, wrapped herself in it, drew her knees up to her chest and was hugging them in her arms.

Tom gasped. It has to be hot enough to kill her, he guessed. I don't see how a body could stand it. He tiptoed to her bed. "You like something to eat?"

She lifted her head to see what he'd brought her.

And when he saw her eyes, Tom knew she was riled. A lot worse 'n he'd ever seen her. Upset, Molly had the hardest eyes a man could ever see. And that morning, had those eyes been stones, Tom allowed she could have killed him, just by looking.

For a long moment she glared, saying nothing, then, in a flat, cold voice, sneered. "You know damn well I wanted oatmeal." She grabbed her pillow and threw it in his face. "Git your ass out! Now!"

Tom wasn't sorry to leave. Noticing she had water, he backed out. Before he reached the landing, he could hear her stomping. He leaned to listen. First came a dull scrape, the dresser, he reckoned, being dragged across the floor. Next, a big thud, as she shoved it against the door.

At that, he had to grin. Molly's just made my day easier, he thought. Now, I got a good chance of getting to town and back without her knowing. He called for Clint. "Go fetch me that coil of wire from the barn, boy. I'm gonna fix this door so she has to stay there. In case she changes her mind."

Frightened, Clint watched Tom wrap the heavy wire around the bedroom doorknob, run it down the hall to another bedroom door, and wrap it around the handle. "What if she gets out, Dad?" He whined. "What's I supposed to do?"

"She can't. I've seen to it. If she tries, I want you to talk her down, tell her I said she's to stay upstairs 'til I git back."

"She'll be mad, Dad. Whip me good when she catches me."

"No, she won't. I won't allow it."

Clint threw himself on his father, pounding him with feeble fists. "Why'd you lock her up, Dad? She ain't done nothing. Ain't no reason for this…"

Grasping the boy's trembling shoulders, Tom stooped to look in his face. His voice was firm. "Because of the river, Clint. She says she wants to go to the river. We ain't gonna let that happen. Are we?

Clint shook his head. "No, Dad. I reckon we ain't."

With a chill, he remembered the story his Ma had told about Great Uncle Ben. "Just got sick of livin'," she said. "So, he went to the deepest, fastest part of the river and jumped in. He couldn't swim. They found the old fool ten days later, three or four miles downstream. Them that hauled him out say he was all swelled up and had flies eatin' on him…"

4

The road to town was rutted and bumpy, bouncing the buggy relentlessly, but not hard enough to keep Tom fully awake. He stared through the heat waves, watching them shimmer off the lane ahead, wondering what makes them rise the way they do. Watery little squiggles, climbing, maybe to Heaven. Rather, coming out of Hell, he figured, intending on making him miserable.

He yawned, rubbed his eyes, and looked down on Pearl with a start, suddenly remembering he'd taken her along.

Until then she hadn't spoken. Glad to have him notice her, she asked "Know what? Nelly's got soap on her. Why?"

Tom grinned. "That's sweat, honey. Sweat brings out froth on a horse. Reckon I best slow her down. I'd hate to see her founder."

"What's founder?"

"Goin' down, I guess. The heat wearing her out."

"Oh." Satisfied, Pearl resumed her watch, her curious blue eyes missing nothing.

Renewed by the short conversation, Tom took a few deep breaths and straightened his shoulders, trying to loosen the tightness. "Reckon I ain't never felt such a push to git somewhere and back at the same time," he said. "Be glad to git to Nancy's, little girl. She's got a settlin' way and I need settlin' bad."

He wouldn't admit it, even to himself, but Tom relied on his older sister a great deal. It's like she's stronger'n me, he figured. Such a little bit of a gal, too. But when it comes to sickness, funerals and hard times, it's Nancy I want. She knows how to keep me standing…just something she is.

Her strength, he reckoned, came from overcoming a big mistake. In a small town like Lowell, it hadn't been easy raising a bastard boy. But Nancy'd been smart enough to take that bad situation and turn it good. When their Dad asked who the father was, fifteen year old Nancy said. "It was Jesse James. There was nothing I could do. I tried fightin' him off, but he was too strong."

There wasn't anything their dad could do either. Only a fool would take on a gunslinger like Jesse.

Tom chuckled, remembering. After the fiasco at a bank in Minnesota, Jesse hid out in Harperville and used to ride into Lowell on occasion, to eat at Widow White's Café where Nancy worked, waiting tables. No doubt Jesse had chances to take her. Nancy was feisty, was known to flirt and most folks believed her story.

But their brother, John, happened to learn the truth. And it didn't have a thing to do with Jesse James.

"She went hook, line and sinker for Iry White," John told him. "I caught 'em in the restaurant kitchen. All tangled up, they was, and kissing like they were starving for each another. I didn't like her messing with a married man, but what I could do? Other 'n keep still so Dad didn't find out."

Tom agreed. Their Dad would have taken a gun to Ira and a whip to Nancy. So only he, John, and a few others were aware of the truth.

The Widow White knew. She'd been suspicious of her only son for some time, and when Nancy's belly started to swell, forced a confession. "Don't you ever put a hand on that girl until you do right by her," she warned. "You do, and you get nothing when I go. My grandchild isn't going hungry. You can count on it."

True to her word, the widow took care of Ben and his mother for the rest of her life. Claiming she needed help with the house, she hired Nancy as a housekeeper, gave each of them a room upstairs and helped raise the boy. "With Ira's wife, Edna, being barren, Ben's the only grandchild I'll have," she told Nancy. "I want him growing up decent."

Before the old woman died, she bequeathed the house to Nancy, and set up an account with the bank so the two could live comfortably. Only banker, Bill Fenton, knew the source of Nancy's income, and he wasn't telling. Not with Ira being his biggest depositor.

"In fact," he told his wife, laughing, "with him being so successful, I'll do about anything to convince folks that the bank-robbing Jesse James is a good man. He accepts his responsibilities better than most."

Nancy was sitting on her front porch hulling peas when Tom drove up. She rose quickly to greet him. "Why Tom, what a nice surprise," she began.

She faltered. "My land, Tom, you do look poorly. What on earth is wrong?"

With a deep sigh, Tom dropped to the porch sobbing. "The spell's back on Molly. This time it's bad. I gotta have help, Nancy. We can't hold on much longer."

"I'll come." Nancy lifted Pearl onto her hip, entered the house, turned and looked back at Tom. "Just let me get some things together."

Much of his burden lessened, Tom figured it time to call on the doctor. Luckily, he was in, and his waiting room empty.

Dr. Steve Davis walked out of his office and extended his hand. "You sick, Tom?" he asked. "You look awful. What can I do for you?"

"It's Molly." Tom felt sweat burst out of his skin, pour down his back and sop his shirt. He dropped into a chair. "She's like she was after Pearl was born, only worse. Ain't slept, ain't et for five days. Restless, she is, pacing the floor and talking about dying. She says she's gonna drown herself."

"How about you, Tom? This can't be easy on you."

"I can't sleep either. I been holdin' her down, keepin' her steady. She hates me for it. Scratched me raw a few times, but I don't know what else to do. Clint and Pearl need her, but she pays 'em no mind. Her own babies! How can she do that?"

He looked about the room and coughed. "You don't reckon she's possessed? That the devil took aholt? Or that the curse took over?"

"Absolutely not," Doc retorted. "Far as I know, there's no such thing as demon possession. I've never seen it, and I don't know any doctor who has. I think Molly has something else wrong. I suspected it after she had the little girl. Just hoped it was due to the birthing and not something that would come on her again."

The doctor paused, watching Tom closely. "It's a sickness of her mind. Melancholy, some call it. Folks with it get hopeless. Seems they don't need a reason either. Things can be going well. They might have a restless period before, like Molly did. Most come out of it if they don't do something drastic."

"Like kill themselves?"

"That happens. Get so down they don't want to live. Tell me about the restlessness, Tom. How long did she have that?"

"A while. She went through June working like a horse. Seemed she couldn't plant enough garden or do enough housework, stayin' up late and getting up early. 'Bout the middle of July, she got this awful temper. She'd rage at me for everything or nothing." Tom's looked down at the worn linoleum, fighting back tears. "Mostly, she'd sit in a chair. Just looking. Or she'd cry for hours. 'Bout a week ago, she took to the worse. That's when she started tryin' to get to the river."

Exhaustion seeped into Tom's voice. "I'm tired, Doc. What if I go to sleep? I swear to God, I don't know what I'm to do." He began to sob, hiding his face in his huge rough hands.

Doc placed a hand on Tom's shoulder. "I'll give her some tonic, Tom. If you can get her to take it, it might help her sleep, rest her thinking a few hours. That can clear the mind. Opium is a powerful drug. Sometimes it'll turn on one, making them sadder than they were to begin with. If that happens, you best not give her anymore."

Doc reached to an upper shelf, brought down a large bottle of red syrup and poured some into a smaller one. "If she comes out of it, there's a chance something might keep it from recurring. Joining church has helped some. I reckon when folks believe the world's a bad place, it helps to find faith in something good."

Tom bolted. "Molly won't have no part of that!"

"It's worth trying, Tom. If she's looking for answers, she may change her mind. In the meantime, don't argue with her. She's arguments enough with herself. If she's to get over this, she's got to know you think she's worth saving. It gives her something to ponder when she's fixing on dying."

8

Tom extended his hand to Doc. "Yessir. I thank ye. Reckon I best get back. I been gone too long."

Doc followed Tom as he walked out and called after him. "Tom. I want you to tell Nancy to put the first dose of that medicine into you."

Nancy was waiting for him, her new paisley grip and a basket of food already in place at the back of the buggy. She was singing to Pearl, that silly song about Mary and her lamb. Pearl looked happier than she had in a long time, swaying and smiling and running stubby fingers through her aunt's loose blonde curls.

Tom felt relieved, just watching them, thinking how good it would be for the children to have her around. And wondered if Clint might come to love her the way Pearl did. He never could figure out that boy's disliking Nancy. All the time when she's so good to 'em.

Nancy reached for a wide brimmed hat and looked up at Tom. "Reckon we ought to get going. You got chores." Hoisting the child to the seat of the buggy, she climbed alongside. "You want to talk about what Doc said?

"Just as soon not. I'm tired thinkin' on it."

"I allow that's the truth." Nancy settled Pearl onto her lap and began to hum a lullaby. "I think this baby's tired."

Pearl soon slept in Nancy's arms, with only the clop clop of Nellie's hooves breaking the silence, Tom, frantic, worried over what waited at home, his concern for Molly pushing him on. Fear, just as powerful, was holding him back.

Nancy reached for his arm and gave it a gentle squeeze. "Why I declare, Tom. You're coiled up like a snake ready to strike. If you don't unwind, you're going start twitchin'." Her voice softened. "Tom, If you're tired thinking 'bout it, maybe you ought to talk about something else."

He managed a weak smile. "You're right. I can't do anything now. Best save myself for later. What's Ben been up to?"

"He's working for Iry when he ain't sick half to death from drinking all night at the saloon. He's a wild one, that boy." Unable to stifle a mischievous smile, she looked away. "Like his Pa, I reckon."

Just as mischievously, Tom asked, "You heard from him? Jesse, I mean?"

"Folks say he's dead. A lot say he was kilt over at Saint Joe years ago."

"And folks say he ain't. I asked if you heard from him."

"Nope. Not since it happened. I don't need Jesse or any man to take care of me, 'cept for what I'm rightly owed. Can't help wondering if the same might be true for Ben. With a Pa around, he might be feared to do some of the things he does."

Tom smiled, remembering their Dad, and how strict he'd been. "Didn't do the three of us a whole lot of good, the way we raised Cain. Do you think Ben will be okay with you gone?"

"If he ain't, just as well I don't know. Ain't a thing I can do with a young man that acts like a kid. Right now I figure I'm better off doing something for your boy."

She pointed ahead. "Lookie there, Tom, he's waiting on the porch. He must be mighty glad to see us coming."

༆

Tears of relief flooded Clint's eyes as he spotted the buggy rise over the hill and head toward the lane. Ben isn't with them, he sighed. Thank the Lord. Aunt Nancy was bad enough.

He hadn't left the spot he'd taken on the top stair since Tom drove off. It was shady there, and for a time he amused himself watching a parade of bees buzz back and forth from the orange flowers of the trumpet vine and off to a hive somewhere near the barn.

He was hungry. But didn't reckon he was brave enough to go into the kitchen. The house frightened him. He turned sideways so he could watch the door, just in case anything in there might come at him from behind. It was like he was expecting the bogeyman, even though he didn't believe in him anymore.

'Cept when it was too quiet. Then he wasn't sure.

Silence. No noise a'tall. Reminded him of Ma, deep in her spell. When she's riled and hollering, I know what she's mad at, he thought. When she won't talk, I can't figure out nothin'. Never know for sure if I didn't cause something. He paused to swat a fly resting on the back of his arm. Sometimes, I swear she's in charge of the bogeyman. And he's just waiting for her to tell him to reach out and grab me.

But that day, Clint was able to keep the bogeyman inside. He'd learned how just last week from his friend, Red Donavon, who'd fig-ured it out one night when his Pa was drunk.

"I been all the way to Chicago, Saint Louie and to New Orleans on a steamboat. And never left home. Even if he's whippin' me, or hittin' Ma, I pay him no mind. I just watch pictures."

All afternoon, Clint waited and watched pictures. *Bright moving pictures, with sunshine and happiness running alongside. He and Red at the river, fishing. The afternoon sun glistening on the water, a soft breeze lifting the sweet smell of clover.*

As he caught fish after fish to bring to him mother.

Ma loves catfish. So I'm catching lots. What next? *We're sittin' at supper. Ma bragging on me. Can't stop talking about how happy she is.*

Suddenly he remembered her locked upstairs. Knowing that the only time she'd brag on him was in his daydream. He sighed deeply, wishing she'd be like his teacher, Miz Peters. She praised him almost every day.

Emily Peters was Chariton Township's lone school teacher and had taught Clint and Red through third grade, but allowed them to finish their eighth grade reading books before spring.

Seeming to sense the beauty and meaning both were seeking, Emily gave them *A Collection of American Poetry* for summer reading, and at Clint's request, the fourth grade arithmetic book.

"Reckon you kin give us the answer book too?" Clint had asked. "That way we can make sure we got 'em right."

With Ma hardly noticing what he was up to, Clint had many chances to steal away and play school with Red. They'd memorized Poe's "*The*

Raven" and only yesterday were working on Clint's favorite, *"Woodman, Spare That Tree,"* by George Perkins Morris.

"Miss Peters will be singing our praises come September," Red told him. "Just hope she don't hear about the tobacco we stole from Pa."

Clint snickered. "That and tippin' over George Berky"s outhouse."

Clint was afraid he wasn't going to be seeing Red anymore this summer. With Aunt Nancy here, he'd have to stay close. His greatest hope was that Dad wouldn't need him in the fields so he could start school on time.

With a sigh, he rose to go to the buggy to greet his dad, who handed him the reins and dashed to the house.

"Take care of the mare, Clint," he said. "I gotta go check on your ma."

⌒♡

From her room upstairs, Molly listened to Tom struggle with the wire. Damn fool, she thought. Thinks he can lock me up. Like my skin ain't prison enough. Partly my own fault, she admitted. There ain't no way I'm gonna tell him, though. Every time I try, it comes out something else.

This morning before she sent him off, she'd planned to tell him about her new idea. That she'd figured out what was wrong and what she was going to do to make herself well.

It's a fever, she'd concluded. Pain I got in the middle of my skull's some kind of fever. It being so hot, today's a good time to sweat it out.

With the warm orange of dawn waking the backyard robins, Molly rose and closed the shutters. Thinking if she could break the fever, she might be able to sleep, and stop those awful dreams. She didn't want anything keeping her awake when sleep finally came.

For hours she laid, soaked in sweat, stubbornly determined to purge her body of its merciless poison. A wide band tightened around her temples as racing thoughts attacked. Accusing, then excusing. Hot shame washed her face...a moment's bright glimmer of hope... soon cruelly extinguished.

She'd felt so sure of herself. Up till Tom came and in and ruined the treatment. As he'd looked down on her, strong feelings, rising from deep in her chest had flushed her face. . The hot pain of shame turned quickly to anger.

Son of a bitch felt sorry for me, she recalled bitterly. With that honey drippin' voice of his, full of how good he was to fix my breakfast. He had the same look in his eyes when his dog lay dying. The one he had for fifteen years.

Tossing her braid over a bony shoulder, she laughed dryly. Thinks he's God Almighty, that's what. Bestowing favors on poor Molly. All the while, me never forgetting it was sweet loving pity put that bullet between old Ted's eyes. Now she could hear him, climbing the stairs. She held her breath, wondering what he'd say.

Tom pushed the door, easily moving the heavy dresser into the room. She was sitting in the middle of the bed, knees bent to her chest, hands resting on her ankles. He gasped, shocked by her whiteness.

She looked away and down, as he walked to the bed to sit beside her.

Tom also turned away. And then, began speaking. "I went to see…I talked to…to the doctor. He…he sent you some medicine… thinks it might help."

She collapsed into him, her thin body convulsed by sobs, and for a moment, she rested against him.

Suddenly, she pulled back, leaning to see his face. "How's Clinton?"

"He's good, honey. He's taking care of Nelly."

"I know. I know. I heard it all. Laid here all day listening. Oh Lordy, Tom, how could I do that to him; make him wait hours in the hot sun, all by his self and scared to death. On account of me!" She drew a quick shuddering breath and wept softly.

"Shhhh, Shhhh. The boy's a strong one. Doing what I told him to. Wasn't your fault."

"But it's me caused it. Me! How long I gonna keep doing this to him, Tom? I can't be a mother no more." She rocked back and forth.

"I'm sorry. I'm sorry. I'm so sorry. Poor little Clinton. What's gonna come of my boy?"

Clint tiptoed into the kitchen below, hoping Auntie wouldn't notice him and start asking questions. He'd put the mare up, pulled off her harness, hung it neatly on the stable wall and scooped oats into her feeding trough, all the time thinking he'd make his Dad proud by doing a good job.

Was a good excuse to keep out of the house, too. At first, he figured he might not go in at all. Maybe he'd sleep in the barn and turn this into an adventure.

But he was hungry. Mighty hungry. And Auntie said something about blackberry pie. Clint hadn't had pie for so long the thought made his stomach rumble. He'd eat, he figured, and come back to the barn after.

Nancy greeted him warmly. "There's my boy!" Pearl and I are fixing a picnic. It's too hot to eat in. Want to come with us?" She picked up a platter of sandwiches. "I want you to run this upstairs to your folks. Allow they might want something, too."

Clint stole up stairs, careful to step over that creaky spot on the second step, slipped into the room, and stood quietly waiting for a good chance to offer the food.

With a start, Molly looked up to see him watching her and listening, tears etching flesh colored rivulets into the dirt of his face. She caught her breath. "How long you been here?" She asked.

Pushing his back tight into the wall, Clint stretched his arms and lifted the plate.

Lordy, she thought. Just like a beggar boy, holding his cup. She closed her eyes.

"You hungry, Ma?"

Molly nodded, nudging Tom to take the plate. "You can go now," she whispered.

Almost relieved to have to go back to Auntie, Clint ran from the room.

As he left, Tom rose, ready to fill the hole left in the wake of their fleeing son. "I think you should take your medicine, he said. "Lest you want something to eat first."

She shook her head.

Tom reached for the bottle and poured the thick syrup into a spoon. "A double dose first night. Doc says he wants you to sleep."

He watched as she lay, eyes closed, the drug filling her with a gentle peace. "You're easing," he whispered.

Molly inhaled. A deep sobbing breath, then settled into a pattern of slow, even breathing, her restless eyes finally still beneath their flickering lids. A soft smile lifted the corners of her mouth.

"Well, I declare," Tom said. "Sleep at last." He rose, kissed her forehead, and left, with a sigh of relief that this night wasn't going to be like the last.

⌒◯

Soon after barnyard chores, Tom stripped and climbed into the watering tank for a cool bath. Inside, Nancy had readied his sleeping quarters, spreading a feather mattress on the front room floor, right next to the green velvet sofa they'd bought with their wedding money.

Clint was already fast asleep on a folded quilt next to Tom's make-shift bed, and Nancy would sleep upstairs, keeping one ear out for Molly, the other for Pearl so Tom could get some rest. She stood at the screen door, medicine bottle in one hand, spoon in the other.

In the beginning darkness, the setting sun cast a soft aura over the yard, painting the faded outbuildings a bright shade of pink. She watched tenderly as Tom trudged up the path, grateful, for his sake, this day was ending.

She opened the door, laughing. "Tom Foster, you lucky dog, you gonna get some of this feel good medicine. Sure hope you don't start acting like you did when you used to drink whiskey."

Tom managed a weak grin. "No, ma'am. Ain't enough tonic in all Missouri could get me wild tonight."

⌒◯

He leaned heavily into the pillow. Like an angel of mercy, a soft breeze lifted the curtains, its welcome breath cooling him. *Feels like the room's moving,* he thought. A wave of nausea washed over him. *Hope I don't throw up.* He closed his eyes as his mind began to drift...*up...high over a grass covered hill...Molly's here... Her dark hair hangs loose, falling to her waist. She's got flowers in one hand, the other in mine. We're running down the slope.*

Suddenly they stumble. Tom startled, but couldn't stop the dream. *Then arching their backs, they reach forward to grab their ankles, and roll into a bowl of bright, twinkling stars.*

Chapter 2

The next day

The stifling heat had gone with the night. And when the sun rose over Lowell at 5:15 next morning, Alice Benton was in her kitchen, heating water. Had to get the wash done and hung on the line by the time Warren left for work. Then she'd have until noon to do what she wanted.

The Bentons lived next door to Nancy Foster, in the small white cottage with the red roses out front. Alice, a newcomer to Lowell, moved there with husband, Warren, when he signed on at the bank. Lively and social, she'd joined the Methodist church, not because she was religious, but so she could get acquainted.

And when she saw Nancy leave with Tom Foster after he'd broke down crying on the front porch yesterday, she had to find out what was going on. Clothes flapping on the line and breakfast dishes stacked in the cupboard, she sent her son, Marvin, to Emma Teeter's, to invite her to tea.

Emma was Church of Holiness, the same as Molly's sister, Lillian, and she wasn't shy about sharing information on folks from the congregation. As soon as she walked in, Alice was asking questions.

"Wonder if you heard anything about what's going on out at the Fosters? It's just like Nancy to go off like that and not say a word."

Alice paused, noticing she'd taken Emma by surprise and began to choose her words carefully. She'd suspected the problem was Tom's wife, but didn't want to say so until she knew what Emma thought. One was always safe criticizing Nancy.

"You know something bad is up," she said. "Tom seemed mighty upset."

Alice ushered Emma into her bright little kitchen and offered her a chair at a small table, topped in red checked oilcloth that matched the curtains.

"Probably it's Molly," said Emma. "It seems she has more than her share of sickness."

Alice interrupted. "I heard that. But Nancy never talks about it. I don't mind telling you I'm worried about what Ben might do with her gone. I have to make sure I keep the kids' eyes and ears covered."

Emma laughed. "Ain't that the truth! He'll turn that place into a whore house and saloon before she gets back."

"Oh hush, now. My imagination's bad enough without you making it worse."

"For sure. You hear anything?"

"Tom said something about a spell. I wonder what he meant."

"His wife, you know...Molly...she had a bad one when Pearl was born."

Alice set a steaming teapot on the table between them. "I heard it was a bad case of melancholy after birthing, much more than normal. But Molly doesn't do things like normal folks. Does she?"

"No, she don't. I heard tell she wouldn't have a thing to do with that baby. She wouldn't even hold her."

"And I heard why. At least what Lillian told folks was why." Alice leaned forward. "Because she was a girl! Molly wanted a boy. I hear she told her sister she thought girl babies would be better off drowned."

"She told Lillian that? Why?"

"Because Molly thinks the world ain't fair to women. That life's too miserable for us and we're better off dead."

"She's had a rough life," Emma said, thoughtfully. "Reckon if she was a man she might 'a come out of it different. If I was her, maybe I'd think the same thing."

Arching her eyebrows, Alice looked closely at her friend. Emma wasn't known for giving anyone's actions the benefit of the doubt. "That's a strange thing to say. You know something I don't?"

"I graduated eighth grade with her. She was a smart one. Come from trash, though. Her folks was Jim and Flo Carroll. They lived northwest of town in that old gray shack next to the Berkey place. Jim was a junk man. He did odd jobs, too, when he was sober."

Emma looked down, softening her voice. "Don't reckon Molly ever had a decent meal or a new dress till she started working. She used to do cleaning and warshing over at the hotel before she married."

"What about Lillian?"

"Lillian's three years younger. Sure wouldn't know they were sisters, they was so different."

Alice rose to fill the teacups, cutting thick wedges of cake to serve on her best china. "They are to this day," she answered. "What were they like then?"

Emma cleared her throat. "For starters, Molly was always arguing. She's stubborn as a mule. Lillian? She did anything to get along. If she had a problem, though, you could bet on Molly's being there to set it right."

"Did that happen often?"

"No, not for Lillian. It was just that kids made fun of them. They wore ragged clothes and hardly ever took a bath. Some days they didn't even have any lunch."

Alice gasped. "I can't imagine Lillian Miller dirty."

"Well she was. But being ragged and dirty wasn't the worst thing."

Alice stood, motioning Emma to follow. "Betcha you're warm," she said. "Let's go in the front room where it's cooler."

Emma settled herself into Alice's plump sofa. "Their dad was about the meanest man ever born, so they tell," she began. "Heard he'd hit them just for walking by."

"That why the kids picked on them?"

"Kids didn't bother Lillian. Just Molly. 'Specially the boys. If she came to school with a black eye, they'd tease her. Say she deserved it 'cause she couldn't keep her big mouth shut. Then, she'd swear and fly into them at times, kicking and hitting. But you know how boys are. It only made things worse. I used to lie awake at night wondering what I'd do if they treated me like that. It wasn't fair. She didn't pick her folks. "And I never did anything to help her. Not once. As a Christian, I reckon I can't forgive myself."

Alice reached to pat Emma's knee. "But you go out of your way to be nice to her now. Don't fret, Emma, you were only a kid."

"I know. I know. I ease myself with that now I'm grown. Maybe she'd been a big strapping lad like Tom things would a' been different."

"I hear Tom's good to her."

"He is. I don't know him much. He left school early to help his dad on the farm." Emma looked up, smiling. "Guess he was a wild one before they married."

Alice laughed. "They say Molly was big with Clint, too."

"That's the truth. Lillian told me Molly didn't want to marry him. She figured he'd took advantage of her and she hated him for it. Molly said she'd never marry. She didn't want to end up like her mother."

"How'd she end up?"

"Lucky for her, she died young. Molly couldn't figure out why she stayed. She used to get madder'n a hornet 'cause Flo wouldn't fight back. My Ma said that when Jim beat up on Flo, Molly'd pick up something and start hitting him. She always lost. Guess he'd stop to whip Molly and go finish up on Flo."

Emma sighed. "But that's Molly; she'll go into a fight knowing she'll lose. The only thing that matters to her is being right."

"You think she's fighting something now?"

"Ain't got any idea. I allow Lillian knows, but she don't do much talking. Reckon it makes her feel bad. Lillian has her own life to live, and she's doing good with it."

"I heard a story once," Alice began. "So strange I hate bringing it up. About Molly... that a gypsy put a curse on her. Any truth to that?"

"Oh yes. The story comes from Lillian so it must be true. She came forward at prayer meeting a few years ago to ask the preacher to pray for her sister. Said a gypsy woman with a couple 'a kids came to the door, begging for food. Molly picked up the broom and run them off."

"That's why Molly was cursed?"

"Yes. And a powerful curse, too. That woman stood in the road and pointed at Molly with both hands, asking Satan to bring the power of Hell down on Molly, on her children, and her children's children till the end of time."

Alice was skeptical. Was it possible to harm someone just by cursing? "Do you really think that woman could have caused her melancholy?"

Emma smoothed a wayward wisp of hair from her eyes and thought about Alice's question. She didn't know how to answer. She'd heard gypsy curses couldn't be cured, even by Jesus. With the Lord in her heart, she believed herself safe. But thinking about something strong enough to baffle the Lord made her uneasy.

She paused to think and answered solemnly. "Lillian says it's so. It happened when Molly was carrying Pearl. Lillian figures that's why Molly turns from the girl. She wouldn't even take her to the breast. It left Nancy and the Clint to feed her a bottle. After Nancy went home, that little boy had to look after the baby when Tom was out in the field. The poor man had no choice. He had to keep food on the table."

"Lordy. Those poor kids. Could a preacher cast that out of her, you think?" Alice hesitated. "If something's really there, of course."

Emma fidgeted. "I don't know. It ain't the same as being possessed. Our preacher cast a demon out of a child once. But Molly don't go to church, so he ain't had a chance." Rising, she straightened her skirt and looked through the window. "It's close to noon. This is crazy talk, you know. Sort of gives me the heebies-jeebies. Reckon it's time I go home and fix dinner."

Alice stood and ushered her to the door. "Well, it might be something simple. Maybe she got hurt. You never know."

Emma laughed. "You sure don't." She was watching Ben as he entered his house, flashing a wide smile and a wave before disappearing inside. "And you don't know about that one either. Reckon you'll learn a lot this week."

⌒◯

Ben separated the parlor curtains, peeked out, and watched the two women say their good-byes. Grinning devilishly, he savored his cleverness. "Damn old bitches," he said. "Keepin' the gossip flowin' through town fast as the river in a spring flood. Reckon I outta round up the boys and see if we can't cook up somethin' for 'em to clap their jaws over. Long as Aunt Molly keeps actin' like a lunatic, it oughta be fun."

~○

Out at the farm, his aunt was stirring, scarcely believing her senses. Was that coffee she smelled? Rolling onto her back, she inhaled deeply, pulling the rich aroma into her nostrils, accepting its gentle nudge to consciousness. She stretched her arms over her head and pulled up, dropping her legs over the side of the bed.

"Lordy, she gasped. Feel like my head's full of cotton." Pushing her hands into the mattress, she rose to her feet and fell to the floor.

She came to, minutes later, with Nancy on her knees beside her, lifting her head and holding a bottle of ammonia.

"You okay, Molly? You sure gave me a scare."

"Oh. You're here. Forgot about that." Molly tried to pull away. "Of course I'm okay. Jest dizzy." She shoved Nancy's arm. "Get that stuff outta here. Smells like a stale piss pot."

Nancy drew back to put the cap on the bottle. "You hurt anywhere?"

"Hell no," Molly snapped, "I said I'm okay, didn't I?" Abruptly, she sat up, pulled herself to a squat and tried to stand, only to faint again and fall back, this time, into Nancy's arms.

She shook her head. "What the hell's wrong? I can't even stand on my own two feet."

"I reckon you fainted. You're mighty weak. Tom said you haven't eaten."

"What does he know? Where is he anyways?"

"He's out mowing hay. He'll be back at dinner time." Nancy slipped her arms beneath Molly and lifted her up. "C'mon, let me get you back onto that bed."

Molly gritted her teeth. Damn Tom, she thought, leaving me here with this goddam whore.

But she knew she needed Nancy to get her off that floor. "Okay," she sighed "Let's git there."

With Molly safely back in bed, Nancy left to fix breakfast and almost fell over Clint, hiding at the crook of the stairs.

His voice was timid." She okay?"

Nancy patted the boy's head. "I think so. If she gets some food in her she'll perk right up."

Clint followed her down and went to finish stringing the beans they were fixing to can. Beneath the window, Pearl knelt by a basket, cooing to a small kitten Tom had brought in from the barn. He'd lined the basket with a scrap from an old blanket, and showed Pearl how to feed her, dipping a cloth into a saucer of milk and holding to the little cat's mouth.

Nancy smiled, remembering. Odd, how a big man like Tom come to be so good with critters and young'uns. From time he was a kid, bringing home orphaned rabbits, a stray dog, or a 'coon hurt in a trap. He could hardly swat a fly, he was such a softy. It sure was different with folks who got in his way. When Tom met a bully, he'd fight. And win. Nancy knew a lot of people talked about how Molly stood up to Tom more'n anybody dared. And some laughed behind his back, calling him henpecked.

She poured milk and sugar over a bowl of oatmeal and set it beside the coffee cup on the tray, knowing Tom wasn't being pushed around. His life with Molly was a lot different from how it looked. And no one but Nancy had figured out that if Tom didn't have someone to take care of, his size had a way of forcing his will wherever it had a mind to go. As a kid, it got him in trouble. He had to learn early on to use his heart, instead of his strength to get his way.

Nancy lifted the tray to take it upstairs; figuring she was the only person in Lowell who knew how much Tom needed Molly. Since he keeps his thoughts to himself, she thought, they ain't likely to find out anytime soon.

Molly waited upstairs, talking to herself through clenched teeth. "I'm hungry. Wish she'd hurry. Damn. Have to depend on her for everything." She exhaled through her nostrils, with a snort. "It won't last long if I can help it. If I can just get my strength back." She looked up as Nancy came in, carrying the tray.

Without a word, she wolfed down the oatmeal, and sipped coffee, glaring at Nancy as she tidied the room. She couldn't help thinking how the Fosters always stood by each other, running to one another at the first whimper.

The damn bitch is probably looking down on me, she thought. Running around my house after her baby-ass brother, so's she can butt her nose into my business.

"Damn Tom wouldn't make me nothin' to eat," she said, "all the time I been sick. He tell you he locks me up here? Selfish, mean bastard, that's what he is. A rotten son-of-a-bitch."

Nancy moved quickly about the room, without looking up. "Gonna open this window," she said. "Let in some of that fresh air." As she picked up the dishes, she smiled warmly at Molly's sullen face. "Can I get you anything else, honey? Or maybe you might like to rest a while."

Molly shooed her off. "Just go on. Git. I can take care of myself."

This time, she wasn't so lucky. Falling forward as she tried to stand, she scraped her face against the rough plaster wall, splattering bright drops of blood onto the faded flowers of her nightgown.

When Nancy and Clinton got to her, Molly was begging for help. "Please, Nancy," she whispered. "I-I-I can't get up."

Nancy beckoned Clint. "Run. Get your Dad. Tell him we'll eat early."

༺⊙༻

Clint's mind raced with his legs, pumping terror and hot blood. Face burning, lungs bursting, he pictured himself as he ran through the pasture and over the fence. *Faster, faster,* he thought. *Icy breath breathed on his back.* He ran. Away. Away from the shivers that filled Ma's room.

Tom jumped from the seat of the mower to catch him in his arms. And with Dad's strength now holding him safe, Clint couldn't remember why he was there.

Tom's face was ashen. "What's wrong? Is it Ma?"

"I don't know."

"You don't know? Something bad happened, else you wouldn't be here." Unhitching one of the horses, he lifted the boy onto her broad roan back and climbed up behind him. "Let's get there quick. Is she all right?"

Gasping for breath, Clint couldn't answer.

When he reached the house, Tom leaped from the horse, ran to the house and, two stairs at a time, rushed to his wife. Nancy was at her bedside, cleaning her scrapes with a damp washcloth.

"She's okay, Tom. I didn't mean to scare you. Reckon she fainted and skinned her face." Nancy stepped aside, letting Tom take over.

He reached for her, lifted her up, pressed his mouth to her forehead and rocked her tenderly in thick, sunburned arms. "There, there, Honey," he said softly. You'll be all right. You hurt?"

"Idiot," she shouted. "Can't you see the blood?"

Tom glanced across the room to his sister, who shook her head, mouthing an emphatic, soundless, "No." He sighed with relief.

"There, there," he cooed. Maybe you ought to take some of that medicine. That'll ease the pain. Gets worse, I can get Doc."

Molly groaned. "Do something. I feel like I'm scraped raw."

Offering her a spoon filled with the tonic, Tom managed his best smile. "It ain't bad, Miss Molly Dolly. You're still the purtiest girl I know."

She swallowed the medicine, glared at Tom, and turned away. "And you're a goddam liar," she growled. "Always was."

In a few minutes, she was fast asleep.

"She resting?" Nancy watched Tom mount the horse to return to the field. He nodded, looking glum. She'd watched him through dinner, swallowing food without much chewing and staring into space. He wouldn't pay any mind to Pearl, trying to show off her kitten until she threw herself to the floor in a temper fit. Only then did he pay the poor baby any attention

She leaned over the barnyard fence, unloading a pan of leftovers into a long wooden trough. Two shoats, being fattened for butchering, squealed in appreciation.

"Lookee here, Tom," she said, laughing. "Ain't never seen a hog eat, but what I recollect George Berkey when he came to the restaurant. Used to spread his knees, put his face down to the plate, and shovel it in. Lordy! I wonder if he ever learnt any manners."

Tom looked up with a slight grin, and then smiled broadly. He'd spotted a team of horses coming up the lane. "Well I'll be doggoned if that ain't John and the boys with his best team and another mower. Reckon we outta go meet 'em."

Tom's shorter, lanky brother took off his cap and looked at his feet. "Howdy, Tom," he offered, and then bowed slightly to his left. "Nancy. Thought you two could use some help."

Tom reached to shake his hand. "You must 'a heard about Molly."

"We was in town. Mildred run into Alice at the General Store."

Tom lifted his cap, brushing chaff from his dark hair and managed a wide grin. "That figures. And how's Mildred?"

"Tolerable, Tom. Right tolerable."

Same as always, Tom thought. Ask the same question, get the same answer. Ever since Mildred's run in with Molly, he and John spoke of their wives in careful words. Neither man learned what the quarrel was about, knowing only what his wife told him. By not speaking of it, they managed to pretend it never happened.

Nancy felt good seeing her brothers together and spread her arms wide to embrace them both. Too bad it took problems to bring a reunion. She was glad that John would be lifting some of Tom's burden along with her. Slipping her arm from John's neck she asked, "You 'et, John? How about your boys? Junior? Jim?"

The three nodded in unison. "We did," John answered. "Reckon we best git on to the field."

After supper that evening, Tom joined Nancy on the porch, dropped into an old chair, put his feet on the rail and crossed his ankles. "That was easy," he said. "Molly fell asleep in her chair. I picked her up and put her to bed." "She wouldn't eat for me tonight though. She tried to spit food in my face."

Nancy looked up from her seat on the steps, relieved to see him relaxed. "She can eat tomorrow. Reckon she's tired."

"For sure,"

Tom looked across the yard to the golden sun, dropping behind the old chicken house. From the distance whippoorwills called, coming together to seek refuge from the night. It was almost his bedtime too, and Tom was bone tired. "Glad we got that hay down," he said. "John was a sight for sore eyes."

"He looks good. Those boys are growing fast."

"Junior's 'most tall as John." Tom rubbed the back of his neck and paused for a moment, his thoughts wandering back upstairs. "Guess I like seein' Molly quiet. Think she's better?"

"Don't know. Let's see her rest a day or two. I think she'll be okay."

"You tired? You sure canned a lot of beans. I want to thank ye."

"It's nothing. I'm glad to help. We'll do tomatoes in the morning if everything goes right."

"You want me to stay close and help with her?"

"Think she'd rather have you taking care of her rather than me. But we need more canning jars. Maybe you can run into town when she's resting." Her voice dropped off, her attention drifting to Pearl, who sat close by playing with her kitten.

"Sure." Tom leaned back and stretched his legs. He couldn't get Molly off his mind. He wasn't sure what was going to happen from here on, but today'd been easier than yesterday. For that, he was thankful. He closed his eyes, remembering how life was before the spells.

He'd grown up near Lowell knowing who Molly Carroll was; but since she was two years older, paid her no mind in school. When his dad bought a farm over by Harperville, Tom recalled he'd just finished third grade. He knew his dad needed him and reckoned he was too ashamed to start fourth grade in a new school, big as he was. Folks might think he'd flunked a couple of times.

Tom started noticing girls at fifteen, that and keeping the saloon going. He and John was a couple of scoundrels, getting drunk and in fights 'most every Saturday night. Often he wondered about Donna Rock, questioning if he's the one who fathered her boy. It couldn't be proved, her not being careful who she laid with.

At times, he worried about that boy, if he turned out anything like the Fosters. And Tom reckoned if so, it hadn't been fair to leave him with a whore to raise him. There wasn't much he could have done though, since Donna's folks sent her off to live with an aunt in Kansas City. He never got a chance to find out.

I could have fathered a few more, way I carried on, he thought. Reckon I was lucky. I had so many women, Nancy used to call me "Tom Cat."

Back then, they thought it was funny.

He met Molly again at an Old Settler's Celebration about nine years ago. He'd come with his folks to see the carnival and visit old friends.

In his mind, he could see her again, just as she was that night, standing alone, outside a noisy bunch of youngsters. No bigger than a kid and a mite too thin, her eyes dark as coal against the pale of her face. Wearing a plain brown dress, she'd reminded him of a rabbit, her eyes quick, her movements jerky, and when she'd stare at something, standing stock-still. Like she figured if she didn't move, no one would notice her. In case they did, she was ready to run.

He wondered what it could be that had her so scared. Slowly, he made his way to the back of the crowd till he stood alongside her and then started to talk. "Did you try the food stands?" he asked.

"No."

"I tried one of them cotton candy balls. Almost made me sick." Tom said. "Guess I really liked the fiddle playing at the stand in the middle of the park. Did you go hear them?

'No."

"Bet you didn't see the sideshows yet either."

Molly smiled. "No."

"How about I take you to see the medicine man? He's putting on quite a show. Give you something you can say 'yes' to."

Molly smiled. "Yes."

"Good." Tom reached for her arm and directed her through the crowd to the tents at the end of Main Street. "I thought maybe you'd like to do something," he said, grinning.

From then to now, Tom couldn't get enough thinking about that girl. He reckoned if he could just figure out why she changed one minute to the next, he'd get tired of her. His Ma used to say she had some sort of power over him.

Still does, Tom groaned. A sweet power it is, too. You'd never expect the man who, on a dare, had just out-pulled the best man in the weight-pulling contest to be overwhelmed by anybody. But Molly proved irresistible.

After the show, they'd walked out of town. With a full moon lighting the path, they headed east toward Dog Branch. He wanted to show her where he'd spotted identical twin calves. Thought she might like to come see them tomorrow.

She didn't talk much. Just looked up from time to time, giving him a strange crooked smile, dropping her eyes and looking away. So different from most girls, always chattering. Molly listened. She paid attention to every word. And when his hand reached for hers, he could tell she welcomed it, looking surprised and happy at once, catching her breath a little, and then, that smile.

They'd stopped by the bridge to listen for bullfrogs and he turned her to face him. She turned easily, leaning into his hands as they slipped to her waist, not pulling back when they started to wander.

Each touch, each kiss, quickened her breathing, set her heart pounding so hard he could feel it strong, against his own. She closed her eyes, pressing close, her arms around his neck, holding tight.

Backing her into a small clearing just off the road, he unbuttoned her dress, slid it over her shoulders to drop to her ankles. Underneath, she had on a thin cotton slip. No corset. No underpants.

My kind of woman, he reflected. The kind he could get to. He sat on the grass, easing her down.

She never held off. Figuring she wanted the same thing he did, Tom didn't think it would turn out like it did.

In loving, as in everything, Tom took his time. Practiced enough to know it was better for him when the woman enjoyed it, he never went further than she was ready. And when his searching fingers had opened her thighs and brought her through a soft moaning shuddering, he raised himself over her, entering her forcefully.

Molly screamed! Pressing her hands against his chest and kicking his back with her heels, she tried to push him off. But it was too late. Her struggle excited him, and he plunged, deeper and faster, collapsing in a groan of agonized pleasure.

"Why'd you hurt me?" she sobbed. She sat next to him on the rumpled grass. "I thought you liked me." She pulled her dress over her breasts.

Tom sat shocked. She was a virgin! She didn't even know what was happening. How'd she been so raring to go? So willing?

"I'm sorry," he mumbled. "Didn't know you'd never done it before."

Her voice was trembling. "Was that it? My sister said it felt good. That hurt." She rose, pulled her dress on and smoothed it. "My God, it's started my monthly. It's runnin' down my legs."

Tom stood awkwardly, not sure what to say. No matter what had happened, she still seemed to trust him. Didn't seem angry, just surprised. In the darkness, he stroked her shoulder. "Didn't mean to hurt you."

As he expected, she paused, accepting his hands. Poor little girl, he thought. Just wants someone to hold onto her. He lifted her chin, and gently kissed her mouth. "I'll never hurt ye again, I promise," he whispered. "Let's git you on home."

They walked without speaking to the Elliott House, where Molly had a room.

"Can I come by Sunday?" He asked. "Maybe we can go to the dessert social over at the Methodist church."

She nodded.

"I'll be by about 3:00," he'd said. He turned and left.

From that night on, Tom supposed if he could just figure out the right way to take care of her, Molly'd be happy. He never considered it possible she'd want anything else.

After nine years, nothing had changed. Molly still frightened, and he, still trying. She's never learnt to understand how to accept help, he thought. To let go of her pride and take the hand of another when life get too hard. Thank God for John and Nancy, he had help waiting, if ever he needed it.

It made him feel warm inside, wishing he knew how to put this into words so he could explain it to Molly.

From the barn, a hoot owl called, frightening Pearl. "Daddy," she cried and ran to him. He lifted her to his shoulder. Comforted her, Soon she was laughing, hooting back. Pearl knows how to ask, he thought. And she's only two.

Later, with the little ones in bed, Nancy spoke to Tom. "Maybe you can go by my house when you git to town tomorrow. Pick up that bolt of chambray out of the sewing room. Think I'll make Clint new shirts for school." She paused. "You might ask about Ben, too. Sure would like knowing what he's been up to." She figured Alice knew, and hoped it wasn't something that'd be the talk of the town before she got back.

And as Nancy suspected, Alice was keeping watch on her son. All afternoon, she'd pruned her roses; watching women come, stay about an hour, then leave.

"I counted three of them, Warren. Three! Could have missed some, too, being busy here in the house."

Warren groaned. "I don't reckon you missed any, Alice. What did you hear?"

"Talk for the trash he hangs out with, that's what. Thought he was funny, laughing and hollering. He left the bedroom window wide open. I had to keep the kids in the house. Lordy, Warren, Nancy doesn't get back soon; don't know what I'll do."

"I do," said Warren, wearily. "I do. He walked to the window, looked out and laughed. "It's dark over there now. Reckon he's so worn out he's gone to bed early."

But Ben wasn't home sleeping. Over at Woody's Saloon, he and his buddy, Frank Peters, were standing at the dingy bar, polishing off another round.

Lean, dark and good-looking, Ben was popular with the bar crowd, always doing something to keep them in stitches. He enjoyed attention and had a habit of watching himself in the mirrored wall behind the bar where Woody'd lined up the whiskey bottles, making it look like double the supply.

Brown eyes unfocused, Ben was telling Woody about the trick he and Frank had just played on Pat Donavon. "We was headed back to the outhouse when we saw the old bastard passed out 'longside the path." He stumbled forward, slapping Frank's shoulder, struggling to keep upright. "We dragged him to Preacher Formby's, took off his clothes, and left him in the front yard."

Frank leaned on his elbow, knees buckling, steadying himself. "Just hope he waits 'til mornin' to wake up. Wasn't no way we were leavin' any in that bottle to make it easy on him."

Ben whooped. "Wouldn't you like to be there when that prune-lipped preacher finds him? Old Pat on his back, with that fat belly shaking? Think the preacher can make a sermon outta that?"

Glancing into the mirror to check his effect on the men behind him, Ben spotted a familiar figure walk through the door. His heart sank. It was Ira White. He hunched down and looked in his drink, praying he wouldn't be seen.

In a fine tailored suit and shiny patent shoes, Ira looked quite out of place with the motley saloon bunch. But he hadn't come to join them. He walked straight to Ben and with a firm hand grasped his collar, brought a knee hard to his buttocks and shoved him against the bar. "Thought you were sick, Ben. You were supposed to work today. You've got tomorrow off with no pay to get sobered up. But I warn you Ben, you don't come in Friday, I'll fire your ass."

Ira slammed his fist against the marble top of a mahogany console before pouring himself a stiff drink. He'd returned home after his meeting with Ben, going to his plush leathered office and slamming the door, sending his timid wife, Edna, fleeing upstairs. "That little bastard's going to drive me crazy."

He swallowed his drink, reaching for a crystal decanter to pour another. "He had to end up looking like me, too. Good God! Wonder how many people have noticed?"

He hired Ben two years ago when he'd come looking for work. Figuring Nancy sent him, Ira knew he couldn't refuse.

He stretched his legs beneath the desk, and leaned back, hands locked behind his head. "I have to be rational," he said. "R-a-t-i-o-n-a-l."

It wasn't going to be easy. He liked Ben, couldn't help it. Secretly, was damn proud of him and considered him an asset to the business. The boy was charming and did a good job of convincing local farm-ers to sell land at a good price. A lot of them were pretty hard up and trying to eke out a living on small plots of scrubland or wet marsh. Ira figured he was improving their lot, taking over their payments, share-cropping with the good ones, having them work the land of those who never knew how.

It made sense. Those guys weren't going to make money farming. Be better off working in town. Ben could sell that idea in a heartbeat. Especially to the ones who didn't trust Ira.

"Got his brains from me, no doubt about it," Ira said. "He can do anything. Run the hotel and make a visitor feel like they're Queen of England. He'll even do grunt work at the stable if I ask. He's not rebelling. He's just a damn reckless fool!"

Ira hoped he'd grow out of it, but it seemed he got worse every week. What would Nancy do if Ben were fired? Would she blab their secret? She was manipulative enough. Pretty slick the way she'd wrapped Mother around her little finger, taking more than she needed. It was my money, by God, he thought. Dad meant it for me.

Ira stood and closed the curtains, still grumbling. "A goddam mess. That's what it is. With a kid like him in a town where gossip spreads like wildfire. Only reason he gets by with everything is because of folk's crazy admiration for some goddam outlaw. Folks find out who that kid really is, I'm ruined!"

Chapter 3

September, 1904

He'd suspected it from the first day. Now Clint was sure. Aunt Nancy was putting a spell on Ma and making her worse. It would be no use talking to Dad. All he'll say is to do what Auntie says. And any back talk there'll be a whipping.

He was headed for his hiding place. The spot he and Red had stamped out in the oat field beyond the big oak he called his own. Glumly thinking if he had something to eat he'd stay here all night.

"I'll show 'em," he muttered. "Damn tired of 'em. Always watching. Asking what's wrong with me when it's Ma that's sick."

Earlier, he'd helped set up her bath, hauling the galvanized tub from its peg on the back porch and setting it in the middle of the front room, watching as Auntie poured in hot water and added the bucket of cool water he'd brought from the well.

"Thanks for the help, Clint," she said. Don't want to scald your Ma. Do we?"

"Sure don't." And as soon as she looked away, dipped his hand into the water to check the temperature.

He'd watched Dad carry Ma down the stairs, making jokes. Not seeming to notice that Ma was all floppy, her arms and legs hanging loose as if she was all elbows and knees.

Clint was frightened. He was afraid she might be dead. But he heard her laugh, a wild cackle that brought the bogey man rising out of a dark corner. Knees buckling, Clint thought he felt a cold wind against his face and struggled to breathe.

As Ma turned to look at him, she seemed ready to say something, but a flash of light fell through the curtain onto a face he couldn't recognize. Aunt Nancy was holding her up and suddenly, Clint realized what was going on. It's a spell. Aunt Nancy had decided to put a spell on her to get even. And according to what Ma told him, she had plenty of reason for revenge.

As he reached the clearing beneath his tree, Clint remembered the day Ma told him about Aunt Nancy. "She's wicked, Clint. Evil," Ma said. "Kind 'a person you and me don't want to be with. She pretends to be nice, I know. She helped us out when I birthed Pearl. But everything she does is a damn pack of lies. What she really wants is to cause trouble between me and your dad."

In the dim front room, drawn curtains had muted the sun. "Open the curtains, Clint," she ordered. "I can't see nothing in here."

Turning her back to the window, she watched as he fed Little Pearl. "Nancy runs with trash," she said "Hanging out in the saloon, drinking and chewing tobaccy like a man. She don't fool me none, pretending she's changed. Mess up your life the way she has, it's messed 'til you die."

Clint was puzzled. "How'd she mess up?"

Molly leaned forward, pointing a finger into his face. "By bein' a whore. That's what she is. You might's well hear it now as later. But your auntie just as well had a child by the devil as with that murdering outlaw."

"Ben's a bastard, Clint. A no-good bastard and I want you stayin' away from the likes of the both of 'em."

Clint took the bottle from the baby's mouth and shifted her to his shoulder. "Dad know that?"

"You'll never hear him saying anything's wrong with his family. He goes straight to them when he's mad at me and tells them our secrets." She began to rock, raising her voice. "Thinks if they agree with him, it'll prove him right."

"You and Dad have secrets? What ones he tell?'

"Ha. Everything I've done don't suit him."

"Is Uncle John bad, too?"

"John's dumb. He can't read a word. His folks took him out 'a school, they was so ashamed." She noticed the baby, finally sleeping against Clint's chest. "Carry her to bed, boy. She's had her fill."

As he walked past, Molly reached and lifted the blanket to peer at the baby. "This one's a Foster," she snorted. "You ain't nothing like them, Clint. You're like me. You're gonna get through school and make something of yourself, way my sister did."

But how am I gonna go to school if Ma ends up dead? Clint wondered. Who'll take care of Pearl? A rattle of dry leaves startled him and he turned quickly, expecting to be discovered. But it was only a squirrel, gathering acorns.

After what happened this morning, I can't let Auntie go near Ma again, he decided. The witch! He hated seeing her brushing Ma's hair and rubbing her shoulders. She even holds her on the pot when she gets up to pee! If Dad could see what's goin' on, he'd make it stop.

He could hear Tom's voice in the distance, calling him home. But didn't answer and waited, resting a few more minutes in the strong sureness of the oak...safe from the looks, the questions, and Ma's awful laugh, behind a dense curtain of weeds.

"Git in here. Now." Tom thundered.

Clint rose slowly and began to walk toward the house. "I'm coming" he called. He zigzagged through the corn rows, pushing aside slashing stalks, the damp smell of oak rising as he carefully kicked last year's leaves over his footprints.

Dad was at the hitching post, his team of roans harnessed to the buckboard. "You coming to town with me? He asked. "You'll need shoes 'fore school starts."

Clint shook his head. "Reckon I kin wait 'til frost. Red does."

"Suit yerself. You don't mind the kids making fun of ya, I don't either."

Clint sighed. Reckoned if Dad knew what kids do make fun of, he wouldn't 'a said that. My insides are jumbled enough without having to break in shoes. Besides, he thought, I ain't sure I can leave Ma to go to school.

⌒꙰

In order to hear her every word, Clint positioned himself on the front steps outside the kitchen door with his book. Pausing before opening it, to smooth his fingers over the rough boards and wondered what they'd look like painted. Be nice if it was like Aunt Nancy's front porch. All white, with wicker chairs.

But he hated Auntie's house! Especially the attic. And Ben.

He shook his head, muttering, "No! Ain't gonna think of him." Clint opened his poetry book, trying to forget.

By noon he was finished and looked up to see Tom come up the path, ready for dinner. "Doc gonna come? He whimpered. "She ain't woke up, Dad. I get feared she won't."

"Don't worry, son," Tom answered. "She's gonna be fine. She'll be out 'a bed in a few days."

Fact is, she's better every day. Of that, Tom was certain. She's a bit weak, maybe. But now that she's eating, she'll have her strength back in no time.

It'd been good to be able go to town and not worry. Thinking as he drove how good it was to see her laugh. She hadn't lost her temper. Not once. Tom had clucked to his team, snapping the reins on their red-mottled backs, bringing them to a smooth trot.

With a brief pang in his belly, he took off his cap, lifted his hair and rubbed it between his fingers. She's right, he thought. My hair is getting thin.

"Well lookee you," she'd laughed as he was fixing to leave. "Bald as an old man. Too old for me, that's for damn sure."

And then she started laughing. She couldn't seem to stop, except to catch her breath. Finally, it got to be more than Tom could take. So he gave her another dose of the medicine, hoping she'd fall asleep and forget about it. As he'd filled the teaspoon, he realized there weren't many doses left.

Once in town, he'd turned his team toward Doc's office, intending to get another bottle. But the doctor wasn't in. One of the Elliott girls was in the back room, cleaning. "He's on a call," she said. "Miz Morris is having her baby. Anything I can do fer ya?"

"I wanted to let him know how the wife's doing. I hoped I could get more tonic."

"Know which one it is?"

Tom pointed to the shelf in the laboratory. "It's up there."

"Why not help yourself, Tom. Save yourself a trip back."

Tom filled a mid-size bottle and reached into his pocket for a silver dollar, flipped it onto the tin topped table, and left for Nancy's house, expecting there'd be no one there.

As soon as he strode through the wide front door, he jumped back, not believing what he saw. There, in Nancy's parlor sat Ben, all dressed up in a broad brimmed hat and ruffled dress, and Frank Peters in a blue one, resting their boots on her fancy chairs, with a half-filled whiskey bottle on a small table between them.

"Why, Uncle Tom. Sure didn't expect you." Ben tossed the hat to a corner.

"Reckon that's the most truthful thing you've said this mornin'. Mind tellin' me what you're up to?"

"We're just foolin' around having a little fun with Alice. Frank got hold of some dresses from the girls at the saloon."

"You mean at the whore house."

"We been going down to that shed behind them bushes." Ben pointed through the window. "Putting on a dress and coming in the front door. Leadin' her to believe I'm entertainin' a few ladies. I've got a reputation to live up to, Uncle. Allow Alice can help me out."

Frank guffawed. "She's about cut them roses to the ground, keeping an eye on him."

"Hey, Uncle Tom, you ain't gonna tell Ma are you? We're just havin' fun."

Tom laughed. "Could be Alice'll tell her for me. But why ain't you at work, Ben? I thought you had a job."

Frank set his feet on the rug, spat on his fingers and wiped a smudge from the cream-colored chair. "Iry caught him at Woody's last night after he didn't come in yesterday. He told him to sober up or you-know-what tomorrow."

"That true, Ben?"

Ben gurgled, muffling a laugh. "Yes sir. But I'll be there."

Tom picked up the bottle, slipped it into his pocket, and stood over his nephew. "Yessir, Ben," he began, "I reckon you will. Provided you git to bed and sleep this off. You don't make it to work tomorry you got more'n Iry to worry about. You hear?"

"I hear ya." Ben shot up the stairs.

"And Frank, you don't want me to put you in the wagon and parade you around town in that dress, you better git out of here. I don't want to hear you've been back 'til Nancy gits here. Okay?"

Frank took less than a minute to pick up his things. Tom had a reputation, too. And it wasn't a good idea to stick around to see if he'd live up to it.

Tom had to sit down a while, he was laughing so hard. Remembering how, at their age, he'd a done the same thing. I don't have much time to be wasting on a couple 'a rascals, though. I got to get to the General Store and ain't keen on going. Reckon I've put it off long as possible, afraid I'll have to explain to Alvin Miller what was going on with Molly.

Alvin was married to Molly's sister, Lillian. A nice enough feller, Tom figured, but the kind you'd forget if you blinked twice talking' to him. And his hearing was bad. Tom feared to be shouting his troubles to half the town.

Lucky for him, Lillian was in the store, stocking shelves. "C'mon back to the storeroom," she said. "We can talk where it's private". It seemed to Tom; Lillian wanted to keep things quiet, too.

In a fashionable brown skirt and white blouse, her thick dark hair pulled back in a neat bun, Lillian's only resemblance to Molly was in the contours of her face. She was much taller, poised and sure of herself. Her voice was soft, but firm and confident.

Probably from making Alvin's decisions for him, Tom figured. She's the brains of the two. The reason they've done good. The only thing Tom didn't like about her was that she was saved too much. And set on saving you right along with her, even if you'd as soon burn in Hell.

She followed him to the storeroom and leaned against the closed door, one hand on the knob behind her. "What's going on?" she asked. "I hear it's bad."

Tom brushed against a stack of flour bags, raising a white dust that settled on his overalls. Feeling clumsy, he reached to brush it off.

"She's better now," he answered. "Doc gave her something."

Lillian sighed. "Will she see me? I could come Sunday after church."

"Sure. She's calm with the tonic. Why not plan on eatin' with us?"

"It's never good for me to stay long. We have services Sunday night, so I reckon we'll stay only an hour. Tell her I'm praying for her. And for you, too, Tom. I know this is hard for you."

Tom looked away. He never knew what to say when someone told him they were praying for him. After she got religion, his Ma used to pray for him. She was always trying to get morals into him and praying was one of her ways. Tom hadn't given religion much thought until the day Doc said it might help Molly. Lots of folks went to church. Even Nancy.

And he had to admit, it hadn't hurt Lillian. "Hope the prayers do some good," he offered. "Try anything that could help."

"The Lord heals all things, Tom. He'll heal Molly if she'll let him into her heart. There's a big tent revival in September, at our church-yard. This man, Billy Sunday's supposed to be good. Maybe someone like him could convince her of the truth."

"How'd we get her to go?"

"Through prayer. The Lord will answer. He answers all. Shall we pray together now?"

Tom shifted from foot to foot. When Lillian took his hands and raised them toward the ceiling, she closed her eyes. Stiffly, he followed her lead.

Lillian's strong sure voice filled the room. "Dear Heavenly Father, we beseech you, pour your grace on our dear sister, Molly. Hear us Lord. Look on her suffering and answer our prayer. Remove from her, Lord, the mark of sin, cast by an evil wanderer." She raised her voice. "Come, Lord, Break down the door of her pride that she may surrender to your will. In Jesus' name. Amen.

Tom waited, his hands still in hers.

Lillian looked up. "Amen, Tom?" She asked.

Tom shuffled. "Oh. Aye-men", he said. He sure was glad the prayer was over and reckoned he'd done it right. But the words puzzled him. Wonder what she meant by a mark? If it was something one could see. Like a birthmark? And why was it up to them to pray it off?

Seemed like the Lord shouldn't 'a let it happen in the first place. The gypsy's the one ought to suffer. Allow I don't understand much talk of the Lord, he thought. Reckon I ain't learned the right words.

But, Tom knew, if he asked Lillian to explain, it might mean a sermon. And he wasn't that curious. "Time I go, Lillian," he said. "I'll pick up a few provisions and head out."

After picking out a few candies for the kids and helping Lillian pack the jars in old newspapers, he loaded the wagon. Wondering what he'd say to Nancy when he got home.

Nancy looked up from the stove as he came in, wiping her hands on a tomato stained apron. Seemed to Tom, she was glad to have him back.

"You lookin' for dinner?" she asked. Then called to Clint, "Would you set the table fer us like a good boy?"

She turned to Tom. "Any word of Ben?"

"He said he had today off, gonna work tomorrow."

"That's different." Nancy exhaled, sounding relieved. "At least he's behaving. You get jars?"

Tom shifted. That was easy. "Four dozen. Molly okay?"

"She's good. Think she's beginning to like me."

"Fer sure. I like seeing her happy."

A plate sailed across the room exploding at Tom's feet. "Happy?" Clint shouted. "Ma ain't happy. She's almost dead. And you don't give a damn!" He stormed out of the house, slamming the door.

Tom stared, shocked, as Nancy lifted a wailing Pearl.

"What's he talking about? Lordy. Cussing like his Ma. I been letting him off. But he won't get by with this!"

Nancy positioned herself in the doorway, her hand placed firmly against his chest. "It's okay, Tom, he's jist frettin' over his Ma. Think it's hard on him."

Tom pushed her aside, struggling to follow Clint. "Don't know what's into him. Needs a good licking"

Nancy put a hand on his arm, gently pulling him back. "No, Tom. He don't understand. That's what."

"Don't pick up that broken dish, Nancy. He's got to."

Tom jammed his hands in his pockets and walked off. No need talking to Nancy about handling a boy, something she hadn't been good at. Reckon a boy needs a man around to keep him straight. And I'm gonna fight hard to keep my boy from turning out like Ben.

Soon as he calmed himself, Tom looked for Clint, figuring the promise of dinner and candy might get him to clean up the mess he'd made.

"Not hungry." Clint's voice was sullen.

Angrily, Tom turned back, scolding him. "You won't get a bite 'til you act decent."

Clint whacked a stout stick against the chicken house, beating down weeds that grew alongside. "Decent? Maybe it's you oughta act decent! We gotta stop what's going on with Ma! You don't care. Just leave it all to Auntie."

Tom turned back, speechless. Nancy may be right, he thought. The boy doesn't seem to understand. I don't reckon I can help him much, either. I think I'm puzzled as he is.

Later, that night, Clint heard Ma call out and watched Dad get up from his bed then tiptoe upstairs to see what she wanted.

Clint crept to the landing to listen. Ma was crying. "I'm so scared, Tom," she whispered. "Hold me."

Clint inched to the door and looked in. Dad was in her bed. Kissing her. Hugging, too. And Ma was hugging back. He let go a long breath; relieved he'd had it wrong. Looked like Dad was trying to make her feel good too.

Late next morning, Dad was still in Ma's bed and Clint had to call him twice. "Uncle John's here, Dad," he said. "Says it's time to finish the haying."

⌒◦

Dark clouds came with the last load, threatening rain, the sky turning black and the air still. Nothing moved, not even a leaf.

Suddenly the wind came, whipping dust and trees in a violent, threshing whirlwind. "It's so purty, Dad," Clint shouted. "So strong!"

He looked to his oak, bowing with the wind. "Look at that tree yonder. Think she'll blow over?"

"Not that one. It was standing 'fore I was born. It'll probably be there when we're both long gone."

Behind the oak a dark wall of rain formed, moved through the tree, and aimed straight toward the house. "Here she comes!" Tom shouted. They ran in laughing, split seconds before it slammed into the porch. And with the bang of the door, Molly started screaming.

"Help me! Damn! There's snow blowin' on my bed! Tom! Git in here!"

Reacting to her outburst, Tom dashed to shut the window.

But Molly was as baffled as Tom. She tried explaining it, but couldn't. Hell yes, it's raining, she thought, just turned to snow in the words comin' outta my mouth. Pointing to a wet spot under the window, she tried to tell Tom. "Paper, wall, there. Wet up the ub ub ub wipe."

Tom's face reddened. "What can I do?" he asked.

Molly sat up, raised her arms over her head and began to sway. "Wheee. Meee. See," she crooned.

Tom stood, shocked into paralysis. "What's wrong, Molly. Don't like you acting like a kid."

"You damn fool, help me," she uttered, then fell back and turned to the door, looking for Clint. Thinking he'd been standing there for a long time.

But it wasn't Clint. It was Tom acting bossy. She began to laugh. She couldn't catch her breath. And couldn't stop laughing.

"Dang it Molly. Nothing's funny. So cut it out." Tom snapped. She grabbed his overalls and held on. Disgusted, he reached for the bottle. "It's time for your medicine. I've got things to do."

The aroma of fresh bread lured him back to the kitchen where Nancy was pinning a pattern on the chambray he'd brought back from town. He spotted the bread cooling on the side table, tore off the end of a loaf, spooned on a little honey and started eating.

Nancy glanced up, a smile crinkling her eyes. In the light of the kerosene lamp, her hair glowed orange, spreading warmth through the room like heat from the woodstove.

Tom hadn't felt this comfortable for a long time. He exhaled slowly, trying to let go of his dream. A dream that, someday, Molly might get a bit of Nancy, that woman thing, that way of staying happy while doing chores, singing, as she tended the family.

But it wasn't to be. Tom reckoned he'd just be thankful for the short time his sister would be there. "Miss Nancy, you sure are smart," he began. "Makin' a pattern out 'a them newspapers we packed jars in. Wouldn't 'a thought 'a that."

"I had to iron 'em first, but it works fine. I'm cutting a shirt for Clint."

"That's right nice of ye. Clint, did ye say thanks?"

Clint's fists clenched, his face reddening. "I don't need shirts. When I do, I want Ma makin' 'em."

Nancy kept cutting. "Suit yerself. You don't have to wear 'em."

"Ain't yer job, making our clothes. It's Ma's. And if she can't, I will."

"Good idea," Nancy said gently. "C'mon over here. I'll show you how."

Tom strode across the room, grabbed his son and gave him a firm swat on the behind. "No boy 'a mine's gonna sew. Git to bed and I don't want to hear a word out 'a you 'fore morning."

Later, with Clint asleep, Tom figured he ought to smooth things with Nancy. "I'm sorry, Nancy," he said. "It don't have nothin' to do with you. Times I don't know how to handle that boy. A lot of his mother is in him. More'n I like."

"Reckon he cares for his Ma. He don't want me taking her place. I can't blame him." Maybe school will be good for him. At least it'll keep his mind off her."

"I reckon you're right. I could use him here, but think he ought to go. It'll keep him occupied. Only two days and it'll be starting."

⌒◯

Just two more days! Then school!

Clint woke with the sun and ran out to watch it rise. Morning was his favorite time. Listening to the birds wake one after the other, pretending he was Adam, the only man in the Garden of Eden.

It reminded him of the first day of school. How he'd start over. Get hold of his temper. With last night's anger and this morning's shame, Clint promised himself he'd not get mad again. He could have done something awful. Like grab the shears and poke them into Aunt Nancy's heart. That's what he'd thought of.

Ma's sickness is bad for me, he reckoned. Gotta control it if I'm gonna help her out. Besides, it was causing too much trouble.

With the slam of the screen door, Tom came to join him. Clint looked at the grass, his face suddenly warm.

Tom placed a hand on the boy's shivering shoulder.

"You okay this morning?"

"Yessir. Sorry I got mad."

"So am I. Won't do it agin, will ye?"

"I'll try." Clint looked up. "Still gonna let me start school?"

"Long as you behave."

"I will, Dad. I promise."

The rest of the day, Clint did what pleased Dad most...hard work. It was better, pleasing Dad than fighting him, and Clint figured he'd make up for his wrongs. He cleaned the hen house, put straw in the nests and chopped weeds. He even helped Aunt Nancy wash supper dishes.

Tom watched, hopeful. With Lillian coming tomorry, he didn't want Clint making the visit worse than it should be.

And by the time Lillian arrived late next morning. Nancy had everything in the house clean and polished, including Pearl and Clinton. Didn't want Tom looking bad to "Miss Perfect," she thought.

Lillian arrived on time, looking great. After settling Alvin and her two girls, Faye and Lily, in the parlor with Tom, she went upstairs to see her sister.

"I want to talk to her alone," she announced as she came in the door. "What I have to say to Molly is private." Lillian had made her wishes clear. And all understood that Lillian could handle Molly only when she could control the surroundings. The more people in the room, the greater the chance of fireworks.

Lillian found her awake, propped against the pillows, the blue and white coverlet, their wedding gift, spread over the bed. "Molly, it's Lillian," she began.

"I know who you are. You come to lecture?"

"Of course not. You've been sick and I'm concerned. I understand how hard it's been."

Molly interrupted. "The hell you do! You're healthy as a horse."

"Please. Don't be profane. I want to help."

"Tom says you want me to go to a revival. Did he tell you we might?"

"Praise the Lord!" Lillian leaned toward Molly, her face suddenly animated. "It could change your life. You can't imagine what happiness the Lord can bring. I'm here to give testimony to how much he's brought to me."

"Then you're giving testimony to a goddam lie, Lillian Miller. You telling me you're happy with that gutless husband 'a yours?"

Lillian didn't answer, walked to the window and looked out. Finally, she spoke. "I can be happy with anyone, anywhere, with the Lord in my heart. He lightens my load. When you know Him, He'll do the same for you. Please come. You'll see what I mean."

"I said we might. Tom said the preacher is a healer. Might be fun seein' someone git healed. Heard they smack 'em on the forehead and they fall backwards. Folks ketch 'em or they'll hit the floor."

Lillian turned away, rolling her eyes. She wasn't going to give her an excuse not to go. "Think I best leave, Molly. We have to be at church. Would you like to pray with me?"

Molly hooted. "Hell, no. All I did was say I might go. Might! You ain't saved me yet, Lillian!"

Lillian stooped to kiss her cheek, catching the scent of soap on her skin and a whiff of lavender from her fresh, ironed gown, glad to see Nancy was keeping her washed. And glad she was leaving without getting angry. Molly had a way of bringing her there. Before she found Jesus, it happened a lot.

And anger frightened her. It made her feel like striking back. Like kicking and screaming and throwing things. Cursing. Not stopping until Molly turned into somebody respectable.

But vengeance belongs to the Lord, she reminded herself, and not to Lillian Miller. She had to keep control.

Back downstairs, she quickly ushered her family to the shiny black buggy, made excuses about being busy and said good-bye. Thanking the Lord she had a service to attend, so she could get back to righteousness.

Tom called after her, waving. "Thanks for coming." He was standing with Clinton, seeing them off. As they drove down the lane, he turned to the boy.

"Would you like to go for a walk with me? We'll go to the south pasture and check fences?"

Clint's heart sank, figuring Dad was fixing to give him a talking to.

Tom's plan was to talk to him when both were calm. He stopped to straighten a post. "You like school, don't ye?"

"More'n anything."

"Why? What you like best?"

"Maybe Miz Peters. And seein' Red. And 'rithmatic, reading and poetry. And it makes Ma happy. She keeps tellin' me to git educated."

Tom pulled out his hammer, lifted a sagging wire and nailed it in place. "That sounds good. So, what did your Ma say education will do for ye?"

"She says I can be like Aunt Lillian. Ma says she runs the store and got rich 'cause she graduated high school."

"Reckon you can be rich in a lot of ways, Clint. Ever think about takin' over the farm?"

Clint gasped. "No sir! Ma says that'll make me poor. I hate farmin'. It's hard."

"Work's good for ye. Farming's the finest thing a man can do. Ain't like working for some boss. On the farm, you're in charge. Ever think of that?"

"I don't want no boss neither. But I ain't gonna farm. I'm gonna be a poet. I wouldn't have to git dirty. Just sit at a desk and write poems."

Tom slipped the hammer into its loop on his overalls. "A poet? Who put that in your head? Your Ma? Or that Miz Peters?"

"I-I-I don't know." Clint sputtered. Couldn't see why Dad was so riled. He hadn't done anything wrong.

"You ain't gonna be no poet, Clint. I promise ye," Tom shouted. "You get that idea out of your head right now. D'ya hear?"

Clint nodded and held back tears.

They walked back in silence. At the barnyard fence, Tom could see a lone cow standing, lowing for her calf on the other side. With a lump rising in his throat, Tom opened the gate, freeing the calf to run to its mother.

Some days, he figured, there's more hurt than a man has to take. Reckon that cow's hurting much as I am. He could wean the calf tomorrow. What couldn't be delayed was doing right by his son. Just wish to God A' mighty I knew what right is, he thought. School's gonna start in the mornin'. And I can't figger out whether it's gonna do him harm, or do him good.

❧

"But school don't start for an hour." Nancy was wiping dishes, trying to keep Clint from leaving too early. "Miz Peters won't be there yet. My, but you're impatient!"

"Red might be there. Let me go. Please. I kin wait outside."

Nancy laughed. "Okay. I reckon I can't hold you down. Don't forget your lunch."

He ran to the school, bursting through the door like a gust of March wind. "Howdy, Miz Peters! You're early too. Where's Red?"

"Out back, waiting for you. Go. I'll call when it's time".

Emily Peters smiled. Glad to see her two favorites back. They were the ones who made her job worthwhile. She was at her desk, going over this year's enrollment. Red's sisters, Mary and Colleen were back, even though their mother didn't think school important for them, since they'd only get married. As a result, neither exerted much effort, disappointing her.

And there were five Berkeys this year! Emily made a face. They were the ones who make her want to throw up her hands and quit. The Berkeys were dim-witted, argumentative and smelled bad.

Reaching her arms out, Emily intertwined her long fingers and stretched. Remember you're a teacher, she told herself. This is Dorothy Berkey's first year. Maybe she'll be different.

She rang the opening bell as the children came to take their seats. "Good morning, boys and girls," she began. "All rise as we pledge allegiance to the flag."

School was in session. Clint was so happy he didn't think about Ma all day. If he had, he'd have been glad to know Doc was driving out to see her.

The doctor had been worrying about Molly ever since he learned Tom had taken more opium from his office and hoped he wasn't too late. An overdose could be fatal; taking it too long could lead to dependence and painful withdrawal, and for someone unstable, the hallucinations could cause permanent madness.

50

He found Nancy at the clothesline, Pearl handing her pins from a small bag tied to her waist. "Why, Doc. Good to see you," Nancy said. "Tom's in the barn. Like me to git him?"

"I came to see Molly."

"It's a good time. Hasn't had her medicine, so she'll be able to talk."

"Tell her I'm here. I'll get my bag and be along in a minute."

Nancy called up the stairs. "Doc's here to see ya."

"What the hell for?"

"He wants to know how you are. He's coming up."

"Don't want to see him."

But Steve Davis didn't wait. He'd known Molly long enough to know how to handle her. He had delivered her babies and set a broken arm when she was barely ten. He knew at the time her dad was responsible, but because her mother was with her, Molly wouldn't say anything.

Secretly, Doc admired Molly for the way she'd fought back, and clawed her way out of the mess she was born in. For her fractured dignity, maintained in spite of a town where everyone talked and few understood. It didn't bother him if she got angry. Anything to get her fighting again. Her biggest danger was giving up. To accept what's handed to her, leaving folks to take advantage. And no matter how much that anger inconveniences Tom or anyone else, Doc believed that, without it, she wouldn't get well. And would lose all reason to live.

His trained eyes swept over her, noting her dull eyes, dilated pupils, her heavy motions and deep sigh as she turned away. "How are you, Molly?"

"What you doin' here?" She retorted. "I didn't call for you. Come to tell me I'm crazy?"

"No. Because you're not. But you are in trouble. I came to help."

"Trouble! Shit! As if that's new. How you think you gonna help?"

"First, I have to get you off that medicine. It's bad for you."

"Bad! It's the best damn thing that's happened to me. It makes me sleep. And have good dreams. And my headache's gone."

51

"It was good for a day or so. But take it too long it'll make things worse than ever. It was a mistake, giving Tom that second bottle."

Molly sat upright, wide-eyed. "What'll happen? I can't do it, Doc. I'll git like— like that again." She began to tremble, hugging herself. "I'm afraid, Doc. Scairt I might hurt myself."

He stooped, put his face next to hers, and looked in her eyes. "You won't. I promise. Now that you've rested, you'll be okay."

Doc blamed Tom for the way he'd taken the easy way, giving in to her. Not taking her seriously, knowing it was Molly who had to help herself get well.

"Besides, Molly," he began. "Things aren't going well with your family. You don't know that, do you? Because you're in bed, asleep from the medicine."

She raised her voice. "What you talkin' about?"

"The trouble you're in. How you're losing everything. To that sister-in-law you claim to despise."

"That don't make sense. Losin' what?"

"Getting to run your own house for one thing, and raising your kids. A life with Tom. Is this what you want, Molly? For her to take over?"

Molly stared at her hands, turning them, spreading her fingers and examining her nails as if she'd suddenly discovered they belonged to her. "She's doin' that?"

"She is. But she can't if you make up your mind to take it back. You have two choices, Molly. You can get out of this bed or give everything to Nancy."

Fear flashed behind her eyes. "Think I can?"

"I know you can. Come. I'll go with you."

They joined Tom, who was nervously pacing the front room.

Molly smiled weakly. "Doc says I gotta stay up and get my strength back," she said.

"That right, Doc?" Tom turned to Nancy, who shrugged. Their shared look convincing each other Doc would soon draw them aside and tell them otherwise.

Doc inhaled deeply. Someone has to believe in her. "You tell him, Molly."

"Doc says I can't take that medicine any more. He told me if I get relyin' on it you'll never forgive him."

Doc interrupted. "If Pearl's too much for you, maybe Nancy can take her couple 'a days. I think you ought to be okay by yourself before long."

Tom gulped. "Sure she's ready?"

"Of course." Doc prayed as he spoke. Asking God for enough faith in her she'd sense it in his voice. "Don't worry, Tom. She's stronger than you think. She'll be fine." He winked at Molly. "Won't you?"

She reached for his hand and held it, wishing he'd stay. Something in his eyes was saying she had nothing to fear. She waited, perhaps, for him to say it aloud and make it come true. Tears welled as she watched him back away, her eyes seeking more.

But he's a doctor, and he should know. That simple idea keeping her sure enough to stay downstairs, no matter how Tom and Nancy watched. Even though she was weak and shaky, she ate dinner with them and after, told Pearl the story of The Three Bears.

Later that afternoon, she grew tired, went to the front room and had just settled in her chair when Clint burst in, shouting. "Ma. You're back!"

He peered into her face. "You're gettin' well, Ma. I can tell."

"Clint can tell I'm gettin' well. That's a rhyme, Clint. You gonna be a poet someday." She spread her arms and he fell into them, laughing.

Chapter 4

Autumn, 2004

After talking with the doctor, Molly made up her mind about two things. First, she was going to be nice to Tom. Next, she'd be a better mother. That meant no more hiding in her room. Nancy Foster wasn't going to invade her home again, or take her daughter hostage.

That was reason enough for Molly to insist that Pearl stay with her instead of going with Tom on the drive to town. She watched warily as he loaded Nancy's belongings into the back of the buggy. "Doc didn't say she had to go, Tom," she argued. "Thursday's Pearl's birthday, I want her here."

"No. Auntie don't go." Pearl whined.

Molly watched Tom cautiously, knowing he didn't want her alone with Pearl.

"How about I take her for the ride and bring her back?" He offered.

Face resolved, Molly clutched the child against her hip. "She stays here. That's it."

With his eyes flashing anger, she watched Tom whisper to Nancy, but Nancy didn't respond. Just bit her lip, and shifted her eyes, acting for all the world like someone headed for a funeral.

Molly forced a nervous laugh. "We'll be fine. You get on now. Ya hear?"

Happy and scared at once, she watched the buggy disappear, took a deep breath, straightened her shoulders and set Pearl on the porch. "Now we can start over, Sweetie" she said.

Getting rid of the whore had been the first step, now, to distract Pearl.

"Hey Pearl, where's Puffy?" She began. "Let's get that kitty a saucer of milk." Then we'll play with Dolly."

As she ushered Pearl into the living room, Molly's thoughts were frantic.

"Lordy, I'm glad Pearl's here," she breathed. "I'd be scairt' to death alone, I'm so clenched up."

She leaned back on the couch and tried to relax. Talking to herself, the way Doc told her. Remembering it's the medicine that's jangled her nerves and not something she was 'feared of. Consciously, she watched her breathing. Just like Doc said. "Slow and easy, 'til it loosens up."

Pearl sat at her feet, making a doll house out of a wooden crate. And Molly tried to focus attention on her, just as a mother ought. Surprised to see how much her girl had grown and how much she looked like Tom with big hands and feet and those stocky Foster legs. She believed it was good the girl was large. It might come in handy for her one day, she thought. Size can get a woman the respect she deserves.

Molly lifted her feet onto the couch and stretched out, pulling a long gray skirt over her shoes. "I gotta make it this time," she muttered. "I gotta."

So many things she almost lost, on account of the spell. Of all, Molly reckoned, she'd miss Tom most. He was the first person ever cared for her…maybe the only one.

If he didn't mix caring with meddling, it would be nigh on to perfect. Because at times, Tom could make her wish he'd go off somewhere and never come back.

When they first married, she'd feared him. She used to jump back, thinking he'd hit her when she did something he didn't like. It seemed to Molly a man as big as Tom Foster was free to hit anyone he wanted. 'Cept he never did. He didn't even threaten.

Lord knows I've tested him, she thought, pushed him far as a man'll go. When I can't stop the raging, seems like he ought to. The way Dad did with Ma. Smack me across the face with the flat of his hand.

55

She pulled her knees to her chest, hugging them, considering. But hitting didn't stop me as a kid. So don't reckon it will now. Nothing will. Part of me keeps on raging, no matter what. With a toss of her head, she managed a grim smile. Damned if Tom don't tolerate it better'n I do.

Often, she wondered why he hadn't left her for a better woman. A pretty one in a nice dress, hair pulled up just so, like Emma Teeter's. One that'll lift her chin and flutter her eyelashes when she talks, and never get riled. But since the day they met, she'd never known him to as much as look at one.

'Cause he's watching me all the time, she recalled. I never look up but what he's looking at me. Ain't figured out if it makes me glad, or like telling him to mind his own damn business, to go find something else to look at. Molly reached for her braid, pulled it forward and began to let her hair down. Angry as she'd get with him, she knew in her heart there wasn't one thing she hated him for that didn't disappear the minute he touched her.

She closed her eyes, remembering. There's nothing in the world feels better'n them work roughened hands, movin' on bare skin, scratchy and soft at the same time, bringing on the magic...when everything inside turns liquid, and the hands and the skin can't get enough of each other. And she'd start going wild. But when it was over, face hot, her heart in the pit of her stomach; she'd reach for the sheet. To hide.

How come I make such a damn fool of myself? She wondered. Wish I could just lie there, like I'm s'posed to. Someday he's gonna git up and walk off. It makes me feel like a goddam whore.

Pearl called out, interrupting her thoughts. "Ma. Lookie my house." Molly stood and went to her side.

Poor Pearl, she thought. She had to be a girl. Same as Tom did to me, and Dad did to Ma, some man's gonna come along and show her his hands. And she kin stop being Pearl Foster. Then, have to change her name and belong to him. Just like a horse.

Tom and his mare trotted up the lane, as, arms full of wildflowers, Molly and Pearl stood by the road. He stopped and they climbed into the buggy for the short ride back to the house. Tom didn't speak, keeping his eyes away from her, holding back tears. Molly took his hand in hers and squeezed it. "Everything's gonna be okay," she promised. "Just wait and see."

⁓୭

A soft breeze fluttered the leaves of the back yard trees, loosening yellowed leaves to drift lazily into baskets of apples set on the grass beneath. Molly sat with Pearl on the porch, peeling the fruit for canning, when she looked up to spot Lillian riding up the lane on a beautiful prancing stallion. Dressed in a brown riding costume and matching hat, Lillian had stopped to show her new horse to Tom.

"Come here, Pearl. Molly called. "Lookie there at your Auntie! Just the sight of her takes my breath. I never thought I'd see my Lillian grow up to be so pretty."

When she wasn't upset with her, Molly's feelings about Lillian were proudly maternal. "After all," she said often, "It was me that raised her."

When their ma died, Lillian was ten years old. Molly, thirteen, had just finished eighth grade and since there was no way they'd stay with their Dad, Molly went begging folks for help 'til she finally persuaded the Elliott's to take them in.

Elliott's ran a boarding house, and the girls got room and board in exchange for Molly's work. Later, she got on at the hotel doing laundry and cleaning for spending money, so Lillian could finish school.

They'd been living at Elliott's only a few months when Doctor Davis came by to tell them their father was dead. "They found him at his house. He's been lying there a few days." Doc told them. "I'm not sure what he died of, must have been some kind of sickness. Do you want to set up a funeral for him?"

"Hell no. Let the county take care of him," Molly answered. She wasn't sorry to have him gone. She didn't even ask where they buried him.

They lived in their small room four years, Lillian studying and Molly encouraging her to get good grades. After she finished eighth grade, Molly made arrangements for her to stay with kin of the Elliot's in Harperville and go to high school, working extra hours to pay her expenses.

After she left, we drifted apart, Molly recollected. I sent her money, even in summer, so she could stay in Harperville and be with her boyfriend. It was worrisome, her getting married so soon after graduation and havin' the girls so fast. Left no time for me, that's for sure.

Lillian's husband, Alvin, came from a family of means, and Molly knew her sister would have a good life and she was glad for it. She'd been even happier when Alvin's folks bought the General Store in Lowell for the young couple. But since Lillian came back, Molly didn't see her much. She wished things could change so they could be together more.

"Look at her, Pearl. It was me helped her turn out so grand. Ain't one of them Fosters ever gonna rise to her level. Especially Nancy. Let's go greet your Aunt Lilly."

Lillian rode up, tightening the reins as the spirited horse pranced to a stop. "The revival I told you about is starting Sunday," she said. "Still think you might come?"

Heart swelling with pride, Molly looked to Tom. "You want to go?"

Tom was skeptical. "Reckon we kin. If you want to."

"We'll go. Is it at your church?"

"Yes. Come early and maybe you can meet Mr. Sunday."

"I can't see why not."

"Good. And Molly, I brought along new dresses for you and Pearl, and some britches for Clinton. He got shoes?"

Tom laughed. "No. He won't wear 'em 'til snow falls."

Lillian flushed and looked away. "Well, if you bring him into the store, I'll give him some new ones. Make sure they fit."

At the slap of Lillian's words, Molly reeled back. The same as if her dad had hit her with the back of his hand, the sting of hot blood, rushing to her face; the rage coming on.

All I done and Lillian's ashamed of us, she fumed. "We can pay for shoes, Lillian," she said. "And if the dress don't fit, I have another."

Just you wait, Lillian" she thought. I'll show you what shame is!

Sensing an oncoming storm, Tom interrupted. "Why thank ye, Lillian. That's right nice of you."

Molly stood stiffly, staring at her sister, grinding her teeth into the inside of her cheek, feeling the warm salty blood ooze onto her tongue. "You can go now, Lillian," she said. "Reckon you'll see me Sunday." She turned on her heel and tramped to the house.

True to her word, they drove up to the church in the shabby old buggy on Sunday afternoon, with Molly perched up front on the bench beside Tom, looking like someone who meant to be seen. In a patched, faded dress and an out of-shape hat, Molly's unkempt hair was loose, cascading over Pearl, who sat on her lap. Clint was barefoot. Molly had hidden his new shoes under her bed, so he couldn't wear them, and hadn't bothered to change Pearl into her dress up clothes. Only Tom seemed to be dressed appropriately, wearing the suit he bought for his wedding almost ten years ago.

Lillian's heart sank. She'd been chatting with Emma Teeter and knew from the lull in the conversation Molly had arrived. She saw Pastor Formby look to Molly, and back to her, as if for asking for advice. Face flaming, she lowered her eyes.

Molly walked up, ignoring her sister. "Howdy, Emma." she began. "How you been?" It looked like Emma had a new dress, and Molly wanted to have a little fun over it; at the same time, shaming Lillian. She began to smooth the back of Emma's skirt with her hand. "Looks like a bird must 'a rested on your chair and took a shit. You sat right in it." She cackled. "Least I think it was a bird. Sure ain't gonna say you did it."

Lillian gasped, covering her mouth with her hand. The assembled congregation looking anywhere but at Lillian, as if they hadn't seen anything unusual; keeping quiet though, in case Molly said something they didn't want to miss. Emma was the only one not paying attention, and stood, twisting her neck, trying to see what was on the back of her skirt.

In an attempt to defuse a tense situation, Pastor Formby reached out to Molly and offered his hand. Tall and bony, the pastor's large crooked nose set to one side of a pock marked face. Almost bald, he had swept a few long strands of hair over the top of his scalp with a greasy pomade, unaware the wind had blown the hair straight out, making him look like a clown from the circus.

James Formby knew he was ugly. As a boy, he'd been taunted and teased for it. Now he accepted it as his cross. It was a gift from the Lord and thus, a blessing. He was grateful it had made him humble. Because of his looks, he'd learned to despise himself and to focus his attention from his own conceits onto suffering sinners, like Molly.

"Why Mrs. Foster" he gushed. "Welcome. Mrs. Miller has mentioned you often."

Molly jerked back and stared at him before answering. "For what?"

"That you've been ill. And all of us at First Baptist have been praying for you."

"What'll that do for mĕ, Pastor?"

"Why, look at you! You're up and smiling and at church to learn of the Lord. That's a miracle." He looked skyward. "Praise God."

Jutting her chin upward, Molly backed away. "Doc Davis got me well, Preacher. Not your prayers."

"Of course," he answered. "The Lord works in many ways, certainly through the good doctor. He's a man of prayer, too."

Molly paused, took a deep breath and unclenched her fists. He was making her fume, and she didn't want to lose control. She had him in her trap and she wanted to slam it down on him. *Son of a bitch thinks he's gonna make a fool out 'a me. Well, he's got a surprise coming.* She cleared her throat and began to speak, in a voice loud, clear, and meant to reach everyone present. "I had someone pray for me once, Pastor. It was a beggar woman. She prayed I'd be ruined."

"Oh no, Mrs. Foster, it's nothing like that."

Her eyes flashed. "Shut up and let me finish. Lillian tells me you and her church friends have decided that the gypsy's prayers were good ones. That they ruin't me. Now you're telling me you and these folks are praying for me, too? Well, I ain't sure I like it."

She turned to the assembled parishioners, and, lifting her arms, spread her palms skyward. "Here I am, Molly Foster, living at the mercy of somebody else's prayers. Gonna be mighty interesting to find out who's are most powerful, the gypsy's, or the preacher's."

She began to walk across the churchyard toward her family and the buggy. "Reckon we ought to go home. Tom. Leave the lot of 'em to their goddam prayers." She stopped, turned back, and glared at her sister. "Why don't you pray for Lillian?" She shouted. "And her goddam sin of pride?"

⤳◦

"Poor Lillian, You should 'a seen her face. She nearly fainted."

Emma Teeter was in Alice's living room early Monday morning, reporting Molly's latest escapade. She'd arrived the minute Warren walked out the door for work, delighted to find she was first to reach Alice.

Alice leaned forward, eager to hear. "I would have died, had I been in Lillian's shoes. What else did she do?

"Well, as they was walking off, Pastor went to Lillian to offer her comfort. He told her not to feel bad, that he knew Molly was troubled and that he forgave her."

Emma placed her hand on her bosom and gasped in dismay at what she was about to say. "Molly must 'a heard him. 'Cause she turned around and marched right up to him. Put her fist in his face."

"Oh my. Did she hit him?"

"No. She just shook it at him and hollered. Said, "Who the hell you think you are, forgiving me? For what? For tellin' you the truth? Did you expect me to stand out here with all of them," and she pointed at us, "and lie through my teeth? Tell you I'm gonna praise a God that's so mean he lets other folks decide what's gonna happen to me?'

Alice drew her breath against her teeth. "That's blasphemy."

"Don't I know it. But that don't mean nothin' to Molly. She was laughing at us and called us a bunch of hypocrites. She said 'When I get to Hell, I'm gonna stand at the door and welcome every one of you. And I reckon Satan's got a pit for your ugly little preacher up front so he can go on preachin'. The lot of you, spending forever, having to listen to his bullshit.' Then she howled like a banshee. She said she reckoned that's why they call it Hell."

"My oh my. Poor Tom. What did he do?"

"Just put his arm around her shoulder and left. Them ragged little kids following. As they got to the buggy, something else happened you ain't gonna believe."

"It can't be harder to believe than what you've just said. C'mon. Tell me."

"Well. Doc Davis was standing at the back of the crowd, listening. And went after Molly and put his arms around her. He held on to her, swaying from side to side, hugging her, laughing so hard, she and Tom started laughing, too. 'Molly,' he told her. 'I want you to know I've never seen you better.'"

"What did he mean by that?"

"I can't imagine. Reckon he's not as religious as he pretends. Maybe he's actually one of them atheists, going to church to impress us."

"Well, I wonder too. It makes no sense." Alice stopped and looked through the window. "Speaking of atheists, I wonder if Nancy knows about this."

"She ain't atheist. She meets with them United Souls," Emma snorted. "If there's any difference. Speaking of Nancy, what's goin' on with that boy 'a hers?"

"Did you hear about his carrying on when Nancy was out to Tom's? It was all over town, Ben having women at the house. Heard Tom came and put a stop to it."

"He did. Of course, Nancy acts like she doesn't know."

"Maybe she don't care. Who knows what Nancy Foster thinks? Nobody ever knows what she's up to."

⌒◯

In her house next door, Nancy sat at her kitchen table, having a late breakfast with Ben. He'd stopped at the house to let her know that Ira White was fixing to make an offer on Tom's farm, and that he'd been asked to ride out and see if Tom was interested.

Nancy slammed her fist on the table, spilling her coffee. "What makes him think Tom will sell?"

"Cause the bank let him know Tom's behind in his payments. Iry's got a deal with the banker. He knows they all have payments due when harvest is done, and he likes the bank to give him notice of who might be in trouble."

Nancy pulled to her feet and went to the stove for more coffee. "They ain't got a right to do that. Do they?"

"I don't know. Iry's fer sure gonna get Pat Donovan's place, and maybe George Berky's. Pat's close to foreclosure, and he's sitting on some mighty good land."

"Pat's drunk away everything. I pity his wife and them kids. What'll they do?"

"Iry has a good idea for her. She's good about keeping money coming in, keeps some hens, sells eggs, and chickens. He wants to set her up with some more birds, and go into shares with her. Iry says there's always a market for fresh eggs and fryers."

"I'm glad Iry wants to give her a chance. But I don't want you talking to Tom. Not yet." She sat down again, pushing her plate to the center of the table.

"I have to Ma. Didn't tell you Iry wants me to get Uncle John and his boys to work some farms for him, did I?"

"No, you didn't. Reckon that would be good for John. Iry's good to his farmers that do a good job."

"I reckon. But what do you think I otta do about Uncle Tom?"

"What you have to, I reckon. Just be sure you don't make him mad."

After Ben left, Nancy went upstairs, put on her new brown and gold plaid dress and a matching hat and set out for the bank. She was going to give owner, Bill Fenton, a piece of her mind. And she wanted to look good doing it.

When she walked in, Warren Babbitt was at a desk in front of Bill's office, shuffling papers. "I came to see Bill," she said.

"He's busy. He can't see anyone."

"He'll see me. Are you gonna tell him I'm here or do I walk in?"

Warren walked to the closed door of Bill's office, and stood in front of it. "I'm not sure he'll talk to you." Putting her head down, Nancy brushed him aside, opened the door and stepped into the room, slamming the door behind her.

As if her noisy entrance were an ordinary occurrence, Bill took his feet off the desk with a wide grin. "Why Nancy, please sit down. What can I do for you?"

She glanced around the room, at its dark paneled walls clustered with large portraits of Bill and his prized Arabian thoroughbreds. A small resemblance of his daughter and a smaller one of his wife were on his desk.

"I'll stand," she said. "To start, I want you to get out Tom's records. Let me know how much he owes."

"You know I can't do that. Our client accounts are confidential."

"Then I want you to tell me how Iry White knows that Tom, Pat Donavon and George Berky are close to foreclosure."

Bill loosened his bow tie and unbuttoned the neck of a stiffly starched shirt. "I'm not aware he knows that, Nancy."

"I am. Reckon that leaves me with two choices. I can find out from you, or I can find out from Iry. Which one you think's gonna tell me most?"

"Why, I think I can help you, Nancy. But it's not exactly on the up and up to do so. You know that." He laughed nervously.

Nancy grinned. "A lot of things in this town ain't on the up and up. Are they Bill? And it probably won't help you or Iry if folks start learning what they are."

"I'm not sure what you mean."

"That's okay Bill" she grinned. "I am."

Bill rose and walked to a tall cabinet by the window to remove a large ledger. "Okay, Nancy. What do you want to know?"

"How bad is it?"

He opened the ledger thumbed through a few pages and stopped to read. "He owes me eight hundred dollars."

"How much is due?"

"His payment this year is four hundred, and he's behind a hundred for last year. We know he's had problems with his wife's being sick. And he owes the feed mill. Quite frankly, I can't see how he's going to catch up."

"He could, if you gave him an extension. Right?"

"Why yes. But we..."

Nancy's voice was firm. "I think you should give him an extension, Bill."

"But there's interest on the loan."

"If it's going to break the bank, I'll cover it. But it's my guess you'd rather work out something agreeable to Tom."

"Okay, Nancy." He sighed. "Have it your way. And what do you expect me to say to Mr. White?"

"Just tell him I said you ain't foreclosing on Tom's farm. I think he'll understand that. Don't you?"

"I think so. But don't you think he's gonna be upset at Ben, knowing he had to be the one who told you this?"

She leaned back and whooped, clapping her hands. "Only if you tell him, Bill. Only if you tell him."

Still rattled, Bill slumped into his chair and watched Nancy leave. Knew damn well he wasn't going to lose any money on Tom. Tom would pay off his debt and was good for the interest. He shook his head. No, Tom wasn't a problem, Ira was.

Ira wanted Tom's land. And how in Hell was he going to tell his biggest depositor he couldn't have it without tripping over his tongue?

When Ira dropped by the bank later that afternoon, Bill called him into his office and broke the news. "What do you mean, Tom can't sell?' Ira was livid. He didn't like having made plans on false information. Warren told him just last week that Tom couldn't make his payment. "I've got a guy on his way out there now to make him a deal. We get Tom's farm and we got a six-hundred-and-forty acre section of good land all in one piece. What happened?"

"I'm not sure. But under the present circumstance, we can't foreclose. He's making payments."

"Where the hell did he get the money? He'd have to sell all his cattle to come up with that much. You better not be letting him off the hook."

Bill gulped. He was going to have to play the ace, knowing damn well that Ira couldn't stand losing. "You know that sister of his? Nancy? She used to work for your mother. I think her son Ben is working for you now. Is that right?"

Stunned, Ira leaned back and rubbed his chin. "She has enough money to pay it off?"

Bill nodded. Didn't think he owed further explanation, or that Ira expected it.

Ira got up and walked out, sputtering. "The little shit .Got me again!" He slammed a fist into his other hand, wondering if Ben had got to Tom. If the big man had let him leave in one piece.

⌒♡

When Molly answered Ben's knock, her face whitened. Tom's in the barn," she snarled; then slammed the door.

Ben grinned, muttering. "Old bitch. Reckon I don't want to talk to her either." He headed to the barn, stopping at the hitching post to tie his horse and met Clint, just home from school.

Shocked to see him, Clint stared nervously a moment, then took off running, trying to get past him to the house.

"Hey, you little shit. Ain't you gonna say hello to your cousin?" Ben grabbed him and lifted him high over his head.

"Put me down. I'll tell Dad."

Ben lowered him to the ground, still holding on. "Thought we agreed you ain't never gonna tell anyone on me, Clinton. Haven't changed your mind, have ye?

Clint began to whimper. "No. I won't say anything, Ben. I didn't mean it. Let me go."

Ben laughed, set him back on the ground, and gave him a swat on the seat of his pants. "Didn't think you would, cousin. You go on now."

Clinton tore into the house and dashed to his room. Told Ma he had a headache.

Don't know what I'm gonna do, he thought. Lordy, I hate him!! Reckon I have to wait 'til I grow up, I'll get a gun. Shoot the son of a bitch.

He sat on his bed, leaned against the black iron headboard and remembered the day he came upstairs and found Ben in Aunt Nancy's attic. And why he just couldn't wait 'til he got old enough to get even.

He and Dad had gone to town. Dad had business at the bank, so he was left at Auntie's to wait. Ma'd told him so many bad things about Aunt Nancy; he tried to keep away from her. He sure was curious, though and thought he'd go upstairs and have a look around. See what kind of a house a whore lived in.

He came across the stairs to the attic, climbed it, and when he reached the top, found Ben sitting on an old trunk, playing with a pistol.

"Wow. Ben. Where'd you get that? Know how to shoot it?"

Shit, thought Ben. He'd have to see me. Can't let him tell or Ma's gonna ask where I got it. "Sure do." He pointed the gun at Clint's head. "All I gotta do is pull the trigger."

Clinton jumped back. "No. You ain't spose 'ta play with a gun, Ben, you ain't old enough. I'm gonna tell your Ma."

Ben grabbed him by the collar and pulled him close. "You ain't telling nobody nothing. You get that little boy?"

Clinton struggled to get away. "Let me go. You bastard."

"Where you hear a word like that?"

"Ma. Said you was a bastard."

Ben let go. "Oh she did? And what else did that crazy Ma of yours have to say about me?"

"Aunt Nancy's a whore and you're a devil child."

Ben walked slowly to Clinton's side and stood over him, grinning. "You know what a devil child can do to a dumb little boy, Clint?" He pushed Clint into the wall and put a hand on his jaw, forcing his mouth open.

"A devil child can take a gun and put it down a brat's mouth." He shoved the gun into Clinton's mouth. "You hear me?"

Eyes wide with terror, Clint nodded. He heard a click as Ben cocked the gun.

"And I want to tell you something else." He pulled the gun out of Clint's mouth and lifted it high. "When a dumb little boy tells on a devil, that devil will take his gun, ride out in the country and shoot his Mama"

Ben paused, sneering. "Not unless that boy does what the devil tells him to. And I'm telling you to take off your pants and bend over this trunk."

He was split in two pieces. From the crack of his butt right up his back. Nothing he remembered had hurt like this. And when Ben stopped moving, stood up, and left, he stayed where he was on top of the trunk. He wasn't going to take the chance of seeing Ben's eyes again as long as he lived.

Sure Ben was gone; he reached for his underpants, using them to dry blood from his legs. Later, he'd throw them in the river, not wanting Ma to ask any questions.

For days, he couldn't speak. He made his folks sick with worry, wondering why. They figured he must have laryngitis, that the sickness must 'a taken his voice. Except that laryngitis usually follows a cold. And Clint hadn't had one since winter.

"But I can yell now." Clint punched his fist into the pillow and shouted. "And I hate you Ben. I hate him. I hate him. I hate him."

Suddenly, Ma was at the door. Came to the bed and began rubbing his shoulders. "That's okay, Clinton," she said. I hate him too. Ain't nothin' but a goddam bastard."

❦

Ben wasn't doing any better with Tom then he did with Molly.

"Just get on home before I lose my temper at you, Ben," Tom roared. "You tell Iry I ain't selling. And that's final."

Ben stepped back, palms spread, giving that disarming grin that could win over almost everybody, but was wasted on Tom Foster. Ben wasn't going to argue. "Hey. It's nothing. Iry just wanted me to see if you were willing to talk to him."

Late that evening, Ben long gone, Tom got out his records and went to the table, trying to figure out how much he was going to be able to put toward the payment.

"Reckon I've been puttin' off facing this," he told Molly. "Too 'feared to look and see how bad it is."

He slouched in the chair, rubbing his chin with the back of his left hand, making doodles on the paper with the other. "Thinkin' marks," he called them. There wasn't no way the numbers were gonna add up to enough. He had to come up with something. He reckoned he'd have to sell some of his cattle, then, might be able to pay part of it. Next, see how good he'd be at convincing the bank to extend his loan.

At the opposite end of the table, Clint was doing arithmetic, and Tom couldn't help but notice the boy was doing sums he couldn't start to handle. He swelled with pride. Boy's smart all right. Sure is behavin' better since school started. It probably helps not spending much time with his Ma.

He looked across the room at Molly, thinking how she'd changed, too. She was over the spell it seemed. Still doing a lot of raging though. And too much rage could bring on a spell. He was doing everything he could to keep her settled.

It had been good having her treat him nice. He grinned, remembering the pie she'd made yesterday. Not a very good pie, but leastways, she was trying. And she'd been coming to him now and then, giving him a touch on the back, letting him know she wasn't pulling away. Made bedtime a lot sweeter, not having to win her over.

He watched as she sat sewing by the kerosene lamp, its soft yellow glow falling across her hands and onto Pearl's little face as she sat at Molly's feet. Reckon the way she is with Pearl is the best change of all, Tom thought. Just hope she don't poison my girl's thinkin' the way she's done Clint's. He shook his head, puzzling over what it can be the boy has against Ben. But knew in his heart, Molly'd probably been behind it.

Aware he was staring; Molly looked up and put away the mending. She reminded herself she wasn't going to let that look of his get her riled. Tom was Tom, and she was trying to take him as he was. They'd had fun this week, but he wasn't much fun now. He looked pretty glum going over his books. A smile touched her lips. She knew how to cheer him. "Hey, Tom," she said. "What's say we put these kids to bed and turn in early? Play around?"

"Later Molly" he said as he began to clear the table. "You about done, Clint?" he asked. It's getting late."

Loins swelling with anticipation, Tom thought of the pleasure that waited upstairs

There are times, he reflected, when being married to Molly put him in positions most men wouldn't put up with. Like having to take that long walk to the buggy in front of most of Lowell, or to hear her rage come from the lips of his boy. When he had to walk on eggshells, never guessing what she'd do next.

Yet, there was something about Molly that would turn a lot of men green with envy. And when she was offering it to him the way she was now, he was going to hurry to enjoy it.

Chapter 5

Spring 1909

S he starts out in Montana under a thick skin of ice, moving north, turns east at Fort Benton, meanders through the Dakotas and along Iowa's western border, taking on every bit of rain, mud and melted snow in her path, and arriving in Kansas City sometime in March.

Then, like a giant anaconda, the mighty river slithers her swollen belly across Missouri, leaving a bit of the Rocky Mountains and a whole lot of Nebraska on her low lying bottoms before dumping into the Mississippi at the Illinois state line.

In Lowell, spring belongs to her, when everything that happens depends on the river. If she's calm, life goes on as usual. If she floods, all hell breaks loose. Folks lose their homes, their property, even their lives in her rushing waters. Schools and churches close, as all over Hamilton County, people stay indoors and wait for the river. Praying she'll drop. Instead of rise.

"Lordy. Sure is something. No wonder the Indians called her the Big Muddy."

Clint stood with Red Donavon on a hill overlooking the river, now a slow-moving valley-wide lake, carrying uprooted trees, dead animals and hapless buildings like stately ships on their way to sea.

"It looks like a sliding bed of clay." Red answered.

"Just glad we don't live close to it as some. Looks like that shack comin' down might 'a been someone's house."

"Wow! I wonder if anybody drowned. Aren't you glad we learnt to swim last summer? We could get out if the water got to us."

"Dad says not. He says the river has currents that'll drag you under, 'specially when it's high." Clint grinned and gave Red a soft punch to the shoulder. "Sure hope you ain't told nobody 'bout our swimming hole. The old man would raise hell."

Red laughed and punched him back. "I wonder how deep that hole is now. It looks like it's somewhere out in the middle." He pointed downstream. "And will you look at the bridge? It seems to be risin' out of the water. Sure I'd love to be standin' on it. Should we go?"

"Nossir. 'Fraid I'd fall in."

"You could stay up, Foster. I was the one taught you how to swim."

"Only 'cause you had a smart pupil," Clint retorted, recalling how fast he'd learned that day he finally dared to jump in. "I might be able to swim it. But that water's cold. Besides, how'd we get out there?"

"The water's shallow. It wouldn't cover me boots."

"All the same, I ain't tryin'. Ask me next year when I'm older."

"Next year you'll be sayin' you're too old."

"Next year, we'll be in high school. By then you oughta have some sense."

Red grabbed Clint's arm and held it behind his back. "You keep forgettin I just turned fourteen. Who are you to be talkin' about sense?"

Clint laughed and pulled away. In a month he'd have his birthday. Hoped he'd mature like his friend, with a voice deep and strong. Seemed his own voice sounded like a girl's compared to Reds. He hated the way he'd lose pitch, when a word dropped out and slid around.

Red seemed older in a lot of other ways, too. Since his dad died three years ago, Red had to help his Ma. Took eggs and chickens to town and picked up supplies all by himself. And was the one who dealt with Ira White on the family chicken raising business.

Best thing was Red could spend money anyway he wanted. Soon as he started smoking, he'd buy tobacco for Clint when he bought his own.

"Since you're my partner in crime," Red joked, "It's up to me to be buyin' if I want a buddy to be smokin' it with. Tom sure ain't gonna give you money for tobacco."

Shortly after Red's dad lost the farm and Uncle John took over running it, Red found poor Pat froze to death just outside the barn door, an empty whiskey bottle gripped tightly in his right hand. "Must 'a fell down drunk and went to sleep," Red told Clint. "Can't say I miss him. It's better now, with Ma, the girls and me. We've got a little money to keep, 'stead of it going for booze."

"Can't blame you fer that. I figger his drunks was like Ma's spells. The whole family havin' to change their ways on account of 'em. 'Cause of her, I hate seein' spring come. She gets so restless."

"How's she now?"

"Shut in her room. Lays up there with the door locked, dreaming of getting even with everybody."

Red laughed. "She out to get even with you?"

"Yessir. When I was a kid I used to pay attention to her. Now I walk off if she rails at me. Says I desert her."

"Who looks after her?"

"We all do. Pearl's better at it 'n I am." Clint shook his head. "Just don't figger Dad, how he keeps puttin' up with her. Says she can't help it. That she's like a little kid who can't control her temper."

"How does he know she can't?"

"Because she tries. Least she says she does. He thinks she doesn't want to be mean or mad, but it just comes of her."

"Do ya think he's right?"

"Maybe. Doc explained it that way once. Ain't sure. Sometimes she cries and says she's sorry. Begs us to forgive her. But I reckon if she feels bad as she claims, she wouldn't do it again."

"She looked okay last time I saw her."

"That's 'cause you ain't seen her lately. Nobody sees much of Ma. She don't want to go nowhere and we don't want her goin'. She can put on a show to make you look for a hole to hide. And just when you git used to her being okay, she changes. Reckon it's the way she's gonna be. Whether she can help it or not."

Red remembered his father, how good he was sober and how awful when he drank. "Sounds like she's into the whiskey."

"No, she thinks whiskey's fer sinners and trash. But the medicine Doc gives her makes her drunk."

"Why'd he give her that?"

Clint shrugged. "To calm her. It's hard on everyone when she's wild. We can't wait 'til Doc gives her some so we get a break. Dad gits upset, but I don't pay much attention to her any more. Reckon if she wants to act up or kill herself I can't do nothin' to stop her. Don't take it serious as I used to. Reckon I'm tired worrying."

"Your Dad's been good. Gives you time off."

"You jist reminded me I better git back. There's chores waiting." The boys took one last look at the river and began to walk home. "Dad and I made a bargain when he and Uncle John started working these farms. I help without bitchin' and he gives me time off."

"With your Uncle John working Ben and Junior every day of the week, I'd like to know how you got him to agree to that."

Clint shrugged. "On account 'a Ma, I guess. He don't want me spending time around her when she's riled. So I won't hear her cussin' about folks, especially Aunt Nancy. Thinks it's good I have some fun. That I spend time with you. Reckon that's 'cause he ain't got no idea how ornery you are."

Red laughed. "It's a good thing he didn't take you out 'a school."

"Allow that's true. I've learnt to keep my mouth shut about education. He likes me to take books home for Ma and talk to her about what I've learned. It settles her. She's the one thinks I otta to go to high school. He'd rather I help farm."

Red whooped. "And we're going next year! Ma said I could. Is it for sure Tom's letting your go?"

"Yep. Said he'd get me a riding horse so I can git home in time to do chores. Havin' my own horse will make helpin' out worth it. Glad we got a high school in Lowell now."

"Fer sure. And Miz Peters says we can take Geometry. That otta be fun."

"And history. I want to learn more about them pyramids. Hey, I gotta get back. Don't want to be in trouble with T.F. Be a long time 'fore I git as big as him."

Red chuckled. The boys had taken to calling their parents by their first names lately, their way of letting each other know they didn't consider them very important. But both knew damn well they still had to live by their rules.

"Sure you don't want to go to the bridge?"

"Hell no. I want to live long enough to go to high school."

"Then I'll beat ya to my house. Let's go."

They raced down the road, splattering mud and water as they ran, laughing.

After Red went in, Clint walked home, whistling. Always felt good after being with Red. Reckoned he could talk to his buddy about anything. Even the things Dad made him swear to keep secret. Red wouldn't tell, and never made him feel bad, even if he cried. Red knows what it's like livin' with someone crazy, Clint figured. Knows how it feels havin' folks make fun of you, and to be waiting for somethin' shameful to happen. Red'd had it worse'n he did. Old Pat was mean with fists, Ma, with words.

Clint hoped she was still in her bedroom, because she'd been pretty hard on him lately.

When he walked into the kitchen, Pearl was starting supper. "How's Ma?" He asked.

Pearl turned from the stove where she was lighting a fire. "Same. Think you can help me fix somethin' fer supper, lazy brother?"

"Sure, Pearl. Let me fix that fire." He stirred the coals and put a few sticks on top, reminding himself to go to the woodpile for more before it got dark. "Good thing I'm here. You might 'a burnt yourself."

Pearl laughed. "And so might you. Just 'cause you're older don't make you smarter." She went to the cupboard and reached for plates to set the table. Dressed like a boy, she looked like one, in her striped overalls and blue chambray shirt. Folks had started calling her "Tom's boy" lately, instead of "tomboy" the way they used to and Clint understood she and Tom were crazy about each other, that she loved it when everyone noticed.

Clint dumped a jar of canned chicken into a pan and set it on a back burner, feeling lucky he had Pearl for a sister. Didn't know how he and Dad could get along without her.

Now she was almost as tall as he was. He looked across the kitchen at her stout body, wondered if she outweighed him. Folks always noticed how different they were, her with them thick dark curls and his hair straight as a stick. Lotsa folks say she looks like Dad. And me? Like Ma. Dammit.

He reached into the bowl of boiled potatoes, took one out and began eating it. "You help Dad today?" He asked.

"Just threw down hay for the cows. He wanted me to watch her." Pearl rolled her eyes upward and pointed to the ceiling.

"She need anything?"

"No. But she threw a book at me when I went up to ask. Darn you, Clinton. Why don't you quit bringin' her books?"

Clint picked up a dishtowel and threw it in her face. "Hell, no. Gotta give her something to keep you goin' straight."

"She does like 'em. Least when she's readin' she don't raise Cain."

"You got that right. C'mon sister, git that cornbread outa the oven 'fore it burns up."

They called Tom. Mealtime was fun when Ma stayed quiet.

As soon as he finished eating, Tom pushed his plate back, leaned his elbows onto the table and turned to Clint. "You boys see the river?"

"We did. It's high. Ever been this high before?"

"One year we had water almost to the barn. It's dropping now. Go look for the water line on the marsh trees and you can tell it's down almost half a foot."

"Just so it don't fill up again in Ioway."

"I reckon. But the skies seem to be clearing. Maybe it's over. The south fields are flooded, but we didn't get no damage. Glad you got the cows in the barn and we had enough to feed 'em."

"You gonna be raising more cattle for Iry this year?"

"I think so, Clint. Don't want you two to be tellin' anyone about this, but me and John are thinking of buying out another farm."

"Won't that cost a lot?"

"Well, Nancy wants in on it. Reckon we can share with her easy as we do with Iry."

Clint nodded. Wasn't sure he liked the idea of working more land. Dad was making money now, but this will mean hours in the fields at a time when he was looking forward to spending time in town with Red. Maybe they'd go to the restaurant, or play baseball with new friends they'd make at high school. "You gonna do this fer sure, Dad?"

"Almost sure. George Berky has to sell or the farm goes to the bank. He don't want Iry getting his land."

"What'll happen to the Berkys?"

"George thought he could work at the saw mill. The owner's kin of his wife. Says the boys could work too."

Clint sighed. He didn't care much for the Berky boys. They took all Miz Peters time, her having to teach them when she could have been doing things with him and Red. The little girl, Dorothy, was smart, though. Did the arithmetic for the two who stayed at school. Sometimes, just to get it over with. "Otherwise," she told Clint. "They'll be on it 'til they're forty."

Clint rose to clear the table. "Don't reckon I'll miss them much if they quit school." He looked through the window. "You're right, Dad. It's clearing. Sure hope the river goes down. I want to get back to school."

Someone was screaming, jolting Clint awake. Seemed like it was coming from the back porch. "Dammit it Ma, get back to bed," he grumbled, pulled the pillow over his head and turned over, hoping to get back to sleep.

Tom shouted from the bottom of the stairs, his voice sharp with urgency. "Clint, get down here. Right away!"

Clint stumbled out of bed and met Tom on the stairs.

"You know where Red is?" Tom asked.

"No. Left him at his house yesterday afternoon."

He stepped down to see Red's mother standing inside the kitchen door, a thick shawl tied around her shoulders, her blue eyes wide in an ashen face. "He came and left, Clint. Said you were goin' to the bridge."

With a sharp punch to his stomach, Clint slumped in a chair. "No. No. I told him not to." He looked up at Mrs. Donavon. "When?"

"About an hour or two before dark. I thought you'd be coming back here, so I went to bed. I figured he'd borrow a lantern and come on home. But when I woke up, he wasn't home." She lifted the shawl to her face and began to cry.

Clint felt he couldn't breathe, and fell to the floor, groaning. He could feel Dad's hand on his shoulder, and hear a voice from somewhere asking him to get up.

But he couldn't move. From deep in his belly, a sharp ache began to spread. He stiffened himself against Tom's hands, twisted his body and clenched his face. The pain increased, washing over him, and he began to cry out.

"No. Red, please. Don't drown, Red, please."

Tom reached down and picked him up, held him close, talking softly into his ear. "Don't cry, Clint. Hush, now. It can't be helped. Shhhh. Don't cry boy. Shhhh."

But the crying wouldn't stop. The pain was still inside, tearing parts of him away. He felt it move from his belly into his chest and wrap itself around his heart.

Not knowing what else to do, Tom carried him upstairs and put him on his bed. He tried talking, but Clint couldn't hear. All day and night he laid curled into himself, moaning. And nothing Tom did could make him stop.

Two days later, the water still high on the roads, Emily Peters rode up on her small black mare. She'd heard about Red from her brother Frank. He and Ben had been out looking at the floods and heard about Red. And how it had put a spell on Clint, just like one of Molly's. It wasn't safe to be out riding yet, but she had to get to Clinton.

And it was Emily who got him out of bed, to eat, and to stop crying.

Clint came to her soon as she walked into the room, welcoming her arms. At first, they held each other, crying. But after he seemed in better control, she tried to console him. But it seemed ordinary words had no effect. With all the pain held tight to his body, Emily knew she'd have to reach his soul. Without faith in anything outside the uncertain world he knew, it wouldn't be easy.

But Emily knew she might have a way to get him to get him back. With the thing he loved most, poetry. She lifted his chin. "He isn't dead, Clinton," she said softly." He is just away. Have you heard that before?"

Clint pulled back and looked in her face. "James Whitcomb Riley?"

Emily smiled. "Of course. He wrote it for us, Clint. For times like this." She reached into the large bag she'd dropped on the floor. "I brought you the poetry book. It's yours now. No one else at school seems to like it."

"Thank ye." He took the book and held it awkwardly. "Don't feel like reading right now."

"Of course not. It's for later."

Clint looked down, his cheeks burning, wondering if Miss Peters wouldn't think him strange if he told her the one thing he couldn't stop thinking since he heard about Red.

"Do you remember the poem? Stevenson, I think? Said in one of them verses. 'He is not dead-this friend-not dead?" It won't leave my mind."

He looked up hopefully. "You think it's 'cause he might still be alive? That they outta keep looking for him?"

Emily held his hands, her eyes, bright with tears, looking into his." He wrote another verse, Clint. It goes like this:

"Push gaily on, brave heart, the while
You travel forward mile by mile
He loiters with a backward smile,

Till you can overtake" (Verses Written in 1872 by Robert Louis Stevenson)

"What do you think it means, Clint?"

"That he's—he's in Heaven, maybe? Wants me to keep on without him?"

"I think so. And I, and your Dad, want you to get up and push on, just as Red would. No matter what happens."

"D'ya think he's somewhere waitin' for me? That I'll see him again?"

"I know it. He's waiting for me, too." She rose and motioned him to follow. "Come. We need to let your Dad know you're going to be okay. He's worried about you."

Tom was in the kitchen making soup, and the smell of it whetted Clint's appetite. He took the bowl Tom offered and plopped down at the table.

Emily pushed his chair in, and turned to Tom. "I'll take Clint to the services next week if you agree. If they find the body, there'll be a funeral. If not, they'll have a Memorial Mass at Saint Peter's."

"He can go. Just don't tell his mother. She don't want them kids anywhere near a Catholic Church. I'll come if I can." He slipped his hands on his son's shoulders.

"Funerals are hard, Clint," Tom said. "But they help you get over the hurting. Reckon we'll go into town tomorrow and get you a new suit of clothes."

⌒◌

"You can wear it for graduation, too. It looks good." Aunt Lillian stood outside the General Store and waved to Tom and Clint as they left for Nancy's. Clint was beside Tom in the buggy feeling nice and warm inside, since seeing Aunt Lillian.

She'd put her arms around him soon as he walked in. Even cried with him.

"Oh Clinton." I've never stopped praying for you," she whispered. "But Red's in a better place. Nowhere's better than being with the Lord. You must believe that if you intend to be healed. You know that?"

Clint nodded. Knew darn well what Aunt Lillian thought about Catholics. How she once told him there weren't any of 'em in Heaven. Worshipping statues way they did. But was nice of her to tell him she thought Red made it. Wasn't 'cause of Red she'd said it. It was fer me. He almost smiled. Aunt Lillian had gone a long way, lying like that, trying to make him feel better.

Seeing Aunt Nancy was even better. In her fancy parlor, all she did was hug him and kiss his hair. Kept saying "Poor Clint," over and over, no sermons, and no prayers. He hadn't wanted to see her, thinking he'd feel worse. But being inside her hug like he was, he liked the idée she wasn't full of advice like everyone else. Like she figgered his tears and pain was his that it wasn't up to her to make them stop.

"It hurts so bad," she'd whispered. And when she said that, Clint understood that Aunt Nancy was the one telling the truth.

The Memorial Mass wasn't as bad as Clint feared. He had to drive in alone. Dad didn't come along "cause Ma figured out what was going on and was raising Hell. He didn't want her doing something drastic.

Clint slapped the reins against Nelly's rump and clucked. He was skittery, 'fraid he might make a wrong turn. First time he'd driven to town alone.

But being scared wasn't so bad if it'd keep him from crying. Dad said it was all right to cry at a funeral and not to feel ashamed if he did. Still, Clint hoped he wouldn't. 'Specially in front of folks he didn't know.

Once at church, he didn't feel like crying at all. He knew Red's body lay in the casket, they'd found him only yesterday. But the casket was closed, and for that he was glad. He chose not to look at it because he wanted to remember Red as he was in the poem. Somewhere overhead, beckoning him.

And he couldn't help but keep his eyes on that preacher. Ma'd told him 'bout Catholic preachers wearing dresses. But he hadn't believed her. Yet, there was the parson, wearing a long white dress. And over the top of it, a shiny purple cloak, shaped like a knight's armor.

Hadn't expected he'd see man in a dress for as long as he'd live.

And this preacher was standing up in front of everybody, doing the service. Not a one of 'em laughed. Did most of his preachin' in Latin, too. Kept saying "Ray kwee em in pa chay."

Miz Peters said that meant "rest in peace." But she didn't know what much else meant because she was a Methodist.

And those Catholics sure did strange things during church. They'd stand a while, then sit, or get down on their knees. He couldn't help but wonder how they all knew when it was time to change position. Yet they sure were together on it. And he allowed they must practice it on Wednesday nights, like Aunt Lillian's choir.

Clint got so interested in the Catholic's actions, he forgot about Red. Maybe it was better that way, he told himself. Didn't have to cry once.

Yessir. Got through the day without shaming myself, Clint sighed. Now to face Ma.

She was on the porch, waiting for him. Still in her nightgown, barefoot, her hair going all directions like it hadn't been combed in a week. "You're goin' to Hell, Clint. Gonna burn up with the goddamn Catholics." Thick cords stood out in her neck as she came up, hissing in his face. "Did you have to kneel before the pope's picture and kiss his ass?"

Clint stopped and stared, his arms dropping heavily to his sides. "But, Ma," he began, "what about saying goodbye to Red?"

She didn't answer. Or ask how he felt, the way his Aunts did. Seemed like all she could think of was to say something bad about where Red went to church.

Red was dead. And Ma acted like it didn't matter. Clint swung his right arm back, made a fist and stepped menacingly toward her. "You don't say anything more, Ma. D'ya hear?" he shouted. "Or I'm gonna knock you flat."

Clint sighed. Surprised him how easy it was telling her off. She stood a while and looked at him, not saying anything. Then turned, went into the house and back to her room.

Amazed, Clint shook his head and turned to Pearl as she stood by watching.

"Wonder why Dad never tries that?"

On a warm afternoon a few weeks later, Clint sat in the grass on the hill where he once stood with Red and looked down on the river rolling tranquilly through the valley. A soft breeze fluttered his hair as he sat, still raw with grief.

In the field below a farmer sang as he plowed, unaware that a short time ago, Red's body had floated over the place of his joy. In a blue sky filled with white puffy clouds, birds called Red's name, waiting for his whistled reply.

With the back of his hand, Clint wiped tears, wondering if the hurting would ever stop. If he'd feel better with time, the way Dad promised.

He closed his eyes and listened for the river, its steady distant roar. He began to make pictures. Of Red, lying on his back on the water, his blue eyes closed, a smile plumping freckled cheeks, the shock of orange hair spread around his face, as he drifts with the river. Overhead, branches of willow reach down for him, try to catch him, and bring him back. But he floats away, and at a bend in the river, disappears.

Clint sighed. "......*So that you, too, once past the bend,*
    Shall meet again, as face to face, this friend
      You fancy dead." (Verses Written in 1872-Stevenson)
"But 'til then, Red, I'll miss you.... I sure am gonna miss you."

Chapter 6

November, 1912

A chill November wind howled against the old house, rattling the windows and ripping the last leaf from the backyard elm, shooting it across the yard like a marble out of a slingshot. Gunmetal clouds shrouded the sun, as it glumly watched the arrival of the season's first snow.

Safe inside, Clint perched on a kitchen chair, watching a drop of condensation spiral down a fogged window and vanish into the unpainted sill. Hiding, he thought. Just like my tears, swelling my insides 'til I think I'll bust.

He rubbed his eyes and looked to Pearl, as she heated water on the kitchen stove. Wondering if she'd noticed how hard it was to keep those tears locked in.

"Reckon I picked a bad day to wash," she said. "Gonna have clothes drying all over the house."

"It's gotta be done on the weekend. You can't stay home from school."

Clint looked past her into the front room where Tom paced, moving his lips in a soundless conversation with himself. Ignoring Ma, who sat in her rocker, arms tight to her chest and directing her narrowed eyes through the front window, the tension between them thicker than the steam rolling off the boiler. They'd had a bitter argument. And Clint was the reason why.

Clint stepped across the dim kitchen to help Pearl lift the boiler and pour hot water into the washtub. "Ain't fair," he grumbled. "Every kid going but me. Just bein' pig headed. Not even Ma gonna talk him out of it."

"I heered ye." Tom strode into the room and stood menacingly over his son. "And I won't take your sass. It was okay you goin' to high school here in Lowell, but Harperville's too far. I tolt you that the day of the fire and they ain't nothin' changed."

Two weeks ago yesterday, Lowell High School had burned to the ground. To help its neighbor, Harperville Public School was making room for Lowell students, permitting them to study there until the new school was built. Even though Aunt Lillian found a place for Clint to stay with some of Alvin's family, Tom was adamant. He needed help on the farm and Clint was staying home.

When the fire broke out, Clint was at White's stable getting his horse. It was almost dark and he was in a hurry. Late for chores again, he knew he'd catch hell from Tom.

He'd stayed after school, expecting to take a few minutes with Mr. Wood and get help with a geometry problem, but ended up getting so far into next day's assignment he forgot the time. Knew damn well T.F. wasn't going to accept his excuse. "If I told him I was at the pool hall," he muttered, "He'd probly believe me."

Lately, seemed he'd been doin' nothing but make Dad mad. Ever since Dad partnered with Uncle John and Aunt Nancy, buying more land, there was no end to chores, leaving him little time to study and none for making friends.

He tightened the saddle of the sleek black gelding and patted his rump. "Except for you, Flash, there ain't nothin for me in this deal but the old man's lip. Won't even give me spending money 'cause he thinks I'll spend it on smokes. The more money he gits the tighter he gits. He wants to spend it all on land."

Tonight would be same as usual, Clint figured, another argument and another threat to take him out of school. Hopefully, Ma would butt in and Dad would back off. But when he missed chores last week, Dad said he'd had his last chance.

Wondering how to talk himself out of this one, Clint didn't hear the shouting until someone opened the door, slammed it against the side of the barn and yelled. "Get to the high school. There's a fire!"

Clint raced to the scene, getting there just in time to see flames spread from the rear of the building to the second floor. Then explode, shooting up the walls to the ceiling, blowing out windows and licking along the roof. He saw Mr. Wood, coat over his head, running out of the main entrance and dropping to the ground, coughing and spitting.

He couldn't help but be relieved, for his teacher and for himself. A few minutes more and he'd been in there, too. He might not have been lucky enough to get out alive.

He watched, as within moments, a bucket brigade pulled back, the fire so hot it made it impossible to get close enough to do any good. By the time the fire wagon pulled up, flames shot so high they could be seen for miles.

Eyes burning from heat and smoke, Clint stood speechless. He heard someone say Mr. Woods had been the only one inside and saw a group gathering around him, hoping he might tell them how the fire started. His eyes scanned the crowd, looking for someone he knew, hoping to find out.

Suddenly, he spotted a shadowy figure, standing alone, laughing. Flames lighted a soot-streaked face and Clint realized who it was. "It's Bill Berky," he shouted, and took off running after him. "He burnt down the school."

"You son-of a bitch, stop!" Catching up, Clint grabbed Bill's ankles, pulled him to the ground and started beating his face and kicking him. "Ass-hole. Bastard. I'll kill you, you son-of-a bitch."

By the time the sheriff got there, some of the bystanders had pulled Clint off, and had to keep holding him back.

The boy's like his Ma, they reckoned, cussing, swearing and fighting like a bulldog. If it hadn't been for the fact Bill was guilty; they might have said he went too far, bloodying the boy up the way he did. Molly'd fight for a just cause too…harder than necessary, but most of the time making a bad situation worse.

Lot of the kids told him he'd been a hero catching Bill that way. No one criticized him, each saying he would have done the same thing. But Clint knew better. Face flaming, he finally sidled away, moving toward the stable to get his horse and go home. He wanted to hide. He wasn't a hero, never was. Fact is, he hated Bill. And for a few moments, he had hoped to kill him.

Bill was a moron. And his folks was trash. That's why the kids played tricks on him, laughing at him, calling him names. And that's why, Clint figured, he burnt the school

Truth was, Clint had a deep down unsettlement about how Billy might have felt. Not that the kids made fun of him, the way they did Bill, but they whispered sometimes, and looked at him strangely. Because he was smarter than Bill, he'd learned how to handle them. He'd dream about graduating high school, leaving Lowell and making a name for himself. He'd picture himself coming back and showing them someday.

Bill had brought all this on himself by fighting back. And that's why Clint hated him. It wasn't so much what Bill did, but the way his own face burned when the others made Bill a fool He couldn't explain it, but when the boys disparaged Bill, it shamed him too. And that night, and every night since, Clint waked with a nightmare, burning with rage. Dreaming he'd just killed Billy.

Now, on account of town's dumbest kid, Bill Berkey, with the help of his own father, Clint's high school days were over. It was the beginning of his junior year. More than half-way through high school he wasn't going to graduate. Still seething at Billy and raw with fresh rage at his Dad, he watched Tom go back to the front room and start jamming wood into the heating stove so hard it was shooting sparks all the way to the ceiling.

"And I ain't changing my mind," Tom roared. "You can count on it."

Clint clenched his jaw and began drawing circles on the steamed up window. You better not count on nothin', Old Man, he thought. 'Cause you got a surprise comin'.

Clint had a plan. A damn good one. It might not work, but it was better than doing nothing. Tonight, he was leaving home. He had his clothes and a few belongings in a couple of gunnysacks in the barn. After everyone got to sleep, he was going to leave the house, saddle Flash and head for Aunt Nancy's, knowing she'd stand by and not interfere. At her house, he could get his bearings and figure out where to go.

Lashed by the driving snow, Flash pranced nervously. Clint reached to pat his shoulder, calming him. Sure would be glad when he reached Lowell. It was getting mighty cold. And Aunt Nancy's kitchen was about the warmest spot he could think of. Pulling his collar up to protect his face, he pictured her at the small round table in her kitchen, lifting the blue and white cozy she'd crocheted from the teapot, and pouring a cup of tea. Seemed she'd come to be his favorite person. Clint shook his head. Remembering how much he used to hate her, and how it was her stood by him when Red died.

Quietly he peered through the clear pattern in the frosted glass panel of the front door and watched her come down the stairs to answer his knock. She was wearing a long silk wrap tied at the waist with a narrow sash, the mounds of her breasts spilling over the top. Averting his eyes, Clint blushed at a quick glimpse of the inside of her knee Iry's here, he sighed. I forgot about him.

"My land. Look what the wind blew in!" Nancy picked up a broom and swept snow from Clint's coat. "You look like a walking snowdrift. C'mon in before you freeze. Why don't you put your horse in the shed? I'll fix you a bite to eat." She hesitated a moment, and looked closely at her nephew. "I'll ask Iry if he'd like to join us."

Clint wasn't surprised to find him here. He'd known about them being together for a long time. Since Ben was hurt, Ira had pretty much moved in, leaving Edna alone in the big house on the other side of town. Neither Nancy nor Ira seemed to give a damn about what anyone had to say about it

According to Alice Benton, the only one not gossiping was poor Edna, who kept up her church attendance and Ladies Benevolent Society meetings as usual, pretending nothing had changed.

Dad hadn't mentioned it either. Clint figured he had to know, spending as much time as he did with Nancy. Reckon it's cause he don't want Ma knowing, He thinks if Pearl and me know, we'll tell her. Or he don't think I'm old enough to understand what's goin' on. Clint removed Flash's saddle and scooped oats from the granary. "You'd swear the old man ain't figgered out the birds and bees," he muttered. "Sure won't talk about 'em." He grinned, slyly. "Bet he'd be shocked to find out I've already done it."

He dumped the grain into the trough, and stroked the horse's long velvet nose.

Doing it with trash like Dorothy Berkey wasn't something he was proud of. But he'd wanted to know what it was like and didn't have many choices.

Clint knew she was easy before he tried laying with her. He started walking in the woods by her house about the time she'd be coming home from her job as Aunt Mildred's hired girl. They'd go by the river and lay in the tall grass under a big willow.

Some nights he'd lie awake wondering why she let him do it. He thought about asking her, but didn't know how to bring it up. It seemed they never had much conversation and just got right to it. And Clint couldn't understand what was in it for her since she didn't show any sign of its making her feel good.

But last summer, seems the only thing I could think of was going back for more. All the rest of the guys said they was doing it regular. First damn thing outta their mouth when guys got together…the bragging. Reckon I wanted to be like the rest."

And even though two guys he knew said they'd been with Dorothy, Clint never admitted he had. Wasn't going to let 'em know he had to stoop that low. Figured as soon as he'd tell them, they'd start laughing. Thinkin' he'd never get any better'n trash considering where he came from.

He told them he was going to Harperville with his Aunt Lillian to help pick up stock for the store and said he had a girlfriend there.

And if Aunt Nancy and Iry are laying together every once in a while, it can't be too wrong. She doesn't have to be ashamed of being with a man like him. And Clint liked seeing her happy. He could hear her sing as he walked toward the house and figured she was at the ice box, taking out a pie so she could cut a piece for him.

Nancy set the plate on the table and looked up to see Ira at the door, watching her.

"You going to be okay with this? He asked. "You could be getting in the middle of a family spat." He walked up behind her and put his hands around her waist, nuzzling her neck.

"I'm fine. Reckon he's had a run in with Tom. Being here will give him time to cool off. Think things through." Her eyes twinkled mischievously, "Tom won't fuss at me. He's been scairt of his big sister since he was a young'un."

Ira turned her to face him and drew her close. God, how he loved her! Tenderly, he kissed her forehead. "It's good to have you back," he whispered.

If only they hadn't had to lose so much to find each other again.

Clay's accident happened on a cool summer night in June of 1906. An accident that changed both their lives forever.

Ira'd been at home with Edna eating a light supper of fish and vegetables when Frank Peters burst into the house shouting.

"It's Ben. He's hurt bad."

Ira pushed his chair back and jumped to his feet. "What happened?"

"We was fooling around, had a few drinks at Woody's. Ben decided to ride that young stallion over at the stable. He got throwed off soon as he got on. Damn horse reared up and went at him with its front hooves 'fore we could get him away."

"Oh, my God. How bad?"

Frank looked away. "Doc says he might not make it. Told me to get Nancy, but I thought I'd come to you." He glanced awkwardly at Edna, who sat with her mouth open, staring. "Since you're his boss, I thought you oughta know."

"Anyone go for Nancy?"

"No, everyone's helping Doc get Ben to his office. There weren't no one 'cept me."

"I'll get her. You go back and help Doc. Careful how you handle him." Without a word to his wife, Ira left. He didn't think once about how she might feel. He had to get to Nancy before it was too late. When he reached her front porch, he took a deep breath and, without knocking, opened the door and stepped in. He wasn't going to give her a chance to shut it in his face.

He found her in the parlor, sewing. She stood, scattering the contents of the sewing basket half way across the floor. "It's Ben," Ira began. "He's hurt…bad. Doc's not sure he'll live."

She fell into his arms as naturally as if they'd been together always. He held her a moment, his tears wet on her hair, whispering. "I'm sorry, Nancy. Oh God, I'm so sorry."

She leaned back, reached up and put a forefinger to his mouth. "Shhhh. Later. We have to git to him. You goin' with me?"

He nodded. They'd been together ever since.

Ira moved his eyes around the familiar kitchen resting them on the sink where his mother had stood on the day Ben was born, holding one hand on the pump handle, shaking the other in his face. "It's not just the boy you're doing wrong; it's his mother, as well. No man's got a right to treat a woman like you did her, leaving her with a bad name to raise his flesh and blood. If you were decent, you'd divorce Edna and do right by Nancy. But all you care about is what folks think…what every gossip in this town might have to say about you. Well, I tell you, Ira, what folks think means nothing in the eyes of the Lord. All this will come back to haunt you someday and you'll wish you'd done things differently."

Ira shivered, remembering the gut wrenching days when Ben laid near death. And how much truth there'd been in his mother's words.

After Ben's accident, it seemed Ira's concern about what folks in Lowell thought of him didn't amount to a damn. Together, he and Nancy nursed Ben back to health. And now, wheelchair bound, his son shared a house with Frank Peters and was taking on a greater share of the business every day.

After all she'd been through, Ira wasn't going to let Ben's mother get away from him again. If there were to be justice for Nancy or Ben, Ira figured it'd be done by telling the truth. To make it plain to the folks of Lowell, how wrong he'd been to abandon her.

Doc met them in the waiting room and told them he had Ben on a bed in the back room, unable to move his legs. "He broke his back and the swelling's putting pressure on his spinal cord. And that's a blessing. He can't feel a thing."

Doc slipped his arm across Nancy's shoulders, his voice breaking. "He's got a great will to live, and I think he might make it. But he's in mighty bad shape. I don't think he'll walk again."

Ben had joked as they put him on the bed. "Don't get your hopes up about gettin' rid of me. I refuse to get kilt by a horse...a jackass maybe...but a horse, never."

And when he looked up and saw his mother come in with Ira, he weakened. Tears welled in his eyes, trickling down his temples into thick dark sideburns. "Got a kiss for it, Ma? Make it well?"

She bent over him, kissed his cheek and sat on the bed. Afraid. She reached for his hand and held it to her cheek.

Sensing her anguish, Ben tried to smile. "See you brought my Pa along. Didn't expect that."

Ira fell to his knees, put his head against the mattress and began to sob. "Ben. Son. I've known you as a son. Loved you as a son....Good God, I hope you know that! I..I..I'm so proud of you Ben...Should have said something...just didn't know you knew."

"Looked in the mirror one day and figgered it out," he answered. "Reckon it's her you owe an apology. That right Ma?"

And so it was that in the quiet of her kitchen years later, Ira put his mouth against her hair and kissed her. "I love you, Nancy Foster. I love you."

"I know," she said..."And I love you back."

Clint came in from outdoors, interrupting them. Ira backed away, letting her hand slip slowly out of his to drop to her side. Thinking she was still beautiful and that she was taking better care of him than he ever could of her.

He turned to welcome Clint. "Hello and goodnight," he said. "Think I'll let you two talk while I get some sleep."

"Yessir," Clint mumbled, relieved. It made it awkward with Iry there in case Aunt Nancy started asking questions, except she never asked a single one.

⤿⟲

Clint stared out the window of the *City of Saint Louis* chugging its way to Saint Joe. His first train ride and he was skittery, wondering how it would be to meet up that friend of Iry's who might give him a job.

This morning, Aunt Nancy had packed his clothes into a smooth leather grip that had belonged to Ben, went with him to the depot and before he boarded the train, stuffed twenty dollars into his coat pocket and warned him not to fall asleep on the train lest someone steal it.

He reached into his shirt and fingered a letter of recommendation from Iry. stating to whom it may concern that he, Clinton Carroll Foster, was of honest and trustworthy character, a reliable worker and worthy of a good job. In his left sock, he'd hid another twenty dollars Ira'd paid for his horse. He'd told Clint he could buy him back if he came home.

Steel wheels click-clacked against the metal track, moving past snowcapped houses that puffed dark plumes of wood smoke into a coral sky. One by one, blank windows turned gold with the lighting of kerosene lamps, every mile moving Clint farther from T.F, Molly, and home.

He couldn't help but wonder what Dad was doing right now, and sure hoped he was wishing he'd not been so stubborn. Having all that work and no one to help might make him sorry. Pearl couldn't help him. She'd have to spend more time indoors looking after Ma.

Clint took a deep breath and tried to swallow the jitters that kept rising out of his chest to stick in the back of his throat. "Gotta make it," he muttered. "Don't know what he'll do to me if I go back."

He hoped Pearl was all right. He felt bad about not saying good-bye to her and hoped she'd understand. It wasn't fair, his leaving her with all the worry about Ma and him not there to give her a break.

He leaned back and closed his eyes, behind them, picturing Pearl in the kitchen, fixing supper, looking lonesome. And Ma? She's upstairs raising Hell, carrying on about how I deserted her. T.F.? He's off to the barn, shovelin' snow away from the door so he can open it for the cows.

"Saint Joseph. Saint Joseph, Missouri." The conductor walked through the car, calling the next stop. To the long, slow whistle of the train, Clint reached for his suitcase, wondering if Pearl missed him the way he was going to miss her. If she'd cried herself to sleep when she found out he wasn't coming back.

Chapter 7

November 10, 1914

   Dear Clint,

   Sure was good hearing from you. It's been almost a year since you last wrote. Reckon I was sick with worry that something bad happened. All the time you having a lot of fun following the wheat harvest from Texas all the way into Canada. I'm most jealous you got to go see the Rocky Mountains before you headed back to Kansas City. Are they really purple, the way folks say?

   It's been a mighty good year for Dad and Uncle John. Prices on the crops are highest ever. Dad says it's because of the war in Europe. Guess they don't have time to grow crops with all the men fighting so they're buying a lot of corn from us.

   Ma's afraid you'll have to go. She has Dad get a newspaper every time he goes into town. Lowell has a weekly paper now, thanks to Ira. He makes sure they cover the news of the world along with what's happening in Jefferson City and Washington D.C. Aunt Nancy said there isn't a reason to cover news of Lowell, because Alice Benton does such a good job.

   Ma keeps saying our country might get in the war to help England against the Germans. She's afraid you'll join and get killed. Keeps carrying on about how bad it is she won't see you again.

   I've been going to high school and my grades are at the top of the class. Dad seems to want me to go. He even hired Dorothy Berkey to come help with Ma when I'm gone and that works pretty good. Ma seems to like her.

95

Ma's been good for quite a while now. I took over where you left off bringing her books. She read "Little Women" four times. Said the only thing she hated about it was that Jo got married. Ma thinks she would be better off being a teacher with no man to boss her around.

I was hoping you might come home for Christmas. I heard General Manufacturers give folks a week off at Christmas. Still working there, aren't you? Reckon I'd like to see you. I think you can get along with Dad. He seems satisfied you've decided to leave home for good. Why not come so we can see if you finally got to be good looking as your little sister.

Your Loving Sister, Pearl

January 15, 1915

Dear Pearl,

Reckon I should of let you know I wasn't coming home, but didn't make up my mind till the last minute. Kept thinking about how Ma was the last time I was there and couldn't go through with it. Can't figure it out. Raises hell at me for leaving and being there in the same breath. Wouldn't be so bad if Dad didn't butt in when I tell her to lay off. Guess he thinks I ought to take it. Well, I won't. I'm nineteen years old and man enough not to take her lip. And I reckon he ain't. And that's all I have to say about it.

Still on the same job. It pays good. I live in a rooming house next to the library. The woman at the desk asked me if I was going to read every book they had. Reckon I'd like to, but I'd have to quit my job. Don't think I'm rich enough to get it done.

Tell Aunt Nancy thanks for letting me mail your letters to her house. Just don't want Dad and Ma reading them. Aunt Nancy is a good woman. I don't care what the town says. Your Brother, Clinton

July 10. 1916

    Dear Clint,

    There's bad news. Aunt Nancy died in her sleep last week. I tried to telephone you at the rooming house, but they told me you'd moved to California and gave me this address. Sure hope it gets to you.

    She had been poorly a month or so. Out of breath so much she couldn't climb the stairs. She wouldn't go to the new doctor. Said he was too young to know anything. On the death certificate he wrote she died of a heart attack. Ira was there. He found her dead in the bed when he woke up.

    The funeral didn't go well. Ira made the plans and that didn't set well with Dad and Uncle John. He had the Unitarian Minister say a few words but it wasn't much of a service. After, they went to Ira's lawyer to read the will. She left everything to Ira, except the house. She left that to me. Said what she had was his to begin with and she was glad he let her borrow it a while. Uncle John walked out, but Dad stayed. Said this makes them partners with Ira, and he isn't sure how that will go, especially with this being a bad year. It's been dry and the crops aren't coming in. The pastures are burnt out already. And there's no more hay left over from last year to feed the cattle.

    I taught all year at Chariton Township School. They took me on right out of high school because I took Normal training. I'm supposed to go over to Richville to the college and take some classes but don't know if I can get there this summer. The school board said they'd take me on another year anyway.

    Ma is doing well. Reckon nothing could make her happier than having Aunt Nancy gone. I don't know who she'll spend her time complaining about now. She said she wouldn't go to the funeral because she was afraid she might bust out celebrating. Dorothy stayed with her. Dad and I were both glad she decided to stay home. I think he would have missed it if she had decided to go. I wish you could have been here. It would have helped me a lot. Sure will miss Aunt Nancy.

    Your Loving Sister, Pearl

P.S. Aunt Lillian and Uncle Alvin and the girls were at the funeral. They said to give you their best regards.

July 3, 1916

    Dear Pearl,

    Sure feel bad about Aunt Nancy. Am sending this letter through Ira, asked him to get it to you. I left Kansas City for California in March. Was working for a son of a you-know-what and couldn't take it anymore. I'm in Monterey, working in a canning factory. I like the ocean. Like to go sit by it and read. Listen to the waves and the watch seagulls flying over.

    Got a good rooming house. The landlady is a good cook. She razzes me about being a good eater. Just wish I didn't have to work. Think I might sit by the ocean and read for a year. How's Dad doing without Aunt Nancy? He was mighty fond of her.

    Your brother, Clinton

September 3, 1917

Dear Clinton, Ira said it was good for you to send letters to me in care of him. He's having so much trouble with Dad and Uncle John I think he understands how hard it is for you to get along with them.

Ira went out and bought a herd of purebred cattle from some farm in Illinois. Said they'll make more profit raising purebreds. But he didn't ask Dad or Uncle John first and borrowed money to buy them from the bank. Now, there's not enough feed for them, on account of the drought, and not enough water unless they drive them to the river twice a day, taking the chance they'll run off each time. They lost a few and have to sell some at rock bottom prices to a buyer from Iowa in order to make payment at the bank.

Reckon they'll lose a lot of money. Ira isn't rich as they thought either. Used up a lot of his money to start a hospital. His business is turning down because the farmers can't afford seed. Dad says Ira's ruined. Spent money like he thought it would roll in forever.

I know it would rile Dad something awful to hear me say it, but I think it was good of Ira to start the hospital. That's about all he's doing these days, raising money from everyone that has any. Told me he wanted to make up for everything bad he's done in his life.

I worry about Dad. He and Uncle John are going to lose half of the land if they can't make the payments. Even though Ira is their partner, he doesn't seem to care.

I don't want to worry you. But I can't help thinking things would be better if you were here to help. It would make it easier on all of us.

Your Loving Sister,

Pearl

April, 15, 1918

Dear Mother, Dad and Pearl,

    Wanted to let you know I just enlisted in the United States Army. Figured it was better than getting called up. Reckon you heard they will be making it law we have to go.

    I'll be going to Fort Pike, Arkansas for basic training. That takes six or eight weeks and then I am supposed to have a furlough before I get assigned to duty. Reckon they'll send me overseas, to France. That's where the action is. I expect to be coming home to see you right after I get done training. Clint

Chapter 8

October, 1918

In the midnight blackness of Pennsylvania farm country, a jam-packed troop train came to a screeching halt, slamming Clint against the seat in front of him and onto the floor. "What the hell?" He pulled himself back to his seat and rubbed his eyes. "Just when I got to sleep…"

"This is the Army. They don't allow sleep." Brian Cunningham rose from the floor and pulled himself back to his seat beside Clint. "Wonder what we hit?"

"Damned if I know." Clint looked over his shoulder to the rest of his platoon. Forty-four cursing, laughing, olive clad men, craning their necks out lowered windows, trying to get a glimpse of the track ahead.

"It's a goddam cow," someone shouted. "We hit a cow."

"Move her out," a Sergeant called out orders for his men to clear the track.

"Nice of that squad to do it for us," said Brian. "Think I'll head for the john now the train's stopped. It's hard to aim when the train is weaving."

Alone in the seat, Clint pulled out a cigarette and stretched. He hadn't been this tired as long as he could remember. Not a wink of sleep since they'd boarded three days ago, one hour after being shocked out of a drunken stupor by the blast of a five A.M. bugle call.

The men had been given leave the night before departure, and had spent it raising as much hell as they knew how. Their last chance for fun before God-knows-what waited overseas. No one of them having any idea how little sleep they'd get on the hard benches of the train.

Just glad, Clint thought, I didn't run into a war at home. Fact, it went better than I expected. He'd been pleasantly surprised by Ma. Better behavior than he'd seen in years. She ran to him as he walked to the house on his first day home. With a broad smile lifting the wrinkles of her face, she'd wiped her hands on her apron and reached to embrace him. "Clint. God bless ye!" she shouted. You can't know how I been lookin' forwards to this very minute." She'd hugged him warmly, rising on her toes to plant firm kisses on both cheeks. "C'mon in and eat. Pearl 'n me been cookin' all week, gettin' ready."

With a tight hand on the crook of his elbow, she'd ushered him to the house, asking all kinds of questions. Dad led the way, carrying his bag, and Pearl stood on the porch, looking glad to see him. Each one acting like nothin' bad had ever come between us, he thought, like I'd left here with a smile on my face.

Damn odd. Ma's hair streaked with gray, yet seeming younger than she was six years ago. She was livelier, too. With a spring in her step as she busied herself in the kitchen, making sure he was getting enough to eat. The biggest difference in her, though, was the way she talked, with a lilt to her voice and smiling as she spoke. It was almost as if she were someone else, stopped by for a visit.

After dinner, he'd asked Pearl to join him on a walk. Eager to have a look at his old hiding spot under the oak, he didn't admit to her how often he'd thought about that tree, usually when he was restless and feeling the urge for somewhere else, nor how every night since he decided to come home, he'd dreamed about it calling out to him.

Hell no, didn't make no sense. When he'd wake up dreaming of being missed by a goddam tree! No. He wasn't going to tell Pearl any of it. Better be talking about something she'd understand. He glanced in her direction. "Like I was saying earlier, something's happened to Ma. What's goin' on?"

"She says it's 'cause she's over her monthlies, that she's feeling better. But I think it's because she's went to a church."

"Ma? At a church? Don't believe it." Clint, reached for a juicy stem of grass, stuffed it in his cheek and began chewing.

"Well, it's true. After you joined the Army, she asked Dad to take her to the meeting.

"Well I'll be damned. She don't go on about it. Like Aunt Lillian does."

"Says she took the Lord's name in vain so many times she's going to be careful how she uses it from now on. Besides, Unitarians aren't bent on saving everybody. They just look after themselves."

Clint's eyes moved over the familiar scene as he stepped into the clearing around the oak. "That tree's smaller'n it usta be," he laughed. "Reckon my bein' three feet taller makes a difference."

"I reckon." eyes level with his, Pearl looked at Clint and smiled. "I'm six-one, how about you?"

"Six foot even," he answered. "Tallest in my platoon. It gets me the far right position in the front row when we line up."

"Why's that?"

"Shortest guy gets left end, back row. That way we get our heads in an inclined slope from right front to left rear. It looks good during a parade. Just glad we don't have to march into battle the way they did in the Civil war, I'd be the first to fall." Clint laughed and rubbed his hands against the rough bark of the tree. Forgotten sorrows, left long ago to lie at its roots, rose in his throat, trembling his voice. "Ma still worried I'll die in the war?"

"She ain't brought it up lately. I think she's learned a way to relieve her mind when she's worrying."

"Good. Reckon it's the first time I seen her downstairs in the heat of summer. Think she'll get bad agin come winter?"

"Sure she will, she always does. Maybe it won't be so bad if she keeps going to church. I'll be back at school and can't be watching her. Dorothy Berkey got married so she won't be around to help."

With a gulp, Clint blurted, "Who the hell to?"

"Marvin Benton. Warren and Alice's boy. He got a good job at the bank with his Dad. He and Dorothy are building a new house."

Face flaming, Clint raised his voice. "Why the hell would an uppity town guy like him marry trash like her? His ma bein' the town gossip didn't he know about her past?"

Pearl bent to pick a handful of wildflowers, their sweet smell rising with her as she straightened her back. "They changed, Clint. We all have. You have to get over remembering folks the way they were. It's been a long time." She stepped in front of him and stopped, pulling the bushes aside so he could walk through. "The only one who hasn't changed is you. I swear you're same as the day you left."

"What the hell had she meant by that? The question haunted him. He moved aside to let Brian sit, telling him "Shut your mouth so I can git back to sleep," and tried to return to his thoughts. But Brian wouldn't have any of it.

"So how was the visit home," asked Brian. "Did it make you think twice about joining the army?"

"No. Never want to be a farmer like Dad. Things are going pretty good with him now, but there were a lot of years that he could hardly make ends meet. Last year was one of them."

"What's different for him now?"

"Prices are good, on account of the war, and he's got more land he's farming with my Uncle John and his boys. Guess there's a lot of demand in Europe for crops grown here. Those countries can't even grow enough to feed themselves, they're so busy fightin'."

"That's good news for your Dad. I always thought farming was about taking care of a bunch of cows and pigs."

"You're right about that. There's chickens and horses to tend to as well. When you farm, you work day and night. I don't want to live that way. I want to have time to have a little fun once in a while."

Brian laughed. "So it's a gentleman you'll be, Hillbilly. How in hell are you going to manage that?"

"None of your damn business, Irish. I'll find a way that's legal." He turned away and, pillowing his head on his arm, admonished Brian. "Now leave me the hell alone. Told you I wanted to get some sleep, didn't I?"

With Brian quieted, Clint shifted and tried to sleep, but thoughts of home kept interrupting. He'd been surprised at Dad. The top of his head without a hair, the band left above his ears streaked with gray. He hadn't said much, a few words about the crops and livestock, but nothing about having been left with Clint's broken promise to spend the summer helping out. And not a word about their argument over Ma.

He didn't mention Iry, either. Clint was curious about how they were getting along, but Pearl had warned him to stay away from talk of it. "I don't want him raging the whole time you're here. Her either."

It might have been good to hear some of the old hollering, he thought, especially if it was directed at someone beside himself. Just to be sure they were still his folks and not a couple of strangers.

It seemed Pearl had changed, too. She seemed older. Wiser. Carson Elger, had been calling on her and she'd talked like she was pretty sweet on him. I wonder what'll happen to Ma in case Pearl marries. Dad might have to quit farming.

Yes, they'd all changed, he reckoned. And wondered why it was Pearl who seemed to think he hadn't grown up. Hadn't put it that way exactly, that he wasn't acting his age…but to Clint, it seemed like that was what she meant.

What Pearl don't know, Clint figured, is that I've growed up a lot. 'Specially in the last two months. Ain't nothing in the world like the U.S. Army to make a man out of you. Reckon I'm damn proud to be part of it.

Suddenly wishing to know how Brian felt about it as well, he began to speak "Ain't never been able to git up in the morning and enjoy goin' to work 'til I joined the Army," he said. "Nothing's' worse than workin' for some son of a bitch don't know how to do the job he's telling me to do. Only thing I like about having a job is gettin' paid, savin' my money and takin' off to see the country."

Brian laughed. "It's the same as you I am about money. There are no good times without a dollar in one pocket and a pint in the other. But I'm not carin' for the Army the way you do. How the divil can you like sleeping in a wet tent, spend hours crawling on your belly in the mud and get up at five-o-clock to eat slop? Now they're telling us to go fight a war for a bunch of old men in Washington, maybe die...and you say you like it? How?"

"Ain't sure. It's not that I like takin' orders. But it's easier than it was working. When I know obeyin' orders is for the good of the unit and not for some strawboss struttin' his stuff."

Clint leaned against the dark window and rubbed his chin. "It's darn hard to speak what I'm thinking." He laughed. "Reckon my spea-kin' words ain't the same as my thinking words. Got myself all fouled up with too damn much reading." He paused, deep in thought, want-ing to share this revelation with Brian without sounding silly.

Clint cared a great deal for Brian, loved the long conversations they'd had about things never discussed with anyone since Red. He had been comfortable with the red-haired Irishman the minute he dropped his pack on the nearest cot the first night at Fort Pike. As soon as he introduced himself in a thick Irish brogue, Clint was reminded of Red. This was a man to be trusted. Much as he'd trusted Red.

Through six weeks of basic, they'd shared the same pup tent and become good friends. Clint wanted more than anything to tell Brian what a positive change the Army had made in him. "It's bein' with your buddies," he began, "the squad being as one man and the platoon a bigger man. And a regiment was like a powerful God. There's some-thing about the order of it that settles me. Reckon I've always liked bein' alone 'til now. Ain't never been where I didn't stick out like a thorn on a rose or be hid somewheres in the back row. Can't explain, but it's like all of a sudden I'm important," he laughed. "Because I ain't too damn important...You git what I mean?"

Brian roared, slapping Clint's thigh with his left hand and giving him a sharp punch to the upper arm with his right. "So the hillbilly's thinkin' deep, is he? Before long he'll be fallin' in love with the whole stinkin' company. Just don't start kissing any of 'em."

Then, he paused, becoming quiet, leaning back so he could see Clint's face, his blue eyes soft with knowing. "Sister Mary Joseph used to call that humility. She spent all her time trying to fill me and every kid at Saint George Academy with it. The old witch had a tongue like a knife and used it to cut up little boys. She'd hit me with this long pole she carried, makin' remarks about how dumb I was. 'Don't want you leaving school with the sin of pride,' she'd say."

Brian looked down at his tall military boots and crossed his ankles. "It's humility I've had me fill of," he said. "And I want no more of it. Think it's why I'd probably break your arm to get to the front of crowd, just to make 'em laugh...so they'd like me."

"No," he continued. "I'm not made for the Army. It's glad I'll be when it's over. I've got a sister I'd gladly die for, me Ma, too. Poor woman broke her back raisin' us after Dad died and I did nothin' to make it easy on her."

Tears welled at the corners of his eyes as he turned away. "The army isn't about making us heroes, me friend. If I die, it won't be because I'm dying for one of them. Shit, this war's across the ocean. I'll be dying for the goddam French." He clenched his fist and pounded it against his knee. "I feel like a slave. I'm in it because I'm young, poor, and have no choice. I'll do me duty 'cause I don't want to be called a coward. Like it if you want, Clint, but I'll not be joining with any of your good feeling over it."

Bright eyes suddenly flashing humor, Brian laughed. "And not five minutes ago, you were bitching 'cause you couldn't sleep. Now you're trying to make me cry. Get to sleep, Hillbilly. Or I'll kick your ass."

Clint laughed and turned to the window. In the distance he could see a faint strip of amber beginning to nudge the dark sky from a darker earth, clearing a path for the sun.

Reckon he understands, Clint mused. But he ain't gonna let me mope. Sure glad I found him. Reckon I was in need of someone to help me figger things out. Pearl got me thinkin' I been missin' something. It's like I ain't been paying attention.

He scrunched down, pushed a snoring Brian off his shoulder, lit a cigarette and tried to make himself comfortable, recalling his life since he'd left home at sixteen. Wondering how many towns he'd been in? How many trains he'd rode? He'd been always on the move, lookin' for something new. Being a homebody, Pearl can't understand. Hell, it's like I had to be this way. Ain't even sure I've wanted to be.

Someplace new would settle him a while. He'd get a job; find a rooming house with a good cook, and the nearest library. There was nothing like the majesty of a snow-capped peak, the arid beauty of the desert or the relentless pounding of a stormy ocean to stir his senses, make him glad to be alive. "America the beautiful." he would answer when asked why he loved traveling. "I love her. Gonna see every bit of her." And he'd scour every acre of each new location, delighting in its difference.

But before long, he'd get restless. Not something he noticed, but was noticed by everyone around him. A land lady, co-workers or supervisors, people who watched him change overnight from a man who cheerfully did his job to one who resented everyone. Especially the boss. Clint believing he had been treated unfairly or that someone was getting a better deal. Not long after the transformation, he'd pick up his pay and leave town, never to be heard from again.

With one exception, a stout middle-aged landlady in Kansas City by the name of Mary Perkins. "He lived here two times, first in nineteen eleven and again in fourteen. He's a loner, that one," she told Pearl.

It was the night Aunt Nancy died. Mary was on the phone with Pearl, who'd called long distance, looking for Clint.

Pushing down a surge of pity that forced tears to her eyes, Pearl answered. "He's like that. He wants to keep going. Just hope he's still at that place in California you gave me the address to."

"I liked Clint," Mary went on. "He was smart. Read a lot of books when he should have been out having fun. I used to try talking to him, try to open him up a little. Couldn't understand why, old as he was, he was still having nightmares."

"Nightmares? I don't recollect he had nightmares."

"Oh my. He'd wake up hollering and rouse the whole house. One night I walked into his room. I had to. He wouldn't answer my knock and the other roomers was getting fed up with him 'cause they weren't getting any sleep. I thought I could help him and found him sitting on the edge of the bed, crying."

With a pang to her heart, Pearl asked. "Did he tell you what he dreamed about?"

"Said it was one he had often about his horse. Was its name Flash?"

"Uh huh."

"Well, he said he'd dream that Flash would rear up and hit at folks with his front feet. Most nights it was folks Clint didn't care for. Might go after his boss or this boy he said ruined his life when he was in school. But he said this dream was different. Reckon that's why it upset him so much."

"Did he tell you about it?"

"He did. He said he dreamed the horse was going after his Ma; that he reckoned he screamed because he wanted to save her."

"Well I don't blame him for screaming. That was a scary dream."

"Honey, a man his age shouldn't be waking up scared out of his wits every night. There's something bothering him and I can't figure what. I told him he ought to go see his Ma. That he was probably worrying over her and not owning up to it. That he oughtn't to be ashamed missing her no matter how old he is. But he left the next week. Reckon he didn't like my advice."

Pearl paused. Lordy, she thought, the dreams. Just like Ma's. "You sure have been kind," she said. "And I thank you for it. Reckon I ought to be getting off the line, that crackling sound's making it hard to hear."

"Yes'm. Sure hope you find him. Let me know. I still worry about him."

"Thanks again. Bye, now."

"Goodbye."

Pearl never told Clint she'd had that talk with Mrs. Perkins. She couldn't see how it would do any good, knowing he'd probably be ashamed. Besides, the woman could have been exaggerating. But on the night before Clint was to go back to Fort Pike, his groaning waked her. And when she tiptoed to the hall and pressed her ear to his door, she could hear his sobbing. It took almost an hour for him to get quiet again. Only when she heard him snore did she go back to her room, staying awake the rest of the night praying for him.

She was praying for him, again, that night when Clint's train hit the cow. Wondering how he was, hoping he'd be safe when he went into battle. She turned on her side, bunching the pillow to support her neck. "Wonder if he's as scared as I am," she whispered.

Almost dozing, Clint startled, thinking he'd heard Pearl's voice. She must be thinking 'bout me, he grinned. Through the grimy window, factories and large warehouses loomed dark against a brightening sky. Trains whizzed by, headed either direction. "Must be getting close to the big city," he said. "Reckon we'll be on that boat tonight."

In New York Harbor, the *USS Des Moines* lay docked, waiting for the troop trains. As she sat, men in flared bottom trousers readied the ship for troop transport, stacking bunks in the lower decks, hauling boxes of food to the galley and setting out bed rolls for each man to pick up as he boarded ship.

Later, after the train deposited the army men next to the ship, rows of sailors in white dress uniform came on deck to stand at attention. As they hoisted *Old Glory,* a single bugle sang out the *National Anthem,* bringing tears to the eyes of every man in company G.

As he stood with his platoon waiting their turn to embark, Clint felt more excited than he could remember. "God, Brian. What a sight. Ain't she purty? "The United States Navy, salutin' us."

"You never saw a ship before?"

"We don't need 'em in Missoura way you do in Shecaga, Irish. Sure a lot bigger than I thought she'd be. Look at that artillery. Lordy. That ought to blow them Krauts outta the water."

"It's the U-boats blowing us out you best be worryin' over."

"Aw, keep your mouth shut," Clint answered. "You're trying to scare me."

"Have it your way, Clint. But submarines are like snakes. You never know when they'll strike. And the Navy doesn't know how to find 'em, much less fight 'em."

"I'll keep an eye out. Blast 'em with my Springfield."

Brian shrugged, turning his attention to the rest of the squad as they gathered, leaving Clint alone to step back and soak in his surroundings.

The ship was much like he'd imagined. Beautiful! The harbor, too, with tall cranes loading crates onto ships, gulls squawking overhead, longshoremen bustling and calling orders, as trains and trucks crawled through a jungle of motion, inching freight to and from the docks.

He took a deep breath, mixing the salt smell of ocean with the rank odor of fishing boats. Pulling it all deep into his nostrils, then grimacing at the taste of coal ash, drawn across the ship's smokestack and into his face by a sudden downdraft.

A small crane lifted an artillery gun with a slender cable, lowering it gently to the deck of the *USS Des Moines*. May be going to the front with us, Clint speculated. Wonder if it's one I'll use?

A slight chill crept up his back and through his body, raising hairs on his arms. I'm so worked up I'm getting goose bumps, he shuddered. Beside him a soldier, weak from a fit of coughing, stopped to blow his nose. Clint sighed. Sure hope I'm not taking cold. At the call to move forward, Clint and his unit filed onto the ship.

Chapter 9

H is first night at sea was of high winds and puking. The next morning, Clint woke with the flu.

"Think I got a fever. D..d..don't know whe..when I've felt this bad." Clint looked up at the tall corpsman standing in the narrow aisle beside his bunk and pulled the blanket over his shivering shoulders.

"Don't have to explain, Private, just got over it myself. This one's a son of a bitch. You thirsty?" The aide poured water into a tin cup and offered it to Clint.

"M.m.might throw up."

"Wouldn't appreciate that," he laughed. "We got a lot of cleaning up to do." From somewhere about four bunks down and two up a soldier called for help. "Gotta go. We got half the company sick. Some are crying for Mama. Only thing the Docs are handing out is aspirin and quinine. You want some?"

"Ssssaid I.I.I'd puke."

"Up to you. I'll check with you later." After a sympathetic pat to Clint's shoulder, the medic moved to the next bunk.

⤳

In the Captain's quarters, the ship's doctor briefed the Captain, and the commissioned officers of Clint's Regiment. "It's a goddam epidemic," he said. "Killing people all over the country. Europe, as well. War's spreading it like wildfire. And these kids from the country haven't been exposed to it yet. There's no room in the infirmary, so we have to leave the sick with the healthy. Be damn lucky if the whole ship doesn't come down with it."

Captain John Walker sighed, leaned forward, and rested his elbows on the table. "How many men down?"

"Ninety-six Army, fifty-two Navy. I'm not positive. They're dropping like flies."

Brigadier General Ben Johnson slammed his hand onto the arm of his chair. "Shit. Just what we don't need. We gonna lose any?"

"We've lost 10 men already. And we'll lose more. But most are young and strong, so casualties should be minimal. Pneumonia's the killer. Some of them will have it." The doctor backed his way to the door. "If I may be excused, sir, I'd like to get back to the sickbay. The medics will have finished their rounds and we'll have more information."

"You are dismissed," the Captain said softly.

After a crisp salute, the doctor departed, leaving the officers to assess the situation.

"Guess it's better having them sick here, than in the trenches," Johnson offered. He laughed dryly. "Maybe we oughta bottle the damn thing and give it to the Krauts. Save us a lot of ammo."

Captain Walker straightened his shoulders and cleared his throat. An Annapolis graduate, he held most Army officers in contempt. Especially men like Ben Johnson, who, lacking a brain, had climbed up the ranks by his balls. "I've got a ship to run, sir," he responded. "My men get this, we're not going to arrive on schedule"

"We got orders from General Pershing to be—"

"To hell with Pershing! We can't keep the engines going we've no choice but to wait it out. I have to get my men healthy. I'll not put the ship or any man in danger. You will be informed."

"Yes, Sir. The General will appreciate the Navy's dedication to duty," sneered Johnson. Without saluting, he turned and strode from the room.

But the next day, neither Captain Walker's dedication to his ship, nor Johnson's devotion to his commanding officer was enough to get either man out of bed. On the Captain's orders, junior officers directed a skeleton crew to pull into Halifax and lay by.

◦◦◦

For four agonizing days Clint lay in his bunk. As soon as he stopped throwing up, it seemed like he was half paralyzed. Afraid to move 'cause he felt like his skull might split, with a cough tearing his insides 'til it felt like they'd bleed. He'd sleep a while, be waked by a bout of coughing, go back to sleep exhausted, only to have the tickle in this throat set off the cough again.

Nightmares roamed his sleep. Ma, in a rowboat, stormy waves sweeping over her. Nearby, Red whirled in a vortex, beckoning. Ben, in a German helmet, his rifle aimed at Clint's chest. On the fifth night he dreamed of the river rising higher and higher, he and Pearl, trying in vain, to hold it back.

Almost as quickly as it came, Clint's headache was gone. He rolled from his bunk, the stench of vomit, stale piss and sour breath searing his nostrils. "Gotta get some air," he mumbled and made his way to the deck.

Men reached out as he passed, begging for another blanket or a glass of water. Lordy, he thought. Everyone's sick. No one takin' care of 'em.

He reached the deck and stood a moment, adjusting his legs to the boat's gentle roll. Squinting in the bright sunlight, he spotted a group of sailors hefting long black body bags over the side with many more to go. How many? He wondered. Twenty? Thirty? How many already thrown over?

He stepped closer, hoping to hear, but the men weren't talking. Just, on the count of three, dumping bag after bag of well-trained United States Military into the water with a loud splat. There was no bugler, playing "Taps." No prayers, nor gun salutes. No sign of *"Old Glory"* being raised for these dead. Men like himself, Clint figured, who'd left port only a few days ago ready to die for freedom and country, now being tossed like garbage, into the sea.

115

The sun glinted from a tangle of metal tags and chains, catching his eye. Amidst the snarl of letters and numbers, one man's name, William G. Warner, stood out.

William G. Warner, a name carved into a thin strip of tin. Was this, Clint wondered, all that was left of a man? Someone whose body was at this minute being swallowed by sharks? Would someone pick up that scrap of metal and take it to his folks? What would he tell them? That their son was a hero? That he defended his country with courage to the bitter end? Or that he was just some poor son of a bitch who died of the flu? Whose death didn't mean a damn thing?

Clint turned and walked away, his old ideas of honor and glory sinking with his comrades, beneath the churning waves.

"It's the whole fucking war doesn't make sense." Brian growled. Next to a makeshift field hospital, he and Clint watched helplessly as litters of groaning American soldiers were brought in to be patched up, or to die, depending on their condition. "God, how many you think the Germans are hauling in on the other side?" asked Brian. "All these men butchered...dying...crippled for life. For what?"

"For the freedom you have to bitch," Clint answered. "Ever stop to think why your folks left Ireland?"

"The Brits were kicking our ass same way as Uncle Sam's kicking mine now. Either place could be where I'm gonna get shot."

Clint sighed, tired of Brian's complaining. He didn't like being here either, now that they'd moved close enough to hear the guns. To see the sky burn orange a few short miles ahead, and watch the wounded stagger back from the front, faces streaked with blood and soot. Wordless. Like their tongues been shot out.

A small group of refugees was passing the camp. Women and kids on top of ox driven carts piled with live chickens and furniture. A few old men walked, carrying sacks, one with his white haired wife clinging to his back, looking like two kids playing piggyback. Clint looked away, avoiding the pleading eyes that begged with expectation, their hope that he, an American soldier, might be their savior.

"God, wonder if they know what's back there? Everything in ruins?" Brian slung an arm over Clint's shoulder and gave him a warm shake. "Hey, Hillbilly, I'm sorry. Just scared, that's all. Wonder when they'll send us up?" He pointed to the front. "Not sure I can do it, Clint. Damn. Wish I'd died of the flu. I was too sick to be scared. Shit. I didn't even remember my rosary."

Clint took a deep breath, trying to keep the lump in the center of his chest from rising to his throat. He was scared, too, but wasn't going to say so. Nobody could ever say a Foster acted like a sissy.

Earlier, they'd watched a guy with a bandaged face limp out of a Ford ambulance, hiding his face in his hands and crying like a baby. He'd shit his pants when the shell hit the trench. Said he couldn't help it. Brian had run to him, hugged him and told him not to feel bad. Said he'd 'a done the same thing.

Will I? Clint wondered. There's a lot of them cowards, dropping their guns and running. Getting themselves shot in the back. What would he do? Was it going to be like he'd dreamed it would, him leading a charge of men into Kraut lines, killing 'em like flies. The way Tennyson wrote it, in *Charge of the Light Brigade, "undismayed... not to reason why, ...but to do or die."*

But seeing men like the one Brian hugged this morning sent dread through him like a bullet. He wished they'd leave for the front before all this made him crazy. And get it to hell over with.

Shortly after midnight, they were rudely awakened to begin the march toward Metz. A full moon reflected off the frosted ground, casting an eerie glow over the ground. Ahead, the sky flashed orange and red, streaked by white screaming shells. Brian walked at Clint's side, for once, speechless. Clint figured that was good, because he didn't have anything to say either.

After sunup, just as they reached Metz, the shooting seemed to slow. Suddenly, the guns were silent, making the men edgy. As they gathered with their platoons to wait for orders, a rumor was whispered that the Germans had spotted the buildup and were pulling back to wait for reinforcements. Nervously, the men eyed a gathering of officers standing near the road; animatedly discussing what all assumed must be a dire turn of events. Clint chain-smoked, pacing in circles.

Suddenly, a car approached, drove up to the assembled officers and stopped. Ignoring salutes, an aide to General Pershing stepped out, turned to the men and raised his arms. "It's over!" he shouted. "The German's have surrendered. Men, we have won the war!"

⤳

Since he'd been denied a chance to be a hero, Clint did the next best thing and decided to stay in France with the Occupation. It seemed like a good chance to see Europe. Brian left late in November, making Clint promise to look him up after it was over. "You can always find work in Chicago. And I got a sister Ma wants me to find husband for. Just wish you were a Catholic." Brian said. "Most guys wouldn't trust you anywhere near their sisters. But they've not met Nellie. Not a guy in the world she can't handle."

"I ain't gettin' married," Clint replied. "Not till I find someone deaf, dumb and rich. Reckon you better look elsewhere."

"Think they're sparin' me the effort. Nell's got more boyfriends than she has brains."

"So bein' dumb runs in the family?" Clint laughed. "Take care of yourself, Irish. And keep your ass out of the saloon."

"Christ. Didn't realize how good it would be leaving you, Hillbilly, you're starting to sound like me Ma." Brian dropped Clint's hand and hugged him, grinning when he stiffened.

"Don't worry, buddy, I'm not going to kiss you." Brian backed toward the train, waving, "and don't lose my address," he called.

As the train chugged from the station, Clint walked away, keeping his eyes from the windows in case Brian was hanging out of one. He was the best friend he'd had since Red and he knew he'd miss the Irishman's cheerful baloney. But he wasn't gonna stand there and wave like a jackass. He'd feel like a damn fool.

Besides, he was in a hurry. He had an appointment for a French lesson with a girl like none he'd ever met. He could hardly wait to get there.

Monique La Blanc was dark-eyed and tiny. Small as Ma, but lively, laughed a lot and couldn't seem to keep her hands off him. Not that she was touching places she shouldn't have, Clint grinned. Not yet.

The thought of that possibility almost made him groan. She had a way of touching his arm, resting a hand on his thigh, or stroking his cheek when he talked that made his crazy. All the while, keeping them black eyes focused right on him. He shivered. Last lesson she'd kissed him. One short kiss goodnight as she said goodbye. His lips tingled, remembering, the warm, sweet, full lips, soft against his own.

He felt like he had to kiss her again, only this time longer, with arms around her back, her small round breasts against his chest. He quickened his step.

He'd met the tiny French girl through one of his barracks buddies, Dwight Bond. She was tutoring one of Dwight's friends. She had told him she found teaching French a good way to support herself and her mother. The money her mother made at the bakery not nearly enough to pay rent or buy enough food.

Monique's father had died in the war. A professor of language at a large university, Pierre La Blanc had been conscripted to interview captive German soldiers. Fluent in many languages, he had taught Monique most of them. English was her favorite.

Clint grinned. She hadn't learned his kind of English. He found her hard to understand. She didn't often understand him either, often going into go into gales of laughter at his "heel beely French."

It embarrassed him. Clint had been aware of his rough dialect for some time. In the Army, he took a lot of teasing, first with the nickname "Hillbilly," next with jokes about being a dumb hick out of the Ozark hills. He'd tried to improve, trouble was, he'd forget soon as he opened his mouth. He met a guy from California told him he'd overcome a Tennessee drawl by learning Spanish. Said it was a good way to be more conscious of his speech. Clint had started studying French in hope of learning to watch his.

She opened the front door a tiny crack and peeked out. Clint caught his breath, lost for a moment in the depth of those eyes. "Bon jure mad a ma zelle," he began.

"*Non. Non,*" she laughed and flung the door wide open. "*Bonjour.* BoNzhoor. Mamzelle. *Oui?*"

"We. Gonna ask me in?"

"*Oui.* But Mamma is out. Gone. Is at work. I theenk so. Yes. At work."

"When will she be back?"

She looked puzzled. "Back?"

Clint reached for his watch and pointed to the dial. "What hour? Madam?"

She laughed and grabbed his hands, leaned back and looked coyly into his face. "Ooooo. Why you ask? You want Mamma to stay to work?"

"You might say that." He pulled her to him. "Know why I asked?"

"*Je ne sais pas.*" She snuggled closer, giggling, reminding him of a soft wriggly puppy.

"You don't know?" Clint lifted her chin and brought his mouth to hers, gladdened by her heated response. "Oh yes you do," he mumbled.

She laughed and backed away, her black eyes teasing, pulling him into wanting her so much his groin hurt. "*Non.* No. I do not understand. *Vous desirez?*"

He caught her by the waist, lifted her and began to nuzzle her neck. "I'd like some of you, Mam zell. *Vous.* Understand?"

Eagerly she wrapped her legs and arms around him in and began to nibble his ear. "*Oui,*" she whispered and pointed to the stairs. "*Mon chambre. La.*"

∽◯

"Reckon she's the best thing happened to me in my whole life," Clint told Dwight.

The two were resting in their barracks after a long day of clearing shells from a nearby battlefield. "Ain't learnt much French. Ain't got much reason to." He lay back on his bunk and looked at the ceiling, grinning. "We don't have much time for talking."

Dwight looked up from the boot he was polishing and laughed. "No need to explain, Clint."

"I won't. But Lordy, she's something! I thought I was through with women before I met her."

Dwight looked startled. "Through with women! Why in hell do you say that?"

"I dunno. My sister says it's because I never settled down. Think I might have if I'd met somebody I coulda cared about."

Dwight set one boot on the floor and reached for the other. "That doesn't explain why you're through with women."

"No, reckon it don't. Wasn't 'cause I didn't choose their company. It's just that I can't figger out what they're up to." Clint sat up, lit a cigarette, took a long drag and exhaled a cloud of smoke. "The so called nice ones giving the come on, but you lay a hand on 'em, getting mad as a wet hen. And the rest whores. Laying with anyone."

Dwight jerked back, surprised by the anger in Clint's voice, noticing how he'd started puffing on the cigarette so hard half of it had turned to hot glowing ash. "You just haven't met the right one yet."

"I have. Pretty sure it's Monique." Clint ground the cigarette into the ashtray. "How'd you know your wife was the right one?"

"Angela? Guess I always knew. We grew up together. We were sweethearts all through school."

"Reckon you knew what you were getting into."

"We did." Dwight paused, watching Clint. "Think it's the best. Marriage is for the rest of your life. A guy ought to take his time, make sure he's made the right choice."

Clint stiffened. "You tellin' me I haven't? That I'm movin' too damn fast?"

"Hey! Sorry I said anything." Dwight stood and moved toward the door, stopped, and looked back at Clint. "Sounds to me like you've had a few bad experiences with women. I'd hate to see it happen again."

Clint watched as Dwight left, feeling angry and growling to himself. "No. Don't know a damn thing about me. What's with this idee I been hurt? Reckon Dwight ain't been in love the way I am." He exhaled in disgust. Growing up with his wife like Dwight did was like marrying your sister. Or he's jealous I got a girl like Monique. A shiver of excitement crept up his back. And she's crazy about me. Lordy, can't get enough of me.

⁓◯

Pretty damn snappy, Clint sighed. He turned sideways to better view himself in the mirror, adjusting his cap till he had it at just the right angle with his jaw. I'm made for this uniform, he thought. No damn wonder I drive her wild.

He glanced at his watch. It was time to get going if he was going to catch the train to Amiens. Today was Thursday and he had extended leave. Was to meet Monique there, and go to Paris. Same as when they'd gone to Cannes, he had reserved a private compartment. He took five or six deep breaths and exhaled slowly, trying to keep from getting too worked up.

Remembering how she'd drawn the curtains and straddled his lap soon as he sat down, lifting her skirt to nothing but a black garter belt holding her stockings. How she'd arched her back when he'd put his mouth on her throat, daring him to unbutton her blouse. Then stood, and lifted her nipples to his mouth, spreading her legs wider across his knees.

Lordy, she'd been right there. In his hands. Wet and shivering and moaning and his to control!

Absolute power. His skin flamed with it.

Deliberately, he'd slowed his hand. Matching the pressure of his touch to the movement of her body, bringing her close, pulling back––close––and back––till she writhed in pleasure." *S'il vous plait,*" she gasped. "Please. Please, Please." Finally, collapsing in his lap, a mass of quivering ecstasy. Clint felt like he owned her.

Then, she leaned back, her eyes bright with mischief. "*Vous desirez?*" Clint groaned, as she dropped to her knees and reached for his zipper. The power had suddenly changed hands.

He saw her once a week. Taking the train to Amiens on Thursday and coming back Friday night. Sometimes Madam was home and would fix supper. He'd felt awkward at first, leaving the table to go to Monique's room knowing her mother was downstairs. But he soon got used to it. Madam seemed to like him, and Clint was sure she knew he was good to her daughter. Probably grateful he was an American and hoping he might provide a better life for her in America.

He had been thinking a lot about marrying the girl, bringing her with him when he went home. He planned to bring Madam, too. She was nice enough, even though he couldn't understand her. But he liked her for never saying anything about what he was doing with her daughter. So, he'd arrive with a gift for her, usually wine, or cheese, to keep in her good graces.

Once he'd brought a fat hen from the market and Madam hid her face in her apron and cried. "Merci. Merci," she sobbed. "Good...too good."

Clint was embarrassed. He hadn't expected so much appreciation and turned to Monique for an explanation. She'd looked down, seemingly ashamed. "We have no meat...*pour cinq jours...*" She held up five fingers. "*Jours*...days."

Clint slipped one arm around her back and put his finger to her lips. "You'll have meat," he said. "Can I give her money...francs?"

"*Non. Non.*" Both women seeming to deny his offer.

Clint wasn't going to let them go hungry again. In spite of their protests, he began leaving a few francs in the sugar bowl before going back to base. .

She was on the platform, a small valise on the boardwalk at her side. Seeing her there, with black hair in smooth waves close to her head, thick dark eyelashes soft against her cheek, Clint choked, thinking he'd never in his life seen a girl so pretty. She was wearing the dress he'd bought her in Cannes, the red one. It looked like she'd short-ened it, showing more leg above the red high heel shoes he'd bought to match. As he stepped down to help her board, he had to smile, wondering how in hell the shape of her calf could make him picture her standing there in nothing but them damn red shoes...and maybe the garter belt.

She lifted her head to meet his kiss and stepped in front of him, leading the way to their compartment. He gulped, noticing how smoothly that dress draped over the mounds of her behind. Lordy. Sure missed that when she tried it on. He sighed in pure pleasure. He had five days leave. And it was just getting started.

"You must have forgotten all about your trip to Paris." Dwight was driving back to base, Clint at his side. They'd spent the day looking for shells. It was Monday, first day after his leave and Clint was tired.

It had been a tense afternoon. In the weeds next to an old bun-ker, they'd come across a pile of unspent German shells that probably contained mustard gas. Carefully, they'd cleared them from the area and placed them in the storage bunkers that had been constructed for holding them.

"Reckon there's nothing like the possibility of breathing poison gas to make you forget about everything but being damn careful," Clint answered. "Glad it's over."

"You mean Paris?"

"Hell no. Had a good time. Went to the Louvre, saw Notre Dame Cathedral and took a boat ride down the Seine."

"Did you do anything else?"

"Nothin' I'd tell you."

Dwight laughed. "So you're still sweet on her."

"You could say that. Or you could say I'm still learning French."

"It's a hard language."

"I reckon. How's your friend, Ralph, doing?"

"Not much better'n you. Did you know Monique's been teaching Lieutenant Williams?"

"She didn't mention it."

"Yeah. He has Tuesdays. Ralph has his lesson Mondays."

"Well I'll be damned." Clint felt a twinge of jealousy run through his veins. Wished she'd told him about the other lessons. He'd been so wrapped up in her he hadn't thought of asking.

"You going in this week?"

"Yeah. Thursday." Clint replied.

"And Friday. You got two days to learn French, Clint. You should be way ahead of everybody."

Clint glared sullenly across the table at Lieutenant James Williams, wondering how a man could believe he knew anything about clearing canister shells when he'd never once risked his precious ass getting anywhere near one! Smart-aleck Massachusetts college boy thinks he knows everything. Damn fool can't even say *R*.

"We expect a full repaht, Corporal. We can't jeopardize our men until we know exactly what we're doing. This is serious. I cannot emphasize that enough."

"Yes sir. We did our best, sir. Corporal Bond's the expert in munitions, sir. I took his advice."

"But you did not have cleahance to handle the gas."

"No sir."

"See that this information is included in your repaht. That you acted without clearance. Do you understand?"

"Yes Sir."

"Good. You are dismissed."

With a brisk salute, Clint turned on his heel and left.

Clint mulled over the conversation. So jealous over her teaching that bastard French, his skin burned. Mind racing with resentment, he pictured her teaching Williams. The lieutenant, stiff as a corpse, and her so lively, wondering if she liked his looks. Him being one of those blond, blue eyed muscle men a lot of women go for, and the son-of-a-bitch always bragging about playing football when he was at Yale, wherever the hell that was.

Boots off, Clint stared at the long row of bunks, growing angrier by the minute. When Dwight walked in, he stood and began to ask questions. "Williams call you in?"

"No. Why?"

"Why not? He was all over my ass for the way we handled that gas."

"I made my report. He never said a word."

Clint picked up a boot and threw it onto the wall. "The son of a bitch," he roared. "The dirty son of a bitch is after my ass."

"What's got into you? What the hell are you talking about?"

"Don't know fer sure," Clint answered. "But I'm sure as Hell gonna find out."

Next morning, as Dwight was getting dressed, Clint pulled the blanket over his head, poked his finger down his throat and puked. "Lordy. Musta ate something bad," he moaned.

"Better get to the infirmary." Dwight answered. "I'll report you sick for duty."

"Yeah. I'll go in a few minutes. See ya later." Clint rolled over and waited for Dwight to leave, then rose from his bed, dressing hurriedly into his civvies, and left to catch the next train to Amiens.

He spotted them soon as he got off the train. Standing by the window of the jewelry store she'd brought him to last week. Where she'd shown him the bracelet that was just like the one her father had given her mother, the one they'd sold to buy food. She'd been so happy it was still there. Clint had already made plans to take her there Friday and buy it for her.

He could see Williams had his arm around her waist, and as she turned to point at something in the window, he saw a big hand slip to her breast and begin to stroke, then, squeeze. Clint clenched with fury. Like she's a goddam cow! She squealed, turned toward the officer, and leaned back, daring him to squeeze the other.

Hot with rage, Clint braced himself for the onslaught. He'd kill them both. He opened his mouth to shout something. But no sound came. A familiar force had grabbed his ankles, punched his stomach and held him motionless, taking his voice. As he watched helplessly, they disappeared into the store, laughing.

Dwight returned from duty to find Clint stretched out on his bunk, a pillow under his shoulders, staring into space. "Feeling better?"

Clint looked away. "Is Ralph fucking her too?" He asked.

"Look, Clint. I didn't know what to say. I tried."

"Didn't want to hear."

Dwight sat on his bunk and leaned toward Clint. "You gonna be okay?"

"Hell yes." Clint reached for a cigarette. "Nothin' but a goddam whore. Just what I figgered. Can't say my Ma didn't warn me."

His enlistment was up in thirty days and Clint would be glad to go home. He thought he'd save his money and buy a car the day he got back. He even quit smoking to cut spending, turning down Dwight's repeated requests to join in a drink.

He quit sleeping much too, waking hours before dawn, his face flaming, berating himself. His thoughts pummeled him. I should have known it. I'm a damn fool...all the rest of 'em, laughing at me.

Off duty, he'd walk. From sunup to sundown, he went aimlessly, the rhythm of his steps and exhaustion finally shutting off his thoughts.

It was the only way he knew to forget Monique.

⌒๑

He got into a poker game on the way back. A pretty good player, he figured he'd increase his savings, maybe get a bigger car. Then, someone passed a bottle of cognac, another passed wine. The sweet glow of forgetfulness he'd found in that first sip, kept him reaching for more.

By the time the ship reached New York, Clint had lost everything and had to get a job on the docks 'til he had enough money to get home.

Chapter 10

November, 1931

In the rear view mirror of a Model A Ford, Clint watched a dim Chicago skyline sink into the stubble of an Illinois cornfield. To his left, a pale sun rose in a gray November sky. On his right sat his wife, Nell, holding their six week-old son. Ahead, a long ribbon of gravel stretched toward Missouri. And home.

It hadn't been an easy decision, making up his mind to go back and try farming again. But he'd lost a good job at the Chicago Stockyards and couldn't find work. After the stock market crashed in October, the country was in a depression. Clint wasn't about to have his family stand in a soup line on skid row. Not with Dad begging him to come home. One can always make a living farming, he figured. This time, he'd try harder. Maybe now, they'd get along. Besides, he didn't have much choice.

It was hard to keep his mind on driving. Nell wasn't talking, which was unusual. She seemed to be making a point of crying though, sniffling and blowing her nose. Clint wondered if he ought to be saying something, see if he could ease her, but wasn't sure if talking things over might make her worse. He sighed with relief when the baby whimpered, distracting her.

Out of one eye, he watched her unbutton her dress and lift the baby to her breast. Sure does change when she's tending little John, he noticed. All smiles and baby talk, no matter what else is going on. He leaned back in the seat and reached to pat her arm. "How's he doing?" He asked.

"Fine. As long as I feed him. Doc says every four hours, but the little divil won't wait."

"Don't reckon the doctor knows as much about it as the boy does." Clint's foot hit the brakes as he shifted down and jerked to a stop. "Damn cows. Forgot how dumb they are, always getting out." He watched a lone cow saunter into the roadside ditch, then drove on. "How 'bout you, Nell? You gonna be able to do this? Go to Missouri so far away from your folks?"

Nell stiffened, raising her chin. "I told you I'll be fine."

"Just want ya happy. I know you'll miss your folks. But I worry about Ma. How she might treat you. She don't like my turning Catholic. She just might take it out on you."

"As if I'd be the first to be persecuted for the faith. You're forgetting why my folks left Ireland. I've put up with more than a few who don't like Catholics."

Clint grimaced. No amount of anti-Catholicism Nell had experienced could compare to the kind she'd be getting from Ma. "We won't stay with her long," he said. We'll get settled. Find a place of our own. We can get a nice big house. Brian and your Ma can visit."

"As if they could afford such a trip. I'll be lucky if I ever see them again." She lifted the baby to her shoulder and began to rub his back. "But I got Jack now. I'll not be lonely."

"Got me, too," Clint muttered, wondering what he'd done since the baby came to make her act like he wasn't around. He drummed angry fingers on the steering wheel and took a deep breath. "Why you keep calling him Jack? I thought we were gonna call him John."

"Because of me Dad, John Joseph Cunningham, called Jack. No one but us kids called him anything else."

Clint put both hands firmly on the wheel and stiffened his arms. So his family's name wasn't going to mean a damn thing. He thought about the night John was born, how he called T.F. and told the proud Granddad they'd named the boy John Thomas after him and Uncle John.

"It makes my heart glad, Clint." Tom said. "There's been a John and a Tom in every Foster family 'cept ours long as we been in this country. If it had been up to me, I'd a named you John. But your ma picked Clinton, just for the sound of it. Promised we'd save them names for our next two boys, but it wasn't to be." Tom cleared his throat. "Good men, them Fosters, they settled this country, and fought for it in every war. I always felt like I let 'em down."

So now it's my turn to let the family down, Clint thought. If my name don't mean nothing, maybe my boy's might. Reckon the army made me realize how important serving this country is. He glanced at Nell, thinking she ought to be damn glad that her son's ancestors had fought off the British. It gave the Irish a place to come get away from 'em. Hell, John's great-grandfather fought in the Civil War to free slaves. He was a helluva lot braver than Nell's ancestors. It took them centuries and American know-how before they broke their chains.

No use arguing with her, though. Brian had warned him. He said his little sister had a way of looking after herself first and wouldn't stop arguing till she got her way. Clint stifled a snort, recalling how she wouldn't let him kiss her till he went to church. Said she couldn't go out with anyone not Catholic. And not too long after that first kiss, took him to the priest to take instructions in the faith.

For that, Clint thought; reckon I'm thankful. Turning Catholic's been good for me. Rules to go by, even if they don't make no sense, like not eating meat on Friday, or fasting during Lent. Like the Army, the Church expects discipline and order. Helps make sense of things. After being baptized, the bad dreams stopped for a while. The priest said it was because of a clear conscience.

His chest warmed as he glanced at Nell. She's a good woman, he thought, just a mite bossy at times. I oughtn't criticize, 'cause I'm not sure I deserve her. Nell's the kind of girl a guy ought to be mighty proud to take home to meet his Ma. He smiled to himself—that is any Ma but mine.

"Like I said," he began, "Ma's probably not ever gonna change her mind about the church. Pearl said she promised not to mention it. But she's made promises before."

"And broke them?" Nell laughed. "Don't worry, Clint. I've not met a soul I couldn't win over."

"You ain't met Ma. When I came back from France, she begged me to stay home. Said we'd be a family again. She even went to church a few times 'cause it might help her with her temper, but that didn't last. Dad was gonna help me start farming. It seemed like a good idea at the time."

"And you were in Chicago six months after."

"You'd 'a left, too," he retorted. "She was still mad 'cause I left home at fifteen. She wouldn't let it go."

"It was good you knew Brian so you had a place to come to. And you were lucky to meet me." Nell dropped her chin, her eyes on Clint, teasing.

"Felt at home in your Ma's rooming house. You folks was good to me. Put me in mind of my friend Red's family. They was Irish, too."

"Is that the boy who drowned? And his Dad died of the drink?"

"Yeah. That's why I'm always after Brian. Know damn well a drinker like him can end up like Old Red Donovan, drunk and mean. They can get so bad the family starts praying he'll die."

Nell laughed. "Brian's a darn fool. It's good he's not married. I'll not have a thing to do with him when he's drinking. He's too much like our dad." Her voice softened as she turned to Clint. "I'm proud you signed the pledge. It means a lot to me."

"Reckon booze never done me any good. Don't miss it, and sure as hell don't need it. The folks don't drink. I heard a few stories about Dad's drinking when he was young. But reckon it's something I never had to deal with. Ma's been enough."

Nell cradled the sleeping baby in one arm and, with the other, wrapped him tightly in his blanket. "I can't wait to meet her. Who knows? Maybe we'll be good friends."

The clock struck ten as Tom hoisted a smoking kerosene lamp high over the table so Molly could smooth out her new blue-checkered tablecloth. He yawned. Two hours past his bedtime and he was bone tired. Molly'd been bustling for days, getting the house ready for the homecoming. She looked to be getting riled and it made him edgy. It wasn't good when Molly got this far into something. She'd have trouble getting to sleep.

He set the lamp in the center of the table, turned her to face him and lifted her chin. "Reckon we ought to get to bed, hon. I got corn to pick in the morning. Clint won't get here till late tomorry."

"Tomorry I'm baking. Going to bake blackberry pies." She leaned back and looked at Tom, her eyes softening. "Clinton loves blackberry pie. This time I'm gonna prove it, Tom. Let him know I want him here."

"He knows. You've already done plenty. And he ought to appreciate us more'n last time. He'll be plenty meek after losing his job. It's hard for man, 'specially with a family."

"It wouldn't 'a happened you let him finish high school," she snapped.

"Thought we weren't going into that again," Tom sighed. "Lot a men in this country who graduated from college are out of work. Learning don't mean much, times like these."

Molly's voice brightened. "Can you help me set up the crib? Get that done, I'll quit for tonight."

"Are you sure? How come you got irons on the stove?"

"I'm gonna iron my dress to go to Lillian's party. I've got to look right for Miss Uppity."

"It's mighty good of her to be putting out a welcome for Clint. She says it's so he can get reacquainted. So everyone can meet his wife."

Molly stiffened, flashing her eyes. "I don't know what they'll say about her being Papist. How the hell he ended up with a Catholic I'll never know."

"You don't have to, Molly." Tom answered sternly. "That's Clint's business. I don't want you bringing it up."

Molly gulped. "I didn't mean to. I swear. It just came out."

He lifted the table with both hands, his knuckles white with strain, his voice rising. "Well, keep it in! If you don't want him to leave; you keep your mouth shut."

"I will. I will." Molly lifted a corner of her apron to wipe her eyes. "I want my boy home. I don't think I could bear it, getting old without him. It'll work this time, Tom. I promise."

Clint leaned against the wall of the First Baptist Fellowship Hall and looked over the assembled guests. Was one hell of a spread. He eyed the long tables loaded with plates of fried chicken, ham, and potato salad, plus every family's favorite dish brought to pass. So many desserts, the table Aunt Lillian had set them on drooped in the middle like an old horse.

Clint had stepped back from talking to folks, looking for Nell to see if she was enjoying herself. It seemed she was doing fine, chatting to people like she'd knowd 'em all her life. He stood a few minutes, watching her. It looked like she was getting plenty attention from Marvin Benton. Them snappy blue eyes and thick brogue drawing him like a fly to the honey jar. Hot blood rushed to his face. I better get over there and bust that up. Damned if she ain't just like Brian, always wanting to be noticed.

That, more than a few times, he remembered, had caused her to stretch the truth. Not that she lied. She just puffed things up a little to make them more interesting, keeping her the center of everything long as she could.

His eyes roamed the room, looking for Pearl, and praying she wasn't noticing him. He spotted her standing next to Carson against a back wall, where the glare of a bare ceiling bulb highlighted a dark purple bruise on her cheek. He whistled through clenched teeth. Damn! Oughta known when I seen that pint in his pocket Carson's a drinker! All them letters from Ma, bragging what a good family Pearl was marrying into. She said they were rich farmers and fine upright people.

Upright my ass, Clint fumed. It's a helluva way for Pearl to have money. I gotta stay clear of them. Don't want to meddle in Pearl's business and I just might kick his ass. He decided it best to go to Nell, thinking it time he pried her from Marvin and get something to eat.

As he swung around, he noticed Alice Benton had settled into a nearby chair and was busily smoothing a short blue dress over her bony knees. "Why, Clint Foster. You're all alone at your own party. I see you're watching that little sister of yours. What do you think of her now? I bet you missed her," she prattled. "I never knew kids as close as you two. And what a pretty wife you have! And a baby already! Aren't you proud to show them off?"

Clint grimaced. Same old Alice, he thought.

"Hear you're going to be farming with Tom," she said. "Are you staying with the folks?"

"We're looking for a place of our own. Be moving out soon as we find something."

Alice nodded. "You need your own place. Don't think it's wise having two women in the kitchen." She glanced across the hall to Molly, "Do you know what I mean?"

Clint looked directly into her face, not answering.

She looked away. "Have you seen Ira White? He just got here. And Edna's with him. She always is, since—" her voice trailed off, then brightened. "I bet he'll know where there's a house you can rent."

"I'll ask. You folks okay? See Marvin and Dorothy got a couple kids."

"They're my pride and joy. They named the girl after me. You see Mary Donovan? She's Mary Richards now. She's got six. And over there," she pointed, "are your cousins, Lillian's girls. Faye has Ida May and Albert. And Lily, she's a nurse at the hospital. A good one too! Your Aunt Lillian's proud as punch of her grandchildren. She spends every minute with them she can. Since Alvin's gone deaf she's got to have someone to talk to. That family gets on better than any I've known. I don't think they've ever had an argument."

"Not that they told anybody," Clint said. He stepped away from the wall, hands rubbing his buttocks, a nervous habit Nell had berated him for. Gotta get away from Alice, he concluded. I'm not gonna to oblige her with any gossip about how the Fosters don'tget along. How often they argue. What she didn't get out of him, she'd probably make up anyway. "Better go see Iry," he said. "It's been years."

Except for a mop of snow-white hair, it looked like Ira hadn't changed a bit. Clint watched as he stopped to shake hands with Uncle Albert and say hello to Aunt Lillian. Odd, Clint thought, how that man fills up an entire room just by walking in, making everyone else look like they might as well go on home.

When he spotted Clint, Ira strode forward, his right hand outstretched. "Clint! Good to see you. Want you to stop by my office, soon as you get settled. Hear what you've been up to all these years." He looked around. "Now, where's that wife of yours? Folks say she's mighty pretty, and Edna and I are looking forward to being introduced."

⌒⌒

It was almost dark as they drove back to the farm, and even though he couldn't see her, Clint could tell by her voice that Nell was excited. She hadn't stopped talking since they'd climbed into the car. She'd seemed reluctant to leave the party, and was now acting almost glad to be heading home so she could talk about everybody.

Nell lifted her chin, tossing thick dark curls. "Hoity-toity," she said. "That Ira White sure is something! Thinks he's king of the hill."

"Iry's a good man," Clint retorted. "Richer than we are, for damn sure, but he's done a lot for Lowell. Folks appreciate him."

"Not as much as he appreciates himself. He and Emma Teeter! La-te-da! She's one of those dumb women who spend half their life getting ready to go somewhere."

Clint interrupted, "You don't know that. Emma's Aunt Lillian's best friend. I think maybe Emma don't think much of herself and tries to make up for it by fussing over her looks."

"Baloney! She wants all the men looking at her and all the women jealous. I know her kind, and I can't stand them."

Clint gritted his teeth. It seemed like Nell was determined to criticize. Especially anyone taking attention she thought belonged to her. He'd been looking forward to having her meet the town folks, and now she was putting them down. "Just don't criticize Aunt Lillian," he snapped. "Was nice of her to put on a party for us."

135

Nell's eyes twinkled. "Wayul, reckon that's so. Raat good of her. Golly! Do they all talk that slow? Ever notice it takes men fifteen minutes to get a sentence out, half of it saying Waaayuuul. And the women talking so fast you can't understand them."

"They're Missourians. It's how we talk. You would too, you grew up here."

"I would not. Mary Richards doesn't talk that way."

"Reckon that's 'cause she's Irish." Stifling his anger, Clint tried to change the subject. "You two seemed to get along."

"We did. She's Catholic, too. She said there's not many of us and that Father Donahue will be glad to see us when we stop by the rectory to join the parish. Is it okay if we drive in tomorrow and get that taken care of?"

"I told Dad I'd help him pick corn. We gotta get it in before it snows." Eyeing Nell's dark silhouette against the car window, Clint chose his words carefully. "You take the car and go by yourself. But don't talk religion with anyone else. Being Catholic ain't too accepted in Lowell. Lot of folks figure we'll all burn in Hell."

"I'll tell them who'll end up in Hell," she snipped. "'Outside the church, there is no salvation'. I've heard it all my life."

"Okay if you believe it. But they don't. No need to mention it. You won't change nobody."

"So they're dumb as they sound?"

"Not dumb, Nell. It's what they believe. Okay with you, I'd as soon drop the subject. Be home in a minute and we agreed we won't talk religion around Ma."

"There you go again," Nell sniffed. "Blaming your poor Ma. She's been good to me. And she's crazy about little Jack. I think you've got a wild imagination. Finding ways to excuse yourself for being a pain in the arse."

Clint screeched tires as he steered angrily into the lane. Enough said. Say more and she'd have another comeback. No way she'd quit without the last word, even in front of Ma.

There's years when a Missouri farmer finds it hard to keep believing in anything. Should he pray to God? Or kneel to the weather? Just in case, he pays homage to both, usually, in hope, sometimes, in thanksgiving, or, as in the year of our Lord nineteen hundred and thirty-two, begging for mercy.

Weather's assault had begun in January; when icy winds blew drifts waist high, making everyday chores a challenge of endurance. With spring came rains, swelling the river and flooding the fields, delaying the planting. Next, came summer, hot and dry, withering tender new plants into stunted yellow stubs. Not until October rose vivid and orange against a clear bright sky, did it loosen its grip.

But as Weather relented, God, it seemed, had ignored him! Throughout the country agriculture was in crisis. With the depression on, consumers at home or abroad weren't buying. And in spite of miserable yields, the farmer had produced more than he could sell. Prices fell, and the easy credit of the past few years left many with a burden of debt that became unpayable.

Yet, with his family gathered around a table groaning with food, Tom's heart swelled with gratitude. It was Thanksgiving. Clint was still living at home. There was not enough money coming in this year for them to afford a place of their own. Molly'd been tolerable. His farm was paid for, and because of last year's plenty, there was food enough in the cellar to last till spring. Best of all, six months ago, Pearl came home. She left Carson, this time for good.

Times like this, Tom figured, he had more than most men could even hope for. He spooned green beans from a glass bowl and passed it to Pearl, not speaking, because he knew the rising catch in his throat might thicken his voice. Seemed he couldn't look at her lately, without crying. Bad circumstances may have brought her back, but for Tom, Pearl's homecoming had been a Godsend. Wasn't anybody knew how to handle Molly better'n Pearl. 'Specially when it came to keeping her apart from Nell.

He watched Nell drop her head, make the sign of the cross and whisper the Catholic blessing, glad Molly's attention was focused on getting the stuffing out of the goose. It ain't good what's going on between those two, he thought. At first, they got along fine. Both seemed to be trying. But ever since the morning Nell started throwing up, Molly's been shutting her out, treating her like she don't belong here. Now, Nell's taken to sulking and won't help out. She says if Molly tells her she does everything wrong, why bother?

Nell looked up to see him watching her and smiled shyly.

"You okay Nell?" He asked. "It won't be long."

"Doc says any day."

Pearl moved little John Thomas to the left side of her lap and offered him a spoonful of mashed potato. "Reckon I can't wait," she said. "Hope it's a girl I can sew for. Clint won't let me put anything but trousers on this boy."

Clint grinned. "Yer right about that. Ain't gonna turn my boy into a sissy."

Molly looked down at the baby. "You ain't no sissy are you John Thomas? You're Gramma's little man. Aren't cha?"

"Gama. Gama," the baby gurgled, reaching for Molly.

"Why lookee here! There's my boy, wanting his Grammy. He knows who loves him most." She lifted him from Pearl's arms and glared at Nell, the smug lift of her chin like a slap, flushing Nell's cheeks.

Nell shoved her chair from the table and stood. "I'm not well," she mumbled. "Maybe I shouldn't eat." She went for her son and wrestled him from Molly's grasp. "Time for a nap, Jack. Let's go." Stopping an instant behind Molly's chair to glare angrily at Clint, she turned and stamped up the stairs.

⌒〜⊙

The pains had been coming for hours. About four or five minutes apart now, and increasing in intensity. But Nell didn't seem to be making much progress. She reached for Clint's hand and bit down on the towel she'd stuffed between her teeth.

"The doctor? Where is he? She gasped. "Oh—Oh—Ooooh GOD!"

Clint patted her softly. "There, there. Think he's here now, just heard him come in."

"Good. Maybe he can make something happen. Oh Clint. I hear Jack. He's crying. Clint, don't let her..." Her voice tapered to a low moan as she sucked in a deep breath and arched her back.

"It's okay, Pearl's got him. He's okay."

Soon as Dr. Evans came in she tried to sit, and pushed Clint away. "Go," she whispered. Send Pearl up. I want you with Jack. He'll be scared, hearing me like this. And don't let *her* near him. You hear?"

Late the next morning, battered, bloody, and screaming with rage, Mona Louise Foster finally came into this world. After placing her in Pearl's able hands, Doc sent for Clint. "Got a fine healthy girl," he reported. "A little bruised, but that'll clear up in a few days. She came out upside down. Breech position we call it. It was hard on Nell, and hard on the baby." He laughed. "She interrupted everybody's Thanksgiving celebration, too. But it looks like she was worth the sacrifice."

"She okay?" Clint looked nervously at Nell. Her eyes were closed, her color wan. He reached down to brush a damp curl from her forehead. She smiled slightly and Clint jumped back. "Thought she was dead for a minute."

Doctor Evans laughed. "She's worn out. I gave her a sedative. With two women here to care for the baby, think everyone will be better off if Nell gets some rest."

"Sure, Doc, fine. Anything I can do?"

"Stay out of the way," he laughed. "And about that birthmark, Clint, don't worry. Where its situated, no one's gonna know it's there till her wedding night."

Chapter 11

1936

A bright morning sun poured through the cracks in the old shed, bounced off the straw covered floor and surrounded the Model A with a soft golden glow. Purrs like brand new, Clint thought. Now I got her off the blocks, put in new oil, primed the carburetor and cranked her a few times, she's working fine. "About the only thing around here that does," he muttered. "Long as I keep taking good care of her, she might last a while."

He was fixing to go to town. He needed some nails and a roll of barbwire to fix the line fence he shared with Jim Richardson. He planned to plant corn there this year and didn't want Jim's cows getting in and eating his crop.

He had to see Iry, too. He got orders from Nell that if he couldn't talk their landlord into putting gravel on the dirt lane leading to the house, she'd see him herself. She swore she was going crazy, trapped here all winter and wasn't going to miss Mass again. When it rained, or when the snow drifted in, there was no way to get the car to the main road without getting stuck.

Last Sunday, she'd harnessed the team, loaded the kids in the wagon and drove in anyway, Clint too ashamed to go along. He figured folks had to be talking about how hard up they were since taking off on their own, but Nell didn't seem to give a damn. Not an ounce of pride in her. Bad enough the way she talked Marvin Benton into lending her money to buy them hens last summer so she could make money selling eggs. But she wouldn't do business with Aunt Lillian and sell them to the General Store. Not when she could make more selling door-to-door.

Leaving the folks' and moving here had been Nell's idea. Clint might have waited a while, till someplace better turned up. But Nell was determined to make it work. It was the only place Iry had available at the time, and he'd let them move in without rent payments provided they fix it up.

The place looked like a damn dump, Clint recalled, but Nell said she'd live in hell before she'd spend another week with Ma. So they moved in, one week to the day after Mona was born.

Clint backed the car out of the shed, stopped, and gazed at the house. He had to admit it looked better. Before they moved, it had been empty for years, the roof leaking, and the back porch collapsed. They couldn't even open the back door till he got it fixed. The first winter, they'd boarded up broken windows and shut off every room but the kitchen, set the bed next to the cook stove and slept there, Little Jack tucked between them.

With Mona crying every minute and Jack into everything, Clint hadn't thought it possible they could make it through the winter. But Nell wasn't going to let anything keep her from doing what she had to do.

First, she made a rope harness for Jack, so she could keep him close while doing chores. Then, went about breaking Mona of crying no matter how many nights they got no sleep. She fed the baby every four hours, and then put her in the crib to cry till she stopped.

It took six months. But Clint had to admit, she'd been broke of it good. Seemed mean to him to treat a baby that way, and when Nell was out milking the cow or fixing up the henhouse, he'd lift Mona to his shoulder and carry her around, doing his best to quiet her. Now, she could behave herself almost well enough to suit everyone but her mother. At three-going-on-four, she didn't cry much, even when hurt. Instead, she'd come to Clint, not her ma, to doctor her cuts and scrapes. Even if he had to pour iodine on, which stung as much as the hurt, Mona wouldn't flinch. Just looked at him with them big blue eyes and depended on him to make her feel better.

Guess I worry over her a lot, Clint thought, ain't right for a kid not to be feeling things. But she sure is my girl. Trusts me with everything. It'll break my heart; I ever have to let her down. And some of the things bothering her ain't anything I can fix. Reckon when she's older, she'll have to figure that out.

Wasn't fair how Nell seemed to favor Jack. So did Ma! Wouldn't have a thing to do with her own granddaughter! All Mona needed was some attention, and damn! Jack was getting it all!

Clint looked up to see his little girl standing by the house and waved goodbye. As usual, she didn't wave back. Maybe this summer I'll start taking her to the field with me, he thought. Talk to her more. Get her smiling.

On the outskirts of Lowell, Clint turned past Aunt Nancy's old place where Pearl lived now, and the Benton house, wondering what Alice might be saying about him now. Supposed it was all over town how Nell had gone to the priest and got the Catholics to give them food that first winter. And how she'd gone to Dad and talked him into giving her a cow so the kids could have milk. She tied it on to the back bumper and led it home behind the car. She drove right past Richardson's house, them standing in the front yard, watching. And her acting all the while, like she didn't give a damn.

Everybody's talking plenty, he figured. About how I failed my family and how Nell runs me. Not that I give a damn. Don't care if I see any of 'em again. Only one shows any consideration's Aunt Lillian. Yet, I can't help wondering what she really thinks.

He couldn't have known that at this very moment, Aunt Lillian was in Alice's kitchen, trying to find out if there was any truth in the wild rumor that really had folks talking!

"Alice," Lillian began, "I'm mighty upset. If there's truth to this, it's a terrible scandal, but I know my sister. She can imagine anything. Tell me, what did she say?"

Alice lifted dirty teacups from the table and put them in the dish-pan. "This isn't easy," she said, "but suppose it's better you hear it from me than someone else,"

"What's better?" Lillian interrupted. "Out with it. I'm waiting."

Alice looked away, her voice almost inaudible. "Well—Molly's been telling everybody the little girl isn't Clint's."

"That's impossible! They'd just moved here from Chicago. Nell didn't know anyone."

⌒⊙

"Molly said she made friends right off with Father Donahue. She'd go visit him alone. She said she was going to confession so Clint couldn't go with her."

Lillian pulled up in her chair and glared at Alice. "You see your pastor for counsel. I do too. I don't see how Molly can say that just because they've been alone together."

Alice walked to the window and straightened the curtain before pivoting back to face her friend. "The priest isn't married, Lillian. Not like Pastor. What you think he does when he wants to—well, you know. Where you think he's going to find it? He can't get a saloon girl. Folk's would find out. And with none of those Sisters here, where you think he's going to go?"

Lillian jerked back, her eyes wide. "That baby's only half-Foster. We haven't met Nell's family. How can you judge?"

Alice stepped behind the chair and put her hands on Lillian's shoulders. "I'm sorry to be the one telling you this. But you asked. Molly's saying it. It must feel awful to you."

"How I feel doesn't matter. It's whether or not it's true. If it's not, don't know what I'll do. Other than choke Molly. I'm so upset."

Alice smiled. "Bet you feel like it often. But, there's something else Molly's saying that might upset you more."

Lillian stood and began pacing the room, her hands clasped tightly behind her back. "What now? It can't get much worse."

143

"It's about a mark on the baby. Molly says it's the devil's sign."

"For God's sake." Lillian looked down. "Forgive me, Lord, didn't mean to say that, but what does she mean by that? Lots of kids have birthmarks."

"Don't be upset. It's just that Emma and I were wondering if maybe it just might have something to do with that curse."

"Emma? What curse? She never said a word of this to me."

"But we talked about it before, Lillian, years ago. About the curse, I mean, could it be possible?"

Lillian clapped her hands over her ears and shouted. "Enough! This can't be true.

Molly doesn't believe in the curse. She'd never acknowledge it exists. She thinks it's something my pastor and I made up to make her look bad."

Alice looked down. Lillian was right. Emma's probably started this story, not Molly…at least the part about the curse. "I never thought of that. I'm sorry, Lillian. It's just that…"

"It's just that you're breathing scandal. Maybe you ought to read your Bible. Look up the Mark of Cain."

"Isn't that a protection? On Cain's descendants?"

"Right. Like a birthmark, Alice. It's not up to us to decide when the Lord overcomes evil. That child's innocent. It's not right to destroy her with talk like this."

Alice sighed. "Guess you're right. Maybe you should talk to Molly. See what she has to say."

Lillian arched her brows. "And what good would that do?" Would my sister ever admit she'd lied?" She reached for her shawl and stepped toward the door. "No, Alice. I learned a long time ago to leave Molly in the Lord's hands or whoever it is that runs her life. God made her. He'll take care of her, much as she's willing. She's not my problem. I just feel bad for Clint. He's trying so hard."

It was almost dark when Clint turned into the dirt lane and headed toward the house. Dark skeletons of trees arched overhead, scraping the top of the car. Won't be long, he mused, and everything will be green. I'll have to trim the branches back so I can get the car through.

Suddenly, in the twisted shadow of light and dark, he saw Mona! Right in the middle of the road! He screeched to a stop, missing her by inches.

He leaped from the car, ran to her, and lifted her to his shoulder. "What you doing so far from the house?" he shouted. "I could have run you over. Ma know where you are?"

"Jack chased me," she answered. "I runned away."

"Why? You two have a fight?"

For a long moment, Mona studied her hands. "Mama said to."

"Your Ma?" Clint shouted. "Your Ma told Jack to chase you?"

Slowly, she began twisting her thumb, watching it closely. "No."

"What you mean, no?" Clint asked. "Did she tell you to run away?"

Mona stared at her hands, not answering.

"Mona, what the hell's going on here? You tell me what happened."

There was no response.

Frustrated, Clint cupped her tiny chin in his hand and turned her stiff little neck until he could see her face. "Look at me, Mona. Tell me what happened."

Her eyes expressionless, Mona gazed over Clint's head, took a deep breath, pressed her lips together and stopped breathing. Terrified, Clint began to shake her, until she fell, doll like, against his shoulder. Then came to, gasping.

Not knowing what else to do, Clint tossed her into the car and sped to the house and her mother.

"Ignore it!" Nell shouted. "She's does it on purpose. She's been doing it for weeks. Lucky for me, she did it yesterday when I was at Doc's office. He says it's nothing but a temper tantrum. He said she can't hurt herself that her body has a way of making her pass out and start breathing again."

"Why didn't you tell me?"

"No reason to. Doc says she's trying to scare us and not to act scared."

"I am scared! She ain't got no temper, Nell. It's you that's mad all the time."

"And what's wrong with letting her know I'm upset? You expect me to give in to her?"

"If it's Jack, you do."

Nell stormed to the house and stood in the door. "And what do you know about it, Clint? You were gone. Fact is, I punished the both of them."

"Why? She said Jack was teasing her."

"She tried to poke his eye out, that's what. He was razzing her for sure, and I made him sit on a chair. While he sat, she came at him with a stick. Thank God it was only his cheek she caught. He might have been blinded."

༄

A week later, on the day Katie was born; Mona held her breath and passed out three times. With Dad, Aunt Pearl and Ma's friend, Mary Richardson, raving over the baby, she couldn't get anyone to stop Jack from running from behind things to scare her. She tried telling Dad, and Aunt Pearl, too. But they didn't seem to understand. They just asked all kinds of questions she didn't know how to answer.

Ma and Missus Richardson thought it was all a big joke.

༄

If Jack was Nell's, and Mona was Clint's, Kate Foster decided early on she belonged to everyone. With breathless enthusiasm, she swept into the world like a tiny wildfire, warming everybody.

With the exception of one person. Mona.

"She looks just like Nell. Got Brian's red hair." Clint argued.

"No, she's big. Like Pearl," Tom answered.

"Something to that. Damn near as big as Mona already, and she's only three."

"Smarter than Mona, for sure" said Nell. "I swear she's reading."

Clint shook his head. "No, I think she's memorized that book. A kid that young can't read."

"Can too!" Kate ran into the room, carrying a well-worn book high over her carrot topped head. She looked grudgingly around the room. "And I's not Mama. Not Aunt Pearl neever. I's Kate." She shoved the book into Clint's hands and climbed onto his lap. "I read it," she began. "Aunt Pearl told me how."

Tracing each line of print with a chubby finger, Kate recited the text perfectly, from cover to cover. Was she reading? Clint wasn't sure. But when she was four, at Pearl's insistence, Clint talked the teacher into letting her start school. At five, she was in second grade and seated two rows behind Mona, who struggled in fourth.

"No! It's mine." Mona whined as she tried to pull her reading text from Kate's firm grasp. "Dad said you aren't supposed to read my books. Give it back."

Laughing, Katie ran from the room, the book clasped tightly against her chest. "Gotta catch me first," she taunted. Besides, Dad's in the barn."

"I'll tell," Mona shouted, running after her.

"Mona will tell and go to hell," Kate chanted. "I am the Gingerbread man. Try to catch me, if you can." She darted through the kitchen door and ran outside, Mona close behind.

Face red with fury, Mona picked up a broom from the back porch. "Give it back, or else," she shouted.

Then, seemingly out of nowhere, Jack appeared and stood before her. "Put that broom down," he said firmly.

"Won't. Get out of my way. This time Kate's wrong."

"You're the wrong one, Mona. I said, put it down." Grabbing the broom, Jack wrestled her to the ground. "I'll tell Mom you tried to hit Kate," he warned.

"And I'll tell Dad on both of you," she retorted.

Jack stood over her, laughing. "It won't do you any good. I'll say you were lying."

Mona stood and spat in his direction. "You can't win, Jack Foster. I'll show you."

"Show me what? That you're a darn fool?" Jack laughed. "Monee, groany, boney, pony. Leave Kate alone. You're just mad 'cause she's smarter 'n you. She's finishing up your reading book and you aren't half way through it."

Mona ran into the house and slammed the door. With Jack taking sides with Kate, there wasn't a chance of getting the book 'til she was done with it. Ma would believe Jack and wouldn't whip him even if she caught him lying. The two of them would make a joke of it.

Mona stamped through the house to the kitchen, "Jack's gonna grow up bad if Ma don't make him mind," she muttered. "I got to tell Dad about this so's he'll believe me." She paused, looked around the room and spotted Jack's prized bag of marbles on the kitchen table, picked it up, tightened the drawstring and put it in her pocket. After slipping out the front door, she ran down the path, through the woods, to the river, where she dropped all twenty-five, one by one, into the swift running water.

After supper that night, when Ma sent her to the pantry to dish up dessert, Mona gleefully spooned an extra-large portion of pudding into Jack's dish, right on top of where she'd spit in the bowl. And when Ma asked if she'd seen where Jack left his marbles, Mona swore she'd not seen them for days.

Punishing Kate would take a lot more doing.

Hoping to spot her doing something that might upset Dad, Mona began to shadow her. And in a few days, discovered what seemed to be the perfect opportunity.

What Mona didn't know was that Kate was well aware she was being spied on. And on that warm summer afternoon, while playing with Bridey Richardson in the back yard, decided she'd had enough.

When she spotted Mona slither sideways around the corner of the house and stand behind the lilac bush to listen, she whispered to Bridey.

"It's Mona. She's snooping." Katie covered her mouth with her hand and giggled. "Let's play a trick on her."

She raised her voice. "And you know about my sister," she began. "Mona. She has a big secret"

"A secret?" Bridey gasped. "Did she commit a mortal sin?"

"I don't know, maybe she did. Grammy says it's an evil thing."

"C'mon. Tell me. Did she touch her bottom or something?"

Katie laughed. "No. But that's where the secret is."

Bridey looked shocked. "The secret's about her bottom? How can that be?"

Katy began to rock back and forth, speaking in a sing-song voice. Loud enough so Mona would hear every word. "My sister Mona is a nut. Has three sixes on her..."

Before she could finish the rhyme, Mona slammed her into the grass, kicking, hitting and shouting. "Shut up, Kate. Ma said we weren't supposed to tell anyone!"

Katie fought back with fingernails and fists, finally shoving Mona off, then jumped up laughing. She looked down at her sister's hot, flushed face. "It's what you get for spying on me, Red Face. You won't let me have secrets, I'll tell yours."

Mona kicked clods of dirt along the ragged path, covering her bare feet with fine gray dust, wondering why her birthmark was such a bad thing. Especially when Mom had said it ought to be a secret. Grammy said that three sixes was the mark of the devil, but Ma said that was nonsense. Yet, if it's nonsense, she wondered, why we have to keep it a secret. It wasn't fair. God wasn't fair to mark her with such a thing. She gritted her teeth and couldn't wait until she got to Dad so he could comfort her.

She was heading to the cornfield, looking for Dad as he mended fence. Pretending she'd come to help and hoping to see a sign that it might be a good time to tell him on Kate.

Her face grew hot, remembering. What if Kate had told someone else? What if she told someone from school? Why does it have to be a secret? Does it mean something bad is wrong with me?

Before she said anything, she realized she wasn't absolutely sure that Dad knew about it. He'd never said anything. That's what made talking to him about it hard. She didn't want to make him feel bad, too.

Mom had told her she should thank God it wasn't on her face. But once, when she was little, it was Ma told her to shush when she mentioned it to Aunt Pearl. And Ma usually told folks everything.

"No," she said to herself. "This time I better not tell. If it's a secret, it's best I keep it. Like the way Ma and Dad argue and Dad's nightmares. Some things are best kept inside."

Chapter 12

1944

Brian was on his way. He had called Nell late last night, drunk and sobbing, saying he thought of her and Clint every minute since their Mother died, that he had time off, some great news, and was coming to Lowell to celebrate. "Can only stay a week" he quipped. "So tell Clint I'll not be helping in the fields. It's a great job I've landed and I'm on me way to being rich!"

Glad that Mom and Dad hadn't forced her to meet the train, Mona slipped into their bedroom to check herself in the big mirror that topped Ma's dresser. If Uncle Brian was rich, she figured she ought to look her best.

She'd been changing so fast lately she hardly recognized herself. She seemed softer, wider. If she pulled her blouse tight enough across her chest she could see two small mounds of breasts beginning to grow. Not enough for a brassiere, she thought, but it won't be long.

Last week, she'd waked with blood in her panties. Afraid she was dying, she ran to Mom, who gave her some pads and safety pins, and told her she could expect to bleed for a few days every month.

"Why?" She asked. "Is something wrong with me?"

"No," said Nell. "All women do it. It's the way we're made."

Mona's voice was shrill. "Why? It doesn't make any sense.

Nell reached forward, clapping a hand over Mona's mouth. "Shhhh, shhhh, Jack's in the next room. He might hear you."

"You mean it's a secret? Does Dad know?"

151

"Okay, Mona, enough questions. All you need to know is that it's up to you to wash your own pads and see you keep an extra in your sock."

Nell rose and walked to the door, then turned back, and addressed her daughter softly. "Me ma used to say it was a cross we bear to purify us for the blessing of carrying a child. And it's many a cross you'll bear in your lifetime, Mona. Most are worse than this. If you bear them right you'll make it to Heaven."

Wondering what her body might look after the Resurrection, Mona dropped her blouse to study her breasts. They sure didn't look like Mama's. Hers were big and brown at the tip, where Kate used to suck. Will mine have milk? She wondered. What if it leaks through my dress when I'm at school? The way Ma's did when it was time to feed Katie? I suppose the kids will make fun of me for that too.

It wasn't any use to ask Mom about all this. She'd just tell me to accept it. Or tell me, again, how kids at school make fun of me anyway. Saying they pick on me 'cause I'm hard to get along with.

When she told Dad about the teasing, he got mad and told her how rotten everybody's folks were. "They're damn fools, Mona," he said. "Don't pay no mind to 'em. Be nice as you can, make the teacher happy, and your day will come."

Then, with a twinkle in his eye, Dad went on. "Catch them doing something wrong, look them straight in the eye, and let 'em see you're better than they are. Ain't nothing makes a fool madder'n knowing you're better'n he is. 'Specially if he thinks you'll tell the teacher!"

Mona buttoned her blouse and smirked at her reflection. Now that she'd got the teacher believing she was a good girl, it was easy to tell that teacher she was being tormented...even when she wasn't. Making a damn fool into a liar felt better than about anything.

Casting a final glance at her reflection, she laughed aloud. I'll fix 'em, she thought. Damn fools better not pick on me again!

The *Kansas City Bullet* belched her way into Lowell at three-fifteen, spitting smoke and ashes high onto the depot roof as it jerked to a squealing stop. On the platform, Clint, Nell, Jack and Kate huddled quietly, waiting for Brian to step off the train.

But not until after everyone else had disembarked and greeted loved ones, did he finally emerge, stumbling down the steps and grinning broadly.

"Damn. He's drunk," Clint growled. "Wish to hell I'd left the kids at home."

"Hush," Nell admonished. "Must have been in the bar car talking to people. You know how he loves to talk. Folks enjoying him so much they buy him drinks." She ran towards her brother, enfolded him in her arms and gave him a loud smacking kiss.

"It's like a sight from Heaven," she gushed. "I haven't been so glad to see anyone in my life. Come. Want to show off my kids. They're right there with Clint."

Clint watched Kate wrinkle her nose and turn from Brian's fumy embrace. Then saw Jack return a kiss and hug back eagerly. All day, the boy had been talking about meeting the uncle his ma said he took after, and Clint was plain damn tired of it.

"Only thing different is the color of his hair. Other 'n that, Jacks the spittin' image of his uncle," Nell said. "Katie may have Brian's red hair, but she's a Foster."

Heartily in favor with Nell's comparisons, Brian spread his arms and stepped toward Clint. "My God, Hillbilly," he began, "Sure got you a fine family."

Clint retreated, recoiling in disgust at the aroma of booze and cigarettes that leached into the space between them.

Brian laughed. "There he goes again, look at him, Nell. Scared to death someone's going to kiss him."

"Damn right," Clint retorted. "Told you before, I don't kiss anyone but women or kids."

Nell laughed. "Come on; let's load up the car she said. "Brian wants to meet Mona."

Like two wary boxers in a fight to the finish, one eyed the other, vying for position. Spying, shadowing, and slipping quietly from room to room and keeping a safe distance.

From first sight, Mona and Brian were adversaries, each trying to figure what it was about the other they didn't trust.

She'd located his hiding place the day after he arrived, and Brian saw her do it. Nell's calla lily bed had seemed a good place to hide a couple spare pints, the thick mat of growth at the roots making excellent cover.

Now that she's found it, I'm not sure what she'll do, he thought. It's so I won't upset Clint I'm hiding it. I have to with him acting like some holy roller. I have a drink, and he leaves the room. He runs off to the barn to shovel cow manure, or some other damn thing he does out there. So, I'll have my wee nip on me way to the outhouse. How's he to know? Unless, of course, the girl tells him. Nosy little brat! Clint never did like drinking, and if he found out his brother-in-law was enjoying a bit on his vacation, Brian knew he'd be angry. Clint was his friend, a buddy, and Nell's husband. The last thing Brian wanted was to cause any trouble.

As he stood at the side of the house debating whether Mona was occupied enough not to be spying on him, he couldn't help thinking about the conversation he'd just had with Nell.

Something strange seemed to have come over Clint since the last visit, and Brian was having a hard time trying to understand what it was.

Most obvious was that Clint seemed to have no use for Jack. Forever yelling at the poor kid, telling him he was lazy, and sending him off to do some chores. Nell wasn't liking Jack's treatment, either. Saying Clint's foul mouth was a bad example for all the kids.

"I'm afraid the kids are like him and his mother. Cussing and swearing, and mad all the time. I've heard each of them use bad language more than once. Soaped their mouths for it, I did. But how can I punish when their dad's mouth is worse?"

She started to cry, "Brian, 'tis the church we're needing. Half the time we've been missing Mass. The lane too muddy to get the car out, it drifts in the winter. There's times the old car won't work or with the gas rationing we don't have any gas. Even if we could get to town, there's no Catholic school. I'm wishing we'd stayed in Chicago. It would have been better for Jack."

With that remark, Brian suddenly realized he might have the perfect solution! Jack would come home with him and go to St. Bernard's High, right on his street. And he'd pay the tuition. With his own radio program, he could afford it. And Jack would brighten his day.

Even with Clint's hillbilly blood, the boy was as Irish as his mother. He can sing with the best of them and spread blarney like butter. And he loves his uncle. Be a great entertainer, that kid. I can get him started. Since me ma died, I'm lonely. Without her to nag, it's easy to drink. A good thing it will be for the lot of us, I take Jack along.

Brian wasn't surprised to find that Clint thought it a good idea. So much, that one had to think he might want to be rid of the boy.

"Weren't much older than he is when I set off on my own," Clint said. "Jack needs to grow up. He's too damn lazy. Gotta get off his ass and get some discipline. Heard them sister schools was good at making kids pay attention." His eyes sought Nell's, seeking approval.

"Ah my Jack," she sighed. "God knows I'll miss him. A big opportunity it is, and I'll not be the one to steal it from him. He's got faith enough to become a priest." Her voice wavered and tears welled in her eyes. "Brian, 'tis a great good you're doing. With God watching over you, you'll get your reward."

"Reward?" answered Brian. "If He's watching me close, it's for penance I owe." He slipped his arm around Nell's waist and gave her a squeeze. "This is Brian remember? You've forgot who I am."

Nell pushed him back, laughing. "If it's the devil who's watchin', give the devil his due. Be off with ya, Brian. Let's go tell Jack."

Mona couldn't remember when she'd been this happy. It'd been easy, adding Jack's chores to hers. No more time wasted arguing. And with Ma demanding Kate help her with the housework, she had Dad to herself. I'm making him feel better, too, she thought. Without Jack, he doesn't have to be mad all the time.

Last night, Dad had waked with a shout, sounding frightened. She ran to his bed. He'd been sleeping in Jack's room, so was close enough she could hear him. Ma sent him there the night Jack left. Said she couldn't rest with the moaning, groaning and kicking. And it didn't seem right to Mona that Ma wouldn't try to help him.

But I can, Mona thought, and placed a hand on his heaving shoulder. "I'm here," she whispered. "Don't cry, Dad. It'll only make it worse."

"Can't get much worse," he answered. Then, he caught himself. He didn't want to place his burden on Mona. "Had a bad dream. It's nothing; you go on back to bed." He watched her back slowly to the door.

"Mona," he said. "Just as soon you not mention this to your ma. She don't understand."

"I know, Dad," she said softly. "Don't worry. I do."

I sure as Hell don't understand it either, Clint grumbled. Same damn dream, night after night. Red's head, bobbing in the river, Bill Berky standing in the hellfire of the burning school. Ben, Brian and Jack doing inhuman things. Me trying to stop them, but can't move. His mother, watching it all.

Shivers swept over him as he sat up and reached for the cigarette pack he'd left on the bedside chair. How come all them dreams are the same, he wondered. All that stuff happened so long ago. Don't make no sense. He shuddered. I'm scairt. Scairt to death. Can't figure what's going on.

With his heart pounding so hard it seemed to be beating on his breast bone, Clint gasped for air, each hair on his body bristling, then, standing upright and pulling on every nerve. He knew better than to try to get any more sleep. The thoughts just wouldn't leave. His agitation was rising. Gotta get away, he thought, else I'll lay here and go crazy.

But where the hell am I gonna go? He asked himself. Don't even know what I'm running from. Am I crazy? Like Ma? Is it true, same as T. F. and Doc argue it, that she's sick? That she can't stop herself? What's that mean to me?

Clint reached for the pants he'd slung over a bedside chair only three hours before. Might's well get dressed, he figured. Gotta get busy; get the hell out of this house.

He walked. In the same way he'd walked last night, the night before, and the night before that. After slipping quietly down the stairs, feeling his way through the cluttered kitchen and out the back door. Then, carefully making his way down the rough dirt lane to the main road, where the white gravel glowed eerily, reflecting the full moon and lighting the path. Two miles east, turn right, one-quarter mile south, to the folk's house, dreading what he knew he'd see.

The house was blazing with lights. Ma was awake, washing windows in the front room. Just like him, running from the night.

Ma had to work, he reckoned, and he had to walk. Both were mired in the same pit, with no way out. How long, Clint wondered, could he go on? With little or no sleep in over a month, and plagued by a gnawing restlessness every waking moment? Would it end, as hers did, in the sadness that begs for death?

Clint stopped. Shook his body, hoping it would shake off the thought. Can't think that! I won't. Got kids to think of. It ain't been fair, my life. Trying to do what's right and losing everything I ever wanted. I couldn't even fight in the war, or the last one, even though I wanted to. Hell, my own wife turns from me, or just lies there, like she'd rather be someplace else.

A rustle in the bushes startled him. Something's behind me! No, it's the same old bogey man stuff. Like when I was a kid. Like he's there, still, wants to-to what? Kill me? Catch me? I can't think this way. What if I do something to myself? I don't want to die. What if I can't stop? Who'll hold me back, way Dad does Ma?

Clint dropped to his knees, shoulders heaving with sobs, and mumbled a prayer. "God, what's happening to me? What'd I do to deserve this? I confessed my sins. Ever since I met Nell, I've tried. Are ye even there, God? Or are ye like Ma says, a damn cruel joke? I'm breakin' in two, I can't go on, I can't—"

He rose, brushed dirt off his pants and looked to the house. She'd blown out the lamps and gone back to bed. Meanwhile, he'd walk on down to his oak tree. There, he hoped, to be able to sleep.

The next morning, Nell was in the kitchen, making oatmeal. Coffee perked on the back burner. She ignored Clint as he entered the room, looking down and busying herself tidying the room. He hadn't spoken to her in days and she seemed to like it that way. Whatever he said, they'd end up arguing. Usually over Jack or Mona, and how he'd treated them, and always ended with the same gripe about what he hadn't done, and that he wasn't going to church.

He didn't want to hear any of it again. Sidestepping around her, he went to the cupboard for a cup and a bowl, to the stove to fill them, and outside to the back stairs. Tail wagging, Tex sat beside him, eyeing the dish.

"Good boy," Clint said. And after two bites, offered the rest of his breakfast to the waiting dog.

"Why's he eating on the porch?" Kate dropped into a kitchen chair for a quick breakfast before leaving to catch the school bus.

"How would I know? He won't say anything." Nell sniffed. "He's fool enough to want to eat on the porch, let him. It's misery he's running on these days, and he seems to enjoy it."

Hands on hips, she turned to Kate. "Why don't you ask him? See if he's got an answer. Sure and I don't know what it is."

"I might ask him if he's going to the dogs if that's who he's eating with." Kate giggled. "We better let Mona do it. She's the one he talks to."

Mona tramped in to the room, glared at Nell, and directed a remark toward her. "You mind your own business, Kate Foster. Did you ever think Dad won't tell you anything because you'd run to Ma and make fun of him? You and Jack cut him out of the family, that's what. It's not fair."

Mona jerked back, surprised by the sting of Nell's open palm against her cheek.

"You talking around me again, Mona?" She asked. "You think I don't know what you're up to? You have something to say, you say it to me, not someone else." She scooped steaming oatmeal into a dish, poured milk on top and handed it to Mona. "Go on with you. Eat with him. I see it's your Dad cutting the family out of his life, not the other way around. Sit out there and tell him how bad it is. Just so you stay away from me."

Mona slammed the door and left the house, shouting over her shoulder as she made her way to the road. "Bye, Dad," she called over her shoulder. "See you at supper."

Kate stood, picked up her books and stepped across the room to kiss Nell goodbye. "She's sideways, Ma," she sighed. "Nothing's ever straight with Mona. It always comes out crooked. We have to stop paying any attention to her. No one can understand what she does."

Late that afternoon, Clint was jolted from a short nap on the front room couch by the shrill ring of the telephone. It was T.F. He needed help with Ma.

"I gotta git to town, Clint. They's bank papers I have to sign."

"What you want of me, Dad?

"Kin ye come by tomorry, stay with her an hour or two?"

"I'm pretty busy with crops, right now Dad. Ain't got all the corn picked. Can Pearl come?

Tom's voice trembled as he answered. "Please, son, just help me out. Pearl's on a teacher's meeting up in Harperville. I can't leave your Ma alone. She's talking killing herself again. I can't take her along; she's in such bad shape. I don't know what she'll do. Folks talk, you know."

Clint stiffened. How in hell can I deal with this? He thought, and then asked, "What time you want me there, Dad?"

"Right after noon. One-o-clock. Come early and eat with us."

"Not this time, Dad. I'll come by. She'll be okay with me.

With a sense of dread, Clint walked outside. The last thing he wanted to do was to take care of Ma. Tired as he was, he realized, that even though he had promised T.F., he might not be able to do it.

Chapter 13

1944

It was only a small patch of ice on the top step. Clint had stepped over it when he came in. Knowing it'd probably melt by afternoon, he didn't pay it much attention. But when Molly ran from the house, it was still early. That's why she fell.

Clint held his breath as he watched her go down. Like watching a slow motion picture show, with no way to control the action. Each frame momentarily frozen, taking its time to etch in his memory.

A door held open to a clear fall morning. Long, white hair brushing his arm. The back of a flannel nightgown, cracked bare heels below. One foot moves off the porch onto the ice, then slips forward, leaves the step, and kicks high, throwing her backward. The other leg stays behind, then curls beneath her. Buttocks hit the porch with a loud thump. Next, a long, agonizing slide down the steps to the ground.

She lies motionless on the frosty earth. Only her hair moves, whipping in the brisk wind. A white heap of strangeness that is his Mother. A strong gust flutters her nightdress, exposing a bony, milk-white leg, jutting outward from her left hip. The foot, twisted inward, rests on the bottom stair.

Clint dropped to the porch, face in his hands, too numb to move, sobs from within blubbered into his palms. "She's broke," he moaned. "Great God almighty... what if she's dead? I can't go down there. God, no, I can't. If I hadn't...."

A soft cry interrupted him. Warily, he moved to her side.

"You hurt?" Clint moved beside her, looking away as he pulled the nightgown over her legs, his face reddened by a glimpse of her drawers.

"Ma. Ma. Kin you hear me, Ma. It's Clint. You hurt?"

Again, she moaned.

He had to get her to the house! Without thinking how, he slid his arms under her, and then pulled back. Can't reach that leg, he thought, gotta straighten it, else I can't pick her up.

She screamed. And screamed again. Each piercing cry an arrow straight through his heart. But Clint had to do what he knew was right. Dad was coming and there wasn't much time.

There's times when life puts one in a situation so horrific the mind refuses to consider it. That's why Clint's senses shut down that day. So he didn't have to hear her cries. Nor see a drop of her blood. Why, later, all he could remember was what his mind chose to see there. Anything else was only a nightmare, watched from a dull, half-sleep.

It's the reason why, once inside the house, he laid her on the kitchen floor and not in her bed. Positioning her right where she might have fallen, at the bottom of the stairs, with her leg splayed out like a snapped wishbone.

Barefoot, she could have run down the stairs, tripped and fell. Same way he had as a kid, dozens of times. Dad would see how easily it happened.

But no matter what the sequence of events, Ma was hurt bad. Clint had to do something so Dad wouldn't blame him for letting her run outside threatening to go to the river.

He stumbled through the kitchen, upsetting chairs and tripping on a table leg, his deafened ears not hearing the crash of dishes hitting the floor. Only one thought was clear. He had to get to the phone. He had to reach Doc.

He stood, pondering the wooden box on the front room wall, the jutting black mouthpiece, the what-you-call-it, hanging on the side. "Damn," he muttered. "Can't figger out how to use it. What the hell's wrong with me? What the hell I doin' here? Oh. I gotta ring it. Yea, ring it."

One long crank to summon Central brought the voice of Mary Lou Teeter chirping into his ear. "Operator," she answered. Suddenly, she changed her tone, "My God! What's happened? Is that someone screaming? Need the sheriff?"

Clint's words dropped like stones. "Must be somethin' on the line," he mumbled. Get Doc Evans. Ma fell."

"Is this Clint Foster? It sounds like you. Is your Ma at your house?

"We're at Dad's. Git the Doc. Please." His voice dropped to a gruff whisper. "Hurry, I-I-I think it's serious."

"You go tend her. I'll send Doc. No worry. I'll tell him to get there fast."

Clint clanked the receiver back into the hanger and, in a trance, made his way to the kitchen, stepped over an upturned chair and his shrieking mother, and made his way to the washstand.

"Gotta find a towel…a wet one. Where the hell she keep 'em?" He plowed through pantry shelves, shoving jars of canned fruit out of the way and onto the floor. "Shit!" He uttered. "My eyes all clouded with bawling. I can't see."

He stopped, took a few deep breaths and prayed God to slow his heart, before it hammered out of his chest. Reeling, he spotted her apron, hanging from a peg by the back door. A strong smell of cinnamon rose from a field of faded roses as he lifted it to his nose, breathing the sweet spice deep into his nostrils. He remembered the little boy, standing on a chair, watching her cook, waiting for his chance to clean the bowl, licking the batter from his fingers as if he were starving. Instinctively, he looked for the hemmed corner to dry his eyes. The same place she used when he'd hide his face in it, so Dad wouldn't see his tears. Like then, like now, he thought. Nothing's changed.

After dipping the apron into the washbasin, Clint stepped outside. Blood had splattered the steps, and even though the dog had licked up the most of it, he had to be sure no sign of it remained.

The clop-clop of Dad's horse in the lane warned him to hurry. Finished, he ran to the car, stuffed the bloody cloth under the seat, went inside and dropped onto a kitchen chair. Exactly where he'd been when Tom left.

⌒꜡

If it were true a curse had been leveled on his family, Tom Foster figured it must have been aimed at him. Most of his life wasted, spending his best years loving a woman that couldn't, or wouldn't, love back. That she'd taken everything good out 'a him leaving him bone dry and empty, with nothing to show for it but a tough layer of skin and bones made of sorrow. Even the heart of him was gone.

How many times did I save her? He wondered. Brought her back from a spell to being a wife? Every time she came out of it, he'd hope it was the last and his happiness lay only a few days ahead. But sooner or later, she'd test him again. Drag him back into that black world of hurt and pain and pour more hate onto his long-broken heart.

This time, he wasn't going with her. Of that, Tom was certain. As he waited with Pearl in the hospital lobby, he wasn't worrying about Molly's being able to come out of the operating room alive. He was holding in rage. Rage that was swelling inside him so fast he feared he'd explode.

It's the last straw, he fumed. If she lives; I won't go through it again. If she dies, I don't have to. Everything I done to help her brought misery. All I wanted was a good life for her and the kids and she's spent it doing her best to tear every one of us down.

Yesterday, she ruined Clint. Made him go bezerk and tear up the house. The boy's going to pieces. Now he's home in bed, just like his mother, won't talk to no one.

He began to think aloud, alarming Pearl, who rushed to his side." Why?" He asked. "Why didn't I do somethin' earlier 'fore she got to my children?

"Shhhhh, Dad," Pearl answered. "Keep your voice down. We're supposed to be quiet here." She glanced around at the stiff leather chairs that lined the stark reception area, relieved no one else was present, and hoped the woman at the admission desk hadn't overheard.

"It was an accident, Dad. No reason. Guess we always knew something like this could happen."

"Better she'd drowned herself, twenty years ago." Tom clenched his fists, sliding them back and forth against the rough denim of his overalls.

Pearl gasped. "Dad, this isn't like you. Let's wait. Everything'll be back to normal in a few days. Doc's going to set those bones and she'll be fine. You'll be living with me. I can help care for her."

Tom face softened as he gazed a long moment on Pearl's dear face, thinking he didn't love anything on earth more'n he loved his girl. He was lucky he had her. And thanked the Lord for her every day of his life.

"Ain't no normal to go back to, Pearl," he sighed. "Ye know that, well as I do. You, me, and yer brother been living in lies all these years, changing our ways to suit her moods. I asked too much of ye. Should 'a put her in the asylum, way folks thought. I was too stubborn. Thought it was something I could fix. Now, it's too late, 'cause, Clint seems to be suffering the same thing."

He paused, reached for her hand and pulled it to his cheek. "We gotta watch him Pearl. We gotta be sure he ain't using her way of getting even with folk. Else he turns it on us."

"Shhhh. Dad. It's going to be all right. We'll talk it over once we see what Doc says."

Tom's voice rose loud and angry as he spotted Doctor Evans come through the door. "She ain't coming home, Doc," he roared. "I've had all I can take. She ain't coming home!" He stood and faced the doctor, his face flamed with rage. "She gonna make it?" he asked.

Shocked, Dr. Evans pulled back. "Don't know yet, Tom. She went through surgery okay. Give her a few days, we'll know more."

Tom's voice softened. "It wouldn't 'a happened if I hadn't left her. It made her mad, so she took it out on Clint."

Dr. Evans shook his head. "No, Molly took her anger out on herself, Tom. She's the one that's hurt."

Tom sighed deeply, his huge shoulders relaxing as if he'd just dropped a load of firewood at the doctor's feet. "I thank ye, Doc. But reckon it's the rest of us hurt most. Think it's time you help us find a place that can take better care of her." Eyes downcast, he studied the toes of his dusty work shoes. "I can't do this no more, Doc. It's got too big."

By noon, she was almost finished. She'd been at it since dawn. Working feverishly at the same chore she'd been responsible for as long as she could remember, cleaning up after one of Ma's tantrums. Pearl's role in the family cover-up was to get rid of the shame by scouring it away. To set the house to rights, in case anyone dropped in. Making it look as if nothing out of the ordinary had ever happened here.

As she sat down to a steaming cup of tea, Nell drove up, forcing her to lift her exhausted body off the chair and go to the door.

"Nell, glad to see you," she began. "Come. Sit a spell. I'll make more tea."

"I've only got a few minutes," Nell answered. "How's Molly?"

"Better than Dad, I think. Been giving her enough pain medicine she's been pretty quiet."

"And neither of them are worse than Clint," Nell retorted. "Darn fool's not spoken a word in three days. He won't eat, except what Mona fixes, and if he's not having a nightmare, he's out walking."

"Do you have any idea where he goes?"

Nell snorted. "I'm not for chasing him. There's livestock to feed, cows to milk, things to get done, and he's not doing any of it."

Pearl's face warmed for a moment, her old wall of defense rising up. She could understand Nell might be having a bad time, but does she have to be angry with Clint when a bit of kindness might help?

But Nell's not flesh and blood, Pearl thought, and couldn't know that an attack on Clint was an equally degrading assault on her; that the mighty pull of Ma's sickness had, at times, drawn her closer to her brother than her own skin.

She lifted her cup and sipped tea, no longer warm enough to give her the satisfaction she'd sought. "Think I know how he feels," she began. "I feel like hiding too, sometimes. Mother's ways can drive you there. She must have been awful to him."

"But you aren't hiding in bed!" Nell countered. "You're over here cleaning up a mess Clint walked away from. Acting like a baby, he is."

165

"Ma can make me feel like a baby, too, Nell. Think if you asked Dad, he'd probably admit to the same feeling."

"It's hard for me to see that," Nell answered. "You'd think with the three of you, one might have found a way to make her behave. She walked over the lot of you, she did. And not one of you would call her bluff."

Pearl bit her lip, then let go the torrent of tears she'd dammed behind her eyes for days. "Not now, Nell," she begged. Please. I can't talk about this..." She raised her eyes to meet Nell's. "Too much has happened. Forgive me."

"Sorry, Pearl. It's just- you've always been so strong. I never knew..."

Pearl waved her hands as if to shoo Nell to the door. "No, Nell. Of the three of us, I'm probably the weakest. Go now. We can talk about this later."

Nell backed to the door with tears brimming her eyes, suddenly unsure of herself. "You're welcome to come see him," she offered. "Maybe the two of you might feel better."

Pearl whispered. "I will."

Seemed he'd just got to asleep when the slam of the kitchen door jerked him awake. The girls must be home from school, Clint reckoned. They was arguing, same as always, with Nell paying no attention. I never could figure how she puts up with their constant bickering," he thought, 'cause it was a thing he couldn't take. It wasn't but a few minutes until he stood and picked up the bedside chair to hammer the floor. In a moment, the house was quiet. "Damn," he muttered. "Ain't no way I'm ever gonna get any sleep." He walked to the door and called for Mona. Thinking if she'd bring him a cup of warm milk, he might be able to get back to relax.

"Hot milk? Yuck!" Kate hissed. "What's she doing taking Dad warm milk? She think he's a baby or something?"

Nell laughed and flipped a sharp retort in Kate's direction. "Maybe 'cause he's acting like one, pounding on the ceiling like that."

Kate ran her fingers through her thick red curls, pushing them back from a freckled forehead. "No, Ma," she said. "Dad's got reason to feel bad after what happened to Grammy. She could die, you know. That'd be awful."

Nell picked up the pan of potatoes she'd started peeling and, handing Kate a knife moved it in front of her daughter. "Okay, Miss Smarty, tell me what you think is going on while you pare these potatoes."

Grimacing, Kate reached for the paring knife. "It's Mona. The way she's acting. Walking around with her mouth all puckered, acting like she's more Dads' mother than Grammy is. Have you noticed, Ma? She's looking down on us. I swear she's trying to keep us away from him."

"Mona's always been Clint's girl. They get along well."

"I'm his girl, too," Kate retorted. "I think I know what Dad wants much as she does. But it's not my job to get it for him. It's weird, Ma. Why are you letting her take him over like that?"

Nell laughed nervously and lifted the lid of the fry pan to turn the chicken. "Ah, Kate, you're looking for things. Mona's better able to settle your Dad than you or I." She shook her head, and then laughed. "And when they're together we're allowed some peace."

"No Ma. It's not like that. Look at me. I'm gonna be Mona." She stood, tucked her chin to her neck, and pointing to herself, urged Nell to watch. "First, I pull in my chin, and bridle. You know, like a horse when you're pulling on the reins. Saw that word in a book I read, and knew right off it was what Mona does. She looks like a horse, chafing at the bit. That's what she does when she doesn't like what we're doing."

Nell sat at the table, unable to hold back a laugh. Kate could mimic anybody, but was at her best aping Mona.

"Now, Ma, See how I walk...a bit crooked, and tight, like I got a cob up my arse." She giggled, slithering sideways around the table, and twisting her right thumb with her left hand. "That's how she winds up so tight, Ma, with her thumb. She turns herself outside in. So we can't see her dirty rotten tricks."

"Okay, Kate. That's enough," said Nell. "You'll not want her hearing you."

Suddenly serious, Katie slouched into an empty chair, crossed her arms, and studied the table. "It's hard being her sister, Ma, with all the kids making fun of her. There's times I get so mad at her I could choke her, the way she tries to embarrass me in front of my friends."

"And what do you do about it, Kate."

With her wide grin bunching freckles into splotches of brown on her porcelain cheeks, Kate shrugged. "I make fun of her too, Ma, just like they do. It drives her nuts."

"Trying to drive me nuts?" Mona sputtered. "Look at 'em, Kate and Ma, laughing at everything, even Dad, especially at a time like this." With strength born of slow burning rage, she filled her shovel behind the last cow stall and heaved its smelly contents out the window into the waiting manure spreader. "I'm done. Now back to the house to let Dad know he can rest. It will be something less for him to worry about."

When she reached the house, Aunt Pearl had arrived, and was sitting at the table with Nell, while Kate busied herself washing dishes. She hadn't even got her boots off before Aunt Pearl approached her, offering a hug.

"Good news for you, honey. I've called our cousins; your great-uncle John's boys are going to come by and help with the chores."

Mona stiffened and drew back. "There's no need for that. I'm the only one does them the way Dad wants. They'll screw everything up."

"I talked with your Dad. He thinks it a good idea. Knows you got a lot of homework and he's afraid you'll neglect it."

"Hmmmmph." Mona glared at Auntie and sidled to the staircase. "I'll see what he has to say before I agree to it. I want to be sure."

Nell's quick slap to her face sent her reeling backwards. "What?" Mona demanded. "What's wrong?"

Nell's response was as abrupt and direct as the finger she had pointed at Mona's nose. "You'll not disrespect your aunt, Mona. And you'll not try to talk your father into refusing help. He can't or won't feed this family, so the decision's mine. Nothing you do is going to change it. Now get on with you, before I lose my temper."

The shrill ring of the telephone sliced into the argument like a sharp knife. Kate ran to answer, hoping it was for her. But soon as she heard Granddad's voice, she could tell it was bad news. "Aunt Pearl. It's for you," she said. "I think it's about Grammy."

After a short, tearful conversation with Tom, Pearl turned to Nell. "I'm going upstairs and tell Clint," she said softly. "Ma's bad, Doc thinks she has pneumonia. She's asking to see us, most of all Clint."

"Kids too?" Nell asked.

"Yes," Pearl answered. "She wants all of us. Someone's going to have to tell her Jack is still in Chicago. She might not like hearing that."

Mona noticed that Kate was first to reach the bed. Threw herself down on Grammy's shoulder and cried like a two year old, flaming Mona's face. Didn't Kate know she could upset Grammy? Begging her not to die is awful. But Grandma just ran her fingers through that mess of curls, and shushed her with a smile on her face.

Then it was my turn, praying to God she wouldn't ask me why I hate her, the way she often does. Or if I'm gonna forgive her so she can die in peace.

She didn't talk to me or anyone. She hugged me, so stiff she felt like she was dead already. I didn't look at her face. I didn't want to know if, like usual, she wouldn't be looking at mine.

After that, we all stood around like statues while Aunt Pearl rubbed one of Grammy's arms and Granddad rubbed the other, both staring at her and not able to think of much to say.

Then Cousin Lily came in, looking like an angel in her starched white cap and uniform. Even her stockings were white. Don't think I ever saw anyone look so pretty in my whole life.

Lily's voice was soft, almost like fingers tracing over your back, and she smiled as if there was nobody in the world she cared more about than Grammy.

"Okay Auntie," she said. "It's time to take your temperature and blood pressure." She tightened the band she'd fastened around Grammy's arm. "You comfy?" she asked. "Anything I can do to help, you let me know." Then pressed her stethoscope against Grammy's chest and listened with a worried look. "You've got a little congestion in your lungs, Auntie. Do you think you can cough for me?"

Grammy was too tired to answer, and I wondered, since we could hear her breathing rattles from across the room, what it must sound like through the stethoscope.

Lily looked sad when she looked at Granddad and shook her head. "My ma was up earlier," she said. "They had a good sisterly talk. I think they enjoyed it."

Finished, she looked down at Grammy and I couldn't help but knowing that our cousin Lily was filled to the brim with goodness. Grammy was almost smiling at her; looking up at her with the closest thing to love I'd ever seen on that sour face.

Lily peeked under the covers for a look at her cast. Then tidied the bed, and kissed Grammy's cheek. And left us behind to whisper to one another about how kind she is.

About an hour later, when Grammy seemed to be sleeping, Ma said we ought to go. But before we got to the door, Grammy called for Dad. Said she wanted to talk to him alone, and for all of us to wait outside. I figured she might want to apologize. It was about time.

Clint shut the door behind him and stood a moment, trying to maintain his balance. I'm so damn tired. Dizzy. Think it's been a week since I had any sleep. Don't know if I can do this, yet.

Ma lifted her arm and beckoned him to come closer. "I gotta talk to ye, Clint. And you gotta talk to me. Got something 'tween us to settle 'fore I go, and from the sound of my chest, it won't be long."

The room was spinning, and Clint reached for her arm to hold him in place. Everything's so damn white in here, he thought, hurts my eyes! The wall, the iron bedstead, sheets. Even Ma, in a sea of whiteness, only thing left of her is them sharp blue eyes and a pink mouth tellin' me off for the last time.

Molly squeezed his hand. "This time, you tried to help me boy. Want to thank you for that. I almost made it. You meant well."

Clint voice was anguished, "No, Ma. I didn't want you to go. Thought you'd get cold and come right back."

"That why you dared me to go ahead?"

He dropped into a bedside chair and began to sob. "No. It's just I was tired. I been sick. You kept going on about killing yourself. It was all I could take."

"You wanted me to jump in the river?"

"No, Ma, no. I was calling your bluff. Didn't think you'd go."

A paroxysm of coughing racked Molly's body, leaving Clint to wonder where she'd find the next breath. "Want the nurse, Ma?" he asked. "See if she can help you?"

"I told you I wanted to see you. I want to know why you held that door open so I could get away."

"Ma, please...I told ya..."

Molly managed a wry laugh. "You told me to go ahead and drown. You said you was sick of my trying. You said for me to go ahead and get it to hell over with."

Clint leaned over and dropped his face into her bed. "I'm sorry, Ma. I lost my head. I didn't mean to say that. Never would I let you kill yerself, Ma. I would 'a stopped ye."

Molly gripped his hair and jerked his head upright so they were eye to eye. "Didn't get the chance though, did ye? It happened in spite of us. I'm planning to die tonight and tomorry, you, Tom and Pearl kin live in peace. Reckon the four of us be better off than we been for years."

"I didn't want Dad to know what happened, that's why I moved you. I know it hurt, but"

"Damn right it hurt Clint. But price enough for me to pay to be dead in hell rather than dragging my family through it on this goddam earth."

"We loved ye, Ma. It weren't your fault. Doc says it's a sickness."

"And Lillian says I'm cursed. You wanna know what it really is?"

He looked up, startled. Not believing she'd ever offer any reason for what she was.

"I do what I damn please, Clint," she whispered. "And you and Mona are just like me."

Chapter 14

The day they buried Molly was the day winter set in, cold, windy, and spitting sleet. But Kate knew the weather wasn't going to stop what had to be done. Grammy had to be put in her grave, to be carried up the hill to the cemetery and planted in the ground just like the tulip bulbs she and Mom had planted last fall.

Unlike the tulips, Grammy wouldn't be coming up next spring. According to Mom, she'd likely drop straight into Hell. She'd never been baptized, was mean, and wasn't a Catholic.

Unconvinced that God wouldn't forget the times Grammy had been nice, Kate wasn't going to give up the possibility for some kind of reprieve. In Catechism, she'd learned one could offer indulgences, paring years of time from a stay in Purgatory. That place you go when your sins aren't serious.

Without telling her mother, she'd already started praying, and knew that someday, she'd pray Grammy into Heaven. Sins of staying in bed, being grouchy or cussing couldn't be mortal. Hell ought to be for thieves and murderers, or folks guilty of impure acts. Sins Grammy couldn't have committed because she never left home.

Whispering Hail Marys as she trudged up the slope, Kate pulled a heavy scarf across her face to keep out the biting rain. It was bad enough she couldn't see, but Mona was insisting on keeping a hand on her shoulder and she was getting impatient.

"Let go of me," she growled, pushing Mona off.

"I won't," Mona hissed. "You have been pretending to cry, so's to get everyone's attention. I'm just giving you what you want."

Kate clenched her jaw and glared at her sister. "Get away from me!" she growled. In spite of the wind, her face was growing warm. She gritted her teeth, trying to ignore the comment. But anger was building fast and control might be impossible. Kate clenched her fists and crossed her arms over her chest, holding herself tight, calling on all her strength to hold back.

It was what Mona did next that broke her will. She isn't looking at me, Kate thought. Her eyes are looking straight down the hill. She's stretching herself tall, and sending her voice out of her nose, speaking down to me loud enough for everyone else to hear at the same time.

"Bitch," Kate whispered. "I know what you're up to."

Mona turned to Kate and whined. "Remember the time you told me you didn't like Grammy. The time she yelled at you. That's why I know you are not really crying."

With an outraged scream, Kate charged, the force of her body sending Mona flat onto the ground. She jumped on top, kicking and hitting.

"Asshole! I'll wring your neck!" she shouted. "How dare you say such a thing at Grammy's funeral?" She came in strong, her bunched fists hammering Mona's face.

With a powerful right, she bashed Mona's mouth, drawing blood. Then jumped to her feet, feeling justified. "Hah, bitch," she cried. "Let's see you smile your eat-shit smile now!"

In the distance, Mona could hear Ma calling them both. Soon she'd be rescued, and Kate would be punished. Ma didn't like it when one of them made a spectacle of themselves. In spite of the pain, she lay quiet. Satisfied that Kate couldn't control herself, Mona figured it was good this happened. It was time everyone knows how dangerous Kate is.

If it wasn't so cold and miserable, it wouldn't be so hard to leave her here, Tom thought. His little Molly, sleeping in her casket, with only a few handfuls of dirt between her and a fast dropping temperature.

In summer, Bigelow Memorial Gardens was one of the most peaceful spots in Missouri. Ringed by a forest of oaks, it sat high on Bigelow hill, folks often calling it the top rung on the stairway to Heaven. Saying when you were carried up that hill and laid to rest, you were almost home.

But on this day, Tom saw nothing but a place of utter desolation. Tall oaks stripped bare, their scrawny arms laughing at the mourners. Below, their roots, still warm and alive, curled beneath the sod, squeezing the dead.

Tom knew he'd worry most 'bout her being here alone, with no one to turn to for comfort, should she wake up afraid. In bed tonight, he'd remember this, he figured, and wake shivering; feeling her chill, hoping the gravediggers had filled the grave. It'd be some comfort if he could know six feet of dirt might keep her from freezing.

Yet, can't help being eased it's over, he reflected. She's finally at peace, resting in Heaven. He shook his head. No matter what folks say, I don't think the Lord would put her in hell without giving her good information on how to stay out of it. Molly didn't believe, but the Lord didn't show her His face, either. If there's blame, let it be shared between 'em, the good Lord and Molly. I don't see it no other way.

It took him a long time to realize that Molly may have had had a sickness, but most times she was downright mean. Playing me, Clint and Pearl, one against the other...on purpose.

I didn't want to see that. He reflected. I didn't want to know. Now I do, reckon it's time I see what's happening to Clint on account of her death.

He looked around and with a pang, spotted him standing with Nell on the other side of the grave. I never saw him so thin, he thought. It looked like he hadn't slept in days, with deep circles under his bloodshot eyes and walking like an old man. Tom hoped folks hadn't noticed Clint needed a shave.

Poor Clint. It had to be him with her when it happened. God knows they weren't much he could 'a done with Molly ranting. Still, the boy's blaming himself. He's been hurt by her words, and hurt by my thinking. Just hope it ain't too late. 'Cause if he's got her ways, I don't know if we can do him much good.

Soon, Lillian would arrive to say some prayers. She'd made it a good service, Tom recollected. It took only a few minutes. It surprised him, Lillian telling the town if it hadn't been for the sacrifices of her sister, she wouldn't be what she is today.

She said it was what they'd talked about the day Molly died. And, with tears brimming in her eyes and a tremble in her voice, had thanked the Lord for making them sisters.

Tom sighed deeply and walked to the graveside, reached for Pearl's arm with one hand and slipped the other into his brother John's. Right now, he needed something solid to hold onto. For the rest of the day, they'd be his strength.

At Fellowship Hall, half of Lowell's population sat, waiting for the family to get back from the burial to join them for dinner, most attending, not because of love for the Foster's, but to see if anything interesting might happen.

Mary Lou Teeter had arrived early. Had to help her ma, Emma, get seated. Emma's rheumatism was bad these days, and she needed Amy's help in getting around.

Spotting Alice Benton at one of the smaller tables, Amy steered her mother there, then slipped away to visit, leaving the two old friends to their usual conversations.

"Wasn't much of a service," Alice began. "It must have been hard to plan one, Molly not being one to attend church."

"Don't think I'd be here if it wasn't for Lillian," said Emma. "It's a nasty day out there. It ruined my hair."

"Did you notice Clint's boy got home?" Alice asked. "He was one of the pallbearers. He's a nice looking boy, looks like Nell. Hear he's in Chicago with his uncle, going to a Catholic school."

"Hah! As if that will be good for him. From what I heard Nell's brother's always drunk."

"No! He's famous! He has his own radio show."

Emma laughed. "That doesn't make him sober, Alice. Sure looks like Kate got her red hair from him too."

"Got her size from Tom," Alice responded. "And got her friendly ways from Pearl, and her brains from Clint. He was smart as a kid."

"That mean he ain't now?" Emma asked. "He don't look good, does he? Skinny as a rail, won't talk to nobody. It seems to me he's grieving more than normal."

"I think Molly's actions bothered him most. With her gone, his time will be easier." Her voice trailed off as she looked around the room. "I wish the family'd get back, so we can get something to eat."

"I reckon," Emma answered. "Looks like a lot of good food there." She shifted in her chair, leaned both elbows on the table and began to whisper. "Want you to take a good look at that oldest girl of Clint's soon as she gets back. Mona, her name is. I finally figured out who she looks like."

"Nothing like her sister," Alice responded.

"No siree! She's the spitting image 'a Molly at the same age. Way her mouth is, with the chin pulled back. Teeth kind of bucked in front. Like a rabbit. Think she's 'bout fourteen, fifteen now. 'Spose she'll be anything like her grandmother?

Alice laughed. "We can hope not."

Emma pulled out a mirrored compact and patted her nose with a soft cotton puff. "The world couldn't take another Molly," she chuckled. "Besides, Mona's Ma is strong and sensible. Even if she's Catholic, I think she'll keep that girl straight." She pointed to the door. "Look, they're back from the burial, probly half froze to death. Reckon we'll be eating soon."

Kate slouched into a chair next to Nell, still trying to make her point. "Ma," she whined. "You weren't watching. She's spent all morning picking at me, touching me. Soon as I'm talking with someone, she'll come up and tell me I got dirt on my face. Or lint on my shoulder."

"And I fail to see what's wrong with that," Nell replied. "You should have come to me with it, instead of hitting her. We'll talk about it no more here, so keep your mouth shut. You've shamed me enough."

"How about her shaming me, Ma?" Kate cried. "She does it every day. Have you thought about that?"

"Kate, I'll be hearing no more. Go fill your plate, and for the rest of the day use that mouth only for eating or it'll be feelin the back of me hand."

Remembering what that felt like, Kate decided she'd pushed Nell about as far as safety allowed. Sulky, she drew her mouth into an exaggerated pout and looked for Jack, knowing he'd take her side. She quickly spotted him behind Ma's chair, waiting for her glance. Mouth open wide, he stuck out his tongue and crossed his eyes, filling her with giggles on top of the temper. It was going to be hard keeping both in at the same time. Now that she'd made one scene, she knew everyone was watching.

Deliberately, she sucked the inside of her cheek between her teeth and bit down hard, hoping to bring tears to her eyes. Today, she figured, she'd far better be seen crying than laughing.

Even though she was at her Grandmother's funeral, had one eye swollen shut and a black, blood-filled blister growing on her lower lip, Mona couldn't remember when she'd felt better. Sharing the spotlight with an angel was a heady matter. And here she was with everyone feeling sorry for her accident, sitting next to Nurse Lily, who was adored by everyone.

The best day in Mona's life began as soon as she walked into the hall, when everyone had turned to look at her face, their mumbled comments rippling through the room like a breeze through a hayfield. Some seemed shocked. All wanting to know what happened.

She knew she had to lie if she wanted this good thing to keep on. No matter what had happened, she wouldn't shame her family the way Kate did.

She cocked her head, gave a wan smile and answered their questions. "It's nothing." she said, meekly, then looked down. "It's slick out there. And I'm kind 'a clumsy." She wiped her hand across her forehead and looked down at the blood on her fingers. "Maybe I need a bandage."

Amy Lou Teeter was first to reach her, and with a sharp cry sent Jack running for Lily, who was in the cloak room removing her boots. "This girl needs a nurse, quick," she exclaimed. "My goodness, will you look here? She's bleeding over her eye!"

Bleeding! Who would believe it would bring such luck. Because of it, Mona had Lily's attention. All that love, kindness, and tender touching she'd seen directed at Grammy was now being lavished on her.

Perched on a stool in the hall kitchen, Mona closed her eyes as Lily cleaned her face with a wet cloth. A sense of warmth rose in her chest, spreading through her body. As if in a dream, she heard folks come in, ask about her, look over her injuries, and offer sympathy. It seemed like no one was thinking about Grammy. They were all talking about her.

It seemed the day's sadness had got up and gone. All because of me, she thought proudly. Reckon I've done a good thing.

Clint pulled open his sand crusted eyelids and tried to focus on Tom's voice, the roaring surf in his head making hearing damn near impossible. Something about selling the farm—day Ma was hurt—moving to town—*what's he saying?*

His eyes dropped shut and for a moment he dozed. Then he jerked awake, startling Nell, who sat by his side. She reached for his arm, but he pulled away. "Leave me alone," he growled. "I'm okay."

After blinking four or five times, Clint pulled his eyes open wide and looked around the room. *A bunch of folks, spinning. A black border 'round 'em.* He looked down at his plate, trying to concentrate. *It's movin'. Gotta eat—chewing— awake—there was a fight. Gotta sleep.*

Deliberately, he stuck his fork into a piece of Dorothy Benton's chocolate pie and watched his hand carry it to his mouth, his thoughts whirling. *Dirt, I'm eatin' dirt. Something about a fight—Alice knows. Jack on the train. A leg, twisted. Cows. Milk the cows.*

Ma. Falling. Gone...

"No!" He shouted.

Do what I damn well please.

He heard his own voice like it was coming from another room. "Do what I damn well please," it said. "I do what I damn well please..."

Dad's hands on my shoulders, someone's got my elbow. Shoes, shuffling. Mona bawling. The inside of a car, a road moving under it. Dad pushing me up the stairs. A sock, slipping slowly over my heel.

Then, Dad's voice. "Take this pill, Son, one of your Ma's. You gotta get some sleep."

⌒◌

With Granddad's help, Kate figured she'd got off easy. After they'd put Dad in bed, he'd pulled Ma aside and told her not to worry about what folks might say about the fracas between me and Mona. "It was only family saw it," Tom said. "And this family don't talk."

Dad's breakdown may have spared her punishment, Kate thought. She was safe from Mona now, who sat upstairs in their bedroom, door opened, listening to Dad snore, to be there if he called. Jack had Ma occupied, giving an occasional wink, as if to let her know he was doing it for his favorite sister.

If only he'd stay, Katie wished. I wouldn't be ashamed of him! Jack's getting handsome. His hair is so black! And his eyes so blue! She giggled. If he didn't look like Ma, he could be a movie star.

It sounded like he really enjoyed living with Uncle Brian. He'd sung with him several times on the radio show and they'd done a few jokes together. Best of all, he was taking dance lessons. Brian's friend was teaching him for free!

"Show me," Nell exclaimed. "Can you do an Irish jig?"

"Not too well," Jack answered. But began to sing "*McNamara's Band,*" put his hands at his sides, and began to move his feet, his body bouncing up and down like a yo-yo.

"That's it Jack. You got it!" Nell cried. "Dad used to jig like that. His brother playing the fiddle. Is Brian teaching you to play piano?"

Jack laughed. "The Uncle says I'm best not hidden behind the piano. Good as am I ought to be out front."

"He did, did he? I wonder why he hasn't told me."

"He will, Ma. Uncle says I'll be doing vaudeville, the way he used to."

"I thought vaudeville was going out. Folks would rather listen to the radio or go to a picture show."

Jack answered excitedly. "There are plays and such. If I could get in a musical play, I'd have to dance. Who knows? Maybe I'll be in movies! Be famous."

Kate interrupted him, laughing. "Horror movies, you mean. Maybe you could play Dracula."

Grinning, Jack moved behind her and tried to pin her arms, the same way he used to when she was little. But Kate easily overpowered him and pinned his behind his back. "Watch it Jack," she bantered. "I'm not the smallest kid anymore."

"But I'm still your mother," Nell interrupted. "You won't be wrestling front of me, any more Kate Foster. You've made enough fool of yourself for today, and I won't see any more!"

Humbled by Ma's words, Kate stepped back quickly and apologized. "Sure Ma, I was kidding-I–

"You'll be going to bed. The two of you. Nearly midnight and Jack leaves tomorrow. It has been a long day."

ᘓᕲ

On the third day after Ma's funeral, Clint got dressed and came downstairs to find Nell fixing breakfast. She turned from the stove, her voice edged with sarcasm. "You decide to join the living?" she asked.

"Needed sleep. That's all." He reached for a loaf of bread, tearing it into chunks with greedy fingers. He was hungry. Reckoned he hadn't eaten in days.

He looked up as Nell set a bowl of hot oatmeal on the table in front of him. "Any gas in the car?" he asked.

"There is," she answered. "You going somewhere with it? I thought you were a walker these days."

Clint ignored her and went on. "Gonna go help Mona finish the chores. Get her off to school. Then, I'm going in to town. Want to see Father Donahue."

Nell gasped. "What the devil for? Are you going back to church?"

Clint pushed his dishes to the middle of the table and rose from his chair. "If it's any of your damn business I'm going to confession," he snapped. "Reckon I'll go in alone."

Father Donahue was in the rectory office when Clint walked in. He rose and extended his hand.

"Clinton," he began. "So sorry to hear of your Mother's death. Anything I can do to help?"

"You can listen," Clint offered, and dropped to his knees." Bless me Father, for I have sinned. It's been almost a year since my last confession. He paused. "Reckon I'm the one kilt my Mother."

He sat back onto his ankles, and began to moan. Tears streamed down his face. "It was my fault. I wanted her dead. I should have stopped her."

When he left two hours later, Clint felt a relief he'd not known in months.

Wanting Ma dead wasn't same as killing her, and according to Father, leaving the house that day was her own doing

"Did you strike her? Do anything to make her fall? He'd asked.

"Nope. I threatened to hit her once when I was a kid. But I was capable of carrying through with it that day"

"But you didn't, Clint. You controlled yourself. Your mother was difficult. What a person might have done is not a sin."

"Thought we could sin in thought, well as word and deed. I told you. I wanted her dead. I sat there, with her carrying on at me, picturing her, my mother, in the river, floating downstream," he continued. "And I reckon I enjoyed the scene."

"You felt relieved? Imagining her like that?"

"Hell yes. 'Scuse me Father. Reckon I cuss too much...."

"Cussing isn't the same as taking God's name in vain, Clint. But thinking you'd rejoice at her death isn't same as being responsible for that death. We all wish for things we only think we want. Thank God, we don't often get them."

Clint managed a weak grin, and then turned serious. "I been missing Mass, Father. I didn't even pray, thinking God wouldn't answer if I did."

"God forgives our sins. You're welcome to come back, Clint. You know that."

"I will. Reckon we'll all be in church this coming Sunday.

On the way home, Clint rounded the corner and turned up the familiar tree-lined lane to his Dad's farm, planning to own up to his role in Ma's death, and to keep Tom from further blaming her for it.

But Tom greeted him with open arms and a big hug. Something he'd not done for years, bringing tears to Clint's eyes.

"Glad you're here," Tom began. "Want you to be one of the first to know I sold the farm the week before your Ma died. I'm moving into town and livin' with Pearl. I plan to be outta this place first of March."

And with Dad being so keyed up about moving into town, Clint saw no way to bring up the subject of Ma's death. Next time he saw him, he'd bring it up. Right now, it seemed best to leave well enough alone.

Chapter 15

1947

"He's just like Ben!" Clint shouted. "Acting like a damn jackass and getting his kicks at someone else's expense."

"He *is* not like any of your relatives." Nell answered. "For one thing, he's smart."

From her perch on the swing under the backyard elm, Mona wasn't sure why Mom and Dad had called a break to their silence and were fighting again. But she had an idea it had something to do with Jack's going into town with Mike Richardson last night, getting drunk, kidnapping old Mrs. Tharp's goat and letting it loose in the Baptist church.

It seemed they were squabbling about something more. And much as she tried to hear, Mona couldn't figure out what it was. She leaned forward to listen.

She heard Clint reply. "Okay. So you're the smart ass. Maybe Jack's more like Brian, a goddam, worthless drunk!"

"You can't know why me brother lost his job. Jack says it was because of a new boss."

"And I say he showed up drunk for work. Brian can't stay sober, and it was Jack told that to Kate yesterday. Mona overheard him. You want to take Jack's word; you have to believe everything he says and not just what you want to hear."

"And maybe you're just like your mother. You always blame it on whoever doesn't agree with you."

"So you had to bring her up again, did ye?"

"Isn't it you that brought in the relatives?" Nell retorted.

"I'm damn worried what he's like, Nell. He thinks he's a big shot 'cause he graduated high school. He was supposed to be helping out this summer. He's hopeless doin' chores. Always singing or playing jokes when he should be busy. Boy ain't nothing but a damn fool, always trying to make someone else look bad."

"And your telling me who's hopeless with chores?" snapped Nell. "Who are you to be talking, Mr. Lay-in-Bed?"

Shocked by the bang of the back door, Mona looked up to see her dad storm out of the kitchen and head to the barn. She rose to follow him.

Clint slipped his arm around her shoulder and gave her a sharp squeeze. "It's okay, Mona," he said. "Just wish you didn't have to do the work of two when Jack is goofing off."

"I know, Dad," she answered. "I just worry what it will be like when I go to nurses' training after I graduate. Think you can handle things alone?"

"That's two years off. Don't worry about that. You're going to be a nurse and ain't nothing gonna get in your way, long as I have any say in it."

Mona sighed with relief. "That's what I want to do most, Dad. I want to be like Lily. I'll make it up to you soon as I graduate.

"I know you will. That's okay. Damn good you have your sights set on something better than going to California with a dancing teacher."

Mona giggled. "I can just imagine him dancing with someone like Ginger Rogers. I bet he'd fall on his face."

"He may have to sometime. I sure can't tell him anything."

"It'd serve him right, Dad," she responded. Mona just wanted him gone; she didn't care what happened to him.

Inside, Jack slumped at the kitchen table and Nell was slamming pans when Kate slipped into the room and eased herself into a chair.

"What you plan to do to for penance?" she asked Jack, "become a priest?"

Jack slammed his fist hard into the table. "Not funny, Kate," he growled. "I'm getting out of here soon as I can." He looked across the kitchen to Nell. "Look Mom," he began. "I'm sorry. I can't take it any-more. It wasn't just last night that Dad's mad at. It's everything I do."

Nell wiped a tear with the back of her hand. "Just when I get my boy back, he says he wants to leave."

"No, Mom. I can't stay here and fight Dad. And I've had it with Mona. Her self-righteousness makes me sick. I've got my future to think about and no matter what Dad says; I know I'm good enough to make it in show business."

"You go, and I may never see you again." Nell put her face in her hands, began to sob, then ran from the room.

"No, Mom—" Jack stood to go after her, but Kate's firm grasp on his arm held him back.

"She's just trying to make you feel guilty," Kate said. "It's something she's good at? We're supposed to feel sorry for her because she can't get along with Dad."

"No. I'm the cause of them arguing," Jack retorted. "If I were gone they'd have no reason."

"Sorry Jack, you're not that important." Kate said. "They fight all the time. Only time they don't is in when we're in church. There, we sit with smiles on our faces pretending we're the happiest family in Lowell."

"How do you handle it?" Jack asked.

"Hell, I ignore them. It's Mona I can't get along with."

"No one can. What's up with her and Dad?"

"She thinks we're all mean to him, so she tags him like a dog, mak-ing sure he knows what she thinks. That's how she keeps the fight going. She keeps him thinking he's right about everything. Far as Mom is concerned, she hardly speaks to her."

"I don't know how you put up with it," Jack said. "She's as much why I want to leave as Dad is. What do you do when she decides to pick on you?"

"She won't. She knows I can beat the crap out of her. She leaves me alone."

Jack laughed and rose from the table. "Got to find Mom," he said. "Make nice with her and see if she'll me give the money to go back to Chicago."

Clint rose early, woke Mona and finished the chores about the same time the sun was rising. He had to go in town and stop at the bank to see if he could get a short term loan and pay it off when the crops come in. He was running short on feed money, and there was no way Nell would give up what she brought in on eggs. She spent the half of it on the church and gave the rest to Jack for all he knew.

It wasn't gonna be easy, Clint figured. Ben had been after him for weeks, looking for him to pay off the loan Iry'd given him for seed this spring. And there was no way in hell he was going to beg that bastard for mercy. Ever since Iry'd let Ben take over the business it had been the same story. Ben wouldn't extend him any credit to buy any supplies until he settled his debt.

He stepped into the bank and immediately spotted Marvin Benton.

Marvin rose to greet him. "Good to see you, Clint. I was planning to drive out to the farm this afternoon. Looks like you saved me the trip.

Clint looked around then waved toward an inner room. "Could we talk in there?"

"Sure." Marvin stepped into a small office and beckoned Clint to follow.

Clint remained standing, slipped off his cap and rubbed his hands on the sides of his overalls. "Any way you could loan me four hundred dollars so I can pay off my bill at the feed store?" he asked.

Marvin settled down at his desk and motioned Clint to sit across from him. "That's a lot of money, Clint. And you're behind on payments already. You have to start paying off the debt you have before taking on any more."

"I'll pay you back when the crops come in."

"Clint, you haven't enough crop acreage to pay your rent and feed your family. I'm sorry. But you've got to start making some payments now."

"My livestock ain't ready to sell, Marvin. Come March I'll be ready."

"Good. We can grant you an extension until then, but we can't loan you anymore." Marvin rose and offered his hand.

Holding back tears, Clint rose, turned and walked from the room. He wasn't gonna give that son of a bitch the honor of shaking his hand. Damn bastard. Ever since he married Dorothy Berkey, Clint knew he didn't have any sense.

He reckoned he'd stop by Dad's. Sure hated bringing up the subject with him, but knew Tom would be agreeable to help him.

As he knocked on the door, he saw Tom coming down the stairs to meet him. He opened the door and stepped in. "How are ye, Dad? It looks like the rheumatism is bothering you, you got a pretty bad limp these days."

"Bothers me when it rains and when the sun shines," Tom said, grimacing. "Don't make no sense. Doc says it's in my hip bad and it seems to be gettin' worse."

He stretched out his hands to Clint. "Lookee here, it's crippling up my hands too. Makes it hard to do a lot of things I used to find easy."

"I reckon," Clint answered. "Can we go someplace where we can sit down?"

"Let's go to the kitchen and warm up a cup of coffee. Meantime you can tell me what's on your mind."

As soon as he got home, Nell was asking questions

"Did you get the money?" she asked.

Clint jammed his hands into his pockets. "Hell, yes. Told you I would"

"And Marvin, he was okay with giving you an extension on the loan?"

Clint turned on his heel and snapped at Nell. "I told you I'd got the money, now let it alone."

Nell sighed deeply and turned back to her mending. "All right, Clint, all right. Now that's done I want you to speak with Kate."

"What now? She blow up again?"

"That she did. She got mad over Jack this time and got sassy with me. With all the cussing and name calling she could come up with, she did. More and more she's just like—"

"That's enough! She's not like nobody, Nell. She's Kate."

"Will you just talk to her?" Nell interrupted. "And I don't care who she's like, she's our daughter and we got to do something about her temper."

"I know. I know. Too damn much on my mind. I'll keep an eye on her. Maybe next time, she'll blow up around me. I'll see what I can do."

Clint strode from the room. Kate's temper tantrum was more than he could deal with after all the humiliation he had suffered during his afternoon in town.

Kate huddled in her bed upstairs, wiping tears. "Damn!" she muttered to herself. "I had to do it again. I can't stop myself. But this time Jack went too far. He can play his jokes on Mona, but he better not play them on me"

Earlier this morning, Jack had frightened her in the outhouse, when he ran by with a lighted firecracker, opened the door and threw it at her feet. Shocked and outraged, she'd chased him to the porch and began pummeling him with her fists.

"Bastard," she yelled. "You dirty son of a bitch. I'll kick your ass."

Nell came out of the house, walked to Kate and slapped her. "You use those words against your brother again, and I slap you twice as hard," she said. "It's me your insulting with those words, not your brother and I'll not hear them in me presence."

"But Mom," she'd argued. "You don't know what he did. He could have hurt me!"

"And now it's me who'll do the hurting. Get to your room. And don't come down until I say you can."

Thirteen year old Kate wasn't sure what was happening. It seemed everything that took place that summer had been shameful. There had been changes in her body; there was all the fighting at home, the problem with her own anger, and the way Jack was behaving.

She'd really wanted him back, and was delighted when he decided to wait until school started to leave for California. But Jack was so stupid! He was always playing tricks on her or making jokes at her expense, not at all like he used to be—fun, and her only ally against Mona.

And Mona! God how she hated her! The bitch! Always into her clothes and personal things, even reading her diary, seeing what she could find so she could run tell Dad. Not that Dad ever said anything. He acted mostly like she wasn't alive, talking only to Mona and, for the most part, yelling at Mom and Jack.

She could hear Mom downstairs, telling Dad about her argument with Jack. He won't do anything to me, she figured. He doesn't care what I do. If it weren't for Mom, I could get by with anything. But I got to be careful; I think I'm getting worse.

But being careful wasn't going to be enough. When it came to her anger; Kate seemed to have no choice. It'd bubble up and then let go with an outburst she had no control over. It wasn't that she didn't try. And God knows how much she prayed to stop, but couldn't. She didn't want to hit anybody; it just seemed such a good idea at the time. She may have been younger than Jack and Mona, but this was one place she held her own since she was bigger than either of them. She could make them back off, so she did, but only when she was angry.

After her outburst at Jack, Nell had come to her room and tried to talk with her. "It's got to stop, Kate," she said. "It's the violence I worry over, the way you hit Jack."

"But Mom—I say throwing a firecracker is violent—" she began.

"There are no buts," Nell countered. "I don't care what he did; you could have come to me."

"And what would you have done, Mom? Laughed with Jack about how scared I was?"

"Of course not. You've got to reason, Kate, and you got none. Only anger, like…."

189

"Like who, Mom?" Kate shouted. "Like you and Dad? It's you two that's mad all the time. When I fight back you are all over me. It seems like if I get into an argument you jump right in the middle of it. Yet when you and Dad fight, we all have to run hide and pretend it isn't happening. Bull shit, Mom, it's all bull shit."

"Kate!" Nell shouted. "Kate! Stop! I'm not having you talk to me that way."

"Oh yeah, well I'm talking to you, Mom." Kate had stepped forward menacingly and held her hands before her face. "And don't try to slap me either, 'cause you say that's violent, Mom. If I can't hit people, why should you?"

Stunned and speechless, Nell turned, and left the room. There was nothing she could do, Kate was too big to punish anymore, and unless Clint started caring, the problem had grown too large to handle.

After that day, everything changed. It's a kind of power I have, Kate thought, and an air about me that all of them are beginning to respect. My actions shouldn't be questioned any more than Mona's. Maybe if I act like Jack and be a jerk everyone will think it's funny.

That's how it goes, she reflected. In this family, the more outrageous someone is, the more we act like nothing is happening. For sure, I went too far with Mom, but long as I went along with her, she'd keep pushing her stupid reasons to punish me for what her precious Jack did. Now maybe she'll leave me alone, and so will Jack, because he doesn't want me besting Mom in another argument. That scares the shit out of him.

Jack left soon after, however, and Nell took to moping and rarely talking to anyone. Dad and Mona seemed almost happy, singing when doing the chores and joking with each other. Kate's days were long, and a dreadful tiredness settled over her as she spent her time angrily thinking, or else, longing for school to start. In spite of herself, she missed Jack and the freewheeling fun they used to have. Mom wouldn't let her see her friend Bridey Richardson as punishment for her behavior, so the only bright thing in her life was the visits from Aunt Pearl. Kate looked forward to seeing her more than about anything. Besides, it was the only time that Nell would talk.

One hot afternoon in mid-August, Nell and Pearl were sitting in the kitchen enjoying a glass of lemonade.

"Kate seems quiet." Pearl said. "Is anything wrong?"

"Kate's not quiet," Nell retorted. "She's become completely unmanageable, she has, got a mouth on her like her grandmother."

Pearl flinched. "Don't you think it could be her age? This is a tough time for some kids. They seem to have trouble with the teen age years."

"She has trouble with me, that's what. I don't know what to do with her. So far this summer, I've been leaving her pretty much alone. Everything I say she has to argue, and she's even threatened me. That's how bad it is. And Clint—" her voice trailed off.

"Can I help?" Pearl asked. "Maybe it would help if she came into town, spent a few days with me and Dad."

"I don't care if she does," Nell answered. "I don't care at all what she does, I am so angry with her."

"Do you think Clint will agree to let her come?"

"Of course he will. He doesn't seem to give a darn. For all I know, he thinks her tantrums are entirely my fault."

"Oh, I'm sure he doesn't." Pearl began. "He's busy."

Nell rose. Sighing heavily, she began to clear the table. "Do you want to take her back with you today?' she asked. "We can pick her up Sunday and take her home after Mass."

Kate was unpacking Nell's old suitcase all the while looking at the floor. She'd hardly spoken on the drive back to town, even though Pearl tried to draw her into some kind of conversation.

Pearl watched her hang her few shabby belongings in the closet, making a mental note to take her to Aunt Lillian's store to buy her a few new dresses for school.

"How does it feel to have a room of your own for a few days?" she asked.

Kate looked up. "It's going to feel good. Mona and I don't get along much."

"Why is it that you and Mona don't get along? Is it just a sisterly spat?"

"Hell, no. Ooops I didn't mean to say that. It's just that Mona and I pretty much ignore each other these days. When we have to be together, we usually squabble. It's best if we don't talk to each other." Kate slammed the suitcase shut and set it on the floor. "Mona's no fun, you know. She's serious all the time. She's always tagging Dad around, worrying about the chores"

"And Jack? You seemed to have a good time with Jack. I bet you really miss him."

Kate sighed. "Jack can be too much at times. He likes to hang out with Mom anymore, making fun of all of us. Guess he's Mom's boy and Mona is Dad's girl."

"And where does that leave you, Kate?" Pearl asked gently. "Don't you know you're their girl too?"

Kate's eyes filled with tears. Almost shouting, she looked into Pearl's face. "No, I'm not," she said. "I'm too awful. I'm always mad and fighting and all of them hate me.

Pearl stood and opened her arms as Kate slipped into them, sobbing.

The late August sky was a limitless blue, and up and down the corn rows long leaves fluttered in the morning breeze. Mona was careful to avoid their slashing edges as she joined her dad in the seemingly endless battle to hoe the velvet leaf from between the plants.

She didn't object to the strenuous task though, because today, Dad was sad and it was up to her to make him feel better. Every day she believed she knew his mood. Whether he was happy or sad, there was something in the way he walked, talked, or didn't talk that would give it away.

Today, he's lonely, she decided. What with Mom not speaking to him except to argue, Jack being such a jerk, and Kate ignoring him, no wonder he's feeling cut off from everybody. Even Granddad and Aunt Pearl seemed distant, visiting occasionally, but talking with him only in polite words, mostly about the weather or the crops, and not understanding how much he needed them to appreciate him.

Everybody's turned their back on him except me, she thought. No worry though, I will help him through this; I just have to find the right way.

"Sure are a lot of weeds this year," she began. "It's been a long summer just keeping up with them."

"Be nice we had some help," Clint said. "Been good to get Jack or Kate here but with both them gone, reckon it's up to us."

Mona grinned. "That's for sure. But we can get it done, Dad. I think today we should be able to finish most of this field."

Clint stopped hoeing and wiped his brow. It was getting warm, the sun almost overhead now and beating down upon their backs. "May have to stop this afternoon," he answered. "It's going to be too hot."

"Not for me Dad. I'd like to see us finish. Even if Jack was here, he wouldn't be helping. Darn Jack anyway, why does he have to be so lazy."

"Jack needs to grow up. Find myself wishing he'd get drafted. The army might be the best thing in the world for him."

"Why's that?"

"For one thing, he wouldn't be singing and dancing," he replied. "He'd be marching and counting."

Mona chuckled. "How'd they make him do that?"

"They have their ways," Clint answered. "They have their ways."

"What kind of ways?"

"Shame you into it. If a guy wants to be treated like a man, he has to act like one. Both the officers and rest of the troops are pretty hard on you if you don't do what you're supposed to."

"But you're hard on him too, Dad."

"Not as much as I should be. Your mother sees to that. Reckon she babies him, Mona. She's making a damn sissy out of him. What I say don't seem to matter."

"Well it should. What about Kate? Why can't she help?"

"Kate's a kid. She should be helping your mother, but seems the two of them are set to argue much as me and Jack." They moved to the edge of the field and sat in the cool shade of an elm tree, sipping water brought in half gallon jars from the house.

"I don't know, Dad. Kate's thirteen. I was able to hoe weeds when I was her age." Mona saw an opportunity and she wasn't going to let Kate off the hook. "She gets a vacation for fighting with Mom; it wouldn't be the same if it was me. Mom would slap me silly if I talked to her the way Kate does."

"How's that?"

"Cussing and stuff like that."

Clint laughed. "A little cussing never hurt nobody, Mona. She just does it to rile her mother. There are times when it takes a little cussing to get someone to listen." He stood and they made their way back to the cornfield.

"No Dad, it's more than that," Mona said, picking up her hoe. "She keeps secrets."

"How do you know about it if it's a secret?" Clint asked.

"I happened to see her diary, she left it open on the bed and I couldn't help but see it."

"Did you read it?"

"Only the part where she wrote about a mortal sin she'd confessed the week before."

"A mortal sin? Reckon that's between her and the priest now, Mona." Clint paused, looking into Mona's face.

"But Dad, she said something awful about us! Said we could all die and go to hell far as she was concerned."

"Maybe she was just mad at us. She reads too much. Got a hell of an imagination."

"No, Dad. That's not all she said."

"So you read a little more than one page?"

"I guess so, Dad. But she left it out. I couldn't help it. After I read that, I wanted to see what she had to say."

"She say anything I should know about?"

"She said she hoped she'd die too. That she hated the family and she just couldn't take it anymore. That's a sin, isn't it? Hating people and hoping you'll die?"

Clint stopped hoeing and straightened his back. "We're going in, now Mona," he said. "Let's pick up these hoes and take them to the barn."

Noticing his abrupt change in gait, Mona breathed a sigh of relief. Kate is going to get it now, she thought. This ought to teach her to treat him better.

But Clint wasn't thinking about punishing anyone. He was planning how he'd talk Nell into letting Kate stay with Pearl through the next school year. He'd left the girl pretty much alone till now, trusting Nell to raise her, and it hadn't worked out. It was time for him to do something. And same as Nell had relied on her family to help when Jack was acting up, now he'd rely on his to lend a hand with Kate.

As they approached the farmhouse, Clint turned to Mona. "I have to talk to your Ma," he said. "And I'd appreciate it if you stayed outside a while. Let us be alone to figger out what we're gonna do about Kate."

"Sure, Dad," Mona replied. "I'll go to the barn and start the chores. I could feed the calves so we won't have to do it later." Disappointed she wouldn't be able to hear the conversation, she started toward the barn. "Let me know when I can come in," she said, with a forced laugh. "I don't want to be out here all night."

"It won't take long, Mona. That's a good girl." He strode to the house, calling back over his shoulder. "Thanks for helping me out."

Before entering, he stood on the back porch and took a few deep breaths. Things hadn't been good between him and Nell, and he had to watch his words so as not to set her off again.

When he came in, Nell was in the kitchen, cooking.

"Nell," he began, "You're right. We gotta do something about Kate and we gotta do it now."

"Glad you finally noticed," Nell retorted, slamming a lid onto a pan. "So what brought this on?"

Clint went to the stove, lifted the coffee pot and poured himself a cup of coffee. "We ain't got time for arguing, Nell. We got to be in this together if it's going to do any good. I'm willing to agree that I ain't been noticing her much as I should have, but I've been busy with the farm and just didn't see how bad it is."

Nell hoisted herself onto a stool and demanded an answer. "I asked what brought this on. Is there something I don't know about?"

"Mona read her diary…"

"Kate's diary is none of Mona's business," Nell interrupted. "What was she doing snooping in there?"

Clint took a long drink of coffee before answering. "It don't matter none to me why Mona read it, it's what she read that has me worrying."

"What did she say?"

Clint drew in a deep breath and exhaled slowly. "Kate was talking about killing herself, that's what. And I know, it's just like my Ma her saying things like that, but I can't forget how many times Ma tried it. We gotta get this trouble with Kate stopped before she does something all of us will be sorry for."

Nell gasped. "So she *is* just like Molly, I've been trying to tell you…"

"She's our daughter, Nell. She's Kate. She's young and maybe we can keep her from getting worse. Ma had no one to guide her as a youngster, and Kate does. I have an idea and I want to hear what you think about it."

"Are you going to take a hand with her?"

"Not right now. I was thinking that, if Pearl is agreeable to it, we could let her stay with Pearl this winter. Give her a break from you."

Nell was shocked. "How will Pearl handle her tantrums if we can't?"

"Pearl's good with kids. After teaching all those years she has a knack for getting the best out of 'em. She was good with Ma too; I reckon if anybody can help Kate right now, it's Pearl. Dad will be a help with her as well. He can talk the temper out of anybody; give him the time to do it."

Nell began to cry. "God knows I've tried everything. Maybe I've done it all wrong, but it isn't for not trying. What worries me is that Pearl isn't Catholic, and we've agreed to raise our kids in the church. Pearl goes to that Unity church, which isn't even Christian. I don't want Kate going there.

"That's the Unitarians ain't Christian, Nell, not Unity," Clint replied. She don't have to go to church with Pearl. We can pick her up on Sunday. Take her to Mass with us. Maybe take her home awhile, long as she holds her temper. Pearl will help make it work, I can promise that. I think we should drive into town right now, talk to Pearl and Dad and see what they say."

Nell rose, pulled a kerchief from her apron pocket and blew her nose. "Guess I might as well get ready and we get it over with. What will we do if Pearl won't let her stay?"

"We'll deal with that when the time comes," Clint answered. "We'll deal with that when the time comes."

Pearl looked up from her needlework as she saw Clint's car come up the drive.

Uh-oh she thought, I wonder what's up with him now. She smiled at Kate, who sat across the room, struggling with a cross stitch, and about ready to give up her efforts.

"Your folks just drove up," she said. "They must miss you already."

"I hope I don't have to go home," Kate replied. "I really like it here."

"I wouldn't worry about that until they get inside," Pearl said, laughing. She rose from her chair. "Let's go to the door and let them in. Then we'll find out what they want."

Clint charged into the living room, before Pearl got to the door. "We got to talk," he said. "Can we go in the kitchen where it's quiet? Where's Dad? I want him there too."

"He's already in the kitchen," Pearl answered. "Having his afternoon cup of coffee."

Clint went into the kitchen, followed closely by Nell, then turned to Kate and said, "You go on upstairs now. This is between us."

From then on, Clint did most of the talking. Refusing to sit at the table and pacing the room like a caged animal, he was brief and to the point. Kate might be suicidal, like Ma, he said, and something had to be done about it. It was clear to him that the problem was because she couldn't get along with Nell. When he asked Pearl if she would let her stay with her during the school year, Pearl promptly agreed. She would be glad to help if she could.

Nell and Tom said very little. Nell was crying softly, and Tom seemed intent on patting her arm instead of contributing to the conversation.

Pearl didn't tell him, nor Nell, that Kate was her favorite, and that she would like nothing more than to love and direct this wonderful, talented girl, and, God willing, be able to help her through her present crisis. Having been deprived of having children of her own, she always looked forward to seeing her nieces and nephew. She had her concerns about Mona and Kate, and was delighted with the chance to be involved with them as she had never been before.

"Shouldn't we call Kate and tell her the news?" she asked. "I don't want her here if she isn't willing to stay."

"No," Clint answered. "I hoped you'd talk with her after we left. I don't want her and Nell getting into it again."

"Well, at least stay and have supper with us."

"No, there's chores to do. And Mona home alone. I reckon we ought to get going right now. We'll see her Sunday, that's soon enough."

Pearl hesitated, looked across the table to Tom, who nodded approval.

She turned to Nell. "Don't worry about a thing," she said. "We'll take good care of her. She'll be fine with us."

Chapter 16

Kate's Diary

August 25, 1948.

Today Dad and Mom came into town and went into the kitchen with Aunt Pearl, closed the door and talked. Then they left and Aunt Pearl called me downstairs and told me I'd be staying with her and Granddad so I won't have to ride the bus to high school. She even promised me that if I get good grades, I can go out for basketball!

I don't know whether I'm happy or sad, but I can't seem to keep from crying.

Aunt Pearl has been good to me, like always. And Granddad too. I have my own room in her big house, and the sheets on the bed are fresh and ironed. When I look around the room, I feel like a queen, but when I think of home, I feel guilty. Did I go too far with Mom? Why did they send me here without telling me why? Why is it okay for Mona to ride the bus, but not me?

I guess I'll never know unless Aunt Pearl tells me. In the meantime, I'll try to enjoy the good things about being here and sure hope I can keep my grades up and play basketball next year. With my height, I ought to be good at it.

August 27.

Today Aunt Pearl took me to Aunt Lillian's General Store and bought me some clothes for school. I almost cried I felt so good. New shoes, too. And stockings and underwear and everything to go with them. She also bought a couple of dresses for Mona. Said she would give them to her when Dad stops by to take me home for Sunday after Mass. I wonder what Mom will say?

I tried to get Aunt Pearl to talk about why I am here, but all she would say was that she and Granddad love me and it would be good to have me in the house to keep them company.

She hugs me a lot. Especially when I cry. But there's not a word about what they talked about in the kitchen and I'd give anything to know.

August 28,

Dad and Mom picked me up to go to Mass with them this morning. I was nervous, but they didn't say anything about the problem. I didn't go to Communion, because I haven't had a chance to go to Confession and tell Father about how disobedient I have been. Or how I hate Mona at times.

I went home with them after and Mona was all questions about what I had been doing, but Mom and Dad still weren't talking about the real reason why I was sent to Aunt Pearls.

We had dinner, and I helped Mom do the dishes. She was very quiet, and then Dad drove me back to town. All the way back he lectured me about helping Aunt Pearl around the house and keeping good company when I go to high school, and not to get into a bad crowd, but not a word about what I wanted most to hear.

Why? Do they want to get rid of me? Or is it really so that I get a chance to play basketball? I only wish I'd left on different terms. That Mom isn't angry with me.

Sept 1,

First day of school. It was fun and I met some people from town I had never seen before. Bridey Richardson was there, too. I've missed her so much and she said she was surprised not seeing me on the bus, and hadn't known I was living in town. She said she was jealous. That it would be nice not to have chores every night after school, the way it is on the farm.

Mona wouldn't speak to me. Just stuck up her chin and pretended she didn't see me. But that's nothing new. I really wonder how she'll treat me now, especially when I get on the basketball team. I'll be popular than and I hope she'll be jealous as hell. That ought to fix her.

Got my books for the courses I'm going to take. Algebra and English, American Literature, World History and Biology. Aunt Pearl says I must take the hard courses if I want to go to college. I scanned through the books and they look interesting. Maybe this will be a good year.

September 2,

School was fun but I'm feeling very sad today. The kids ask me why I'm living with my Aunt and not at home. I lie and say it's because she needs help, but it makes me feel ashamed to lie like that. I wonder what they really think. I was moody when I came home and when Aunt Pearl asked me what was wrong I started crying again. She just hugged me and told me everything would be all right and not to worry about a thing.

Still, I feel like I'm now worth a damn to anyone. No one, not even Auntie really understands me. I wonder what it would like being dead, like Grammy. Being dead and in heaven and not have to feel so bad. Except I probably wouldn't get to Heaven, bad as I've been. Especially to Mom. The commandment says to honor your mother and father and I've got such a temper I don't seem to be able to do that. Besides, Mom hits me a lot. How am I supposed to honor that?

Chapter 17

The late September day was alive with the signs of autumn. Maple leaves flashed golden against a brilliant sky, the crops stood ripe in the fields, and on the horizon the sharp V of a flock of Canada geese headed southward before winter's coming blast.

Clint stood with one foot on a fork, the other firmly planted on the ground as he dug for potatoes, buried beneath mounds of dirt in Nell's garden. Kate and Mona traipsed behind, picking up the fat tubers and depositing them in a bushel basket to be carried to the fruit cellar and stored for the winter.

"We got a letter from Jack!" Nell ran from the house, waving the envelope in her hand. "He finally got a part in a play. It's a musical, too, and he's so excited."

"What the hell?" said Clint. "Never thought it'd happen. I still think he's gonna be waitin' tables the rest of his life."

"Now that's not fair," Nell retorted. "It takes time to break into show business. He's worked hard, he deserves a chance."

"Worked hard taking dance lessons," Clint answered. "I tell you it'll never amount to a damn."

"He could be a success, just look at Brian…"

"Brian's out of work, Nell. Last we heard he was washing dishes in a hospital kitchen. That's where show business got him,"

"You never give our boy a chance. How do you know he won't make it big?"

Oh, oh, Mom is getting angry, Kate thought. Seeing that a heated argument was in the offing, she interrupted. "What else did he have to say?" she asked. "Is he still living at his dancing teacher's house?

"If everyone will shut up, I'll read it to you," Nell said. "Here goes"

"Dear Family, I can't tell you how much I love San Francisco. The hills are gorgeous and the ocean awesome. I love go to the beach just to hear the roar of the waves and watch the gulls fly overhead. It's sure different from Lowell! I'm really happy here and glad I made the decision to come.

And now for marvelous news! I just landed a part in a musical! Not a major role, of course, after all, my career is just beginning, but I do have a small speaking part. Mostly, I will be dancing with the troupe and singing with the chorus. The music is fabulous and great fun to dance to. I can't wait for it to open. It will be a fantastic time.

While the show is on I will be able to quit waiting tables at Woody's Fish House. I absolutely abhor that job! Lance said I didn't have to work, that he would help me out until I become better known, but I feel guilty asking him for spending money, so I try to make enough to cover my other expenses.

Can you believe that Lance Edwards, the great Broadway star, thinks I am going to make it big? He's taught me so much, and to let me stay with him has been phenomenal. I can't thank him enough. He doesn't work much anymore. Since he's already made a killing, I suppose that doesn't matter to him. And just think! I'll be the same someday. I can send for you all and show you my city.

There will probably be press releases later, and pictures of the cast in the daily paper. I'll send clippings as soon as they're printed. Love, Jack"

Nell lifted her chin. "So there, Clint. "Didn't I tell you so?"

"Well I'll be damned. I still don't think he'll amount to anything."

"It sounds like his dancing teacher really likes him, Dad. Maybe he's right," Kate offered. "I suppose we can wait and see what happens."

"I think it's a damn crazy setup. And what in hell is with the fancy talk? I don't remember them talking like that in San Francisco."

Mona giggled. "Maybe he thinks he's already a star. He probably thinks that's how they talk."

"Enough of you," Nell sniffed. "I'm going back to the house. I just wanted to share the good news with you and all you do is make fun of him. Someday he'll show you, just wait and see."

⌒⌒

Imagining himself as a famous movie star was something Jack did often. Adoring crowds milling around him, reading about himself in the tabloids were all parts of his dream. A dream that, now, was beginning to become reality. Lance had told him he had to start small, and actually the part he just got was pretty meaty. In the next, he'd be a supporting actor, and in two years, a star. Hollywood would seek him and his dream would come true. And Dad would beg him for forgiveness, a forgiveness he could not now give.

Sitting in Lance's bright kitchen at a shiny chrome and glass table, Jack surveyed the room with gratitude. Lance is so good to me, he thought. I have to succeed at this, if only to repay him for all he has done.

Lance was a friend of Uncle Brian's, Jack had met him in Chicago and was star-struck immediately. Lance was playing in the long running stage hit "Play Me a Tune" and had shown interest in Jack when Uncle Brian had urged the kid to perform for him.

"The boy's got it!" Lance exclaimed. "He's doing a few things wrong, but tell you what; I'll give him lessons when I have time. "Nothing makes me happier than nurturing a new talent and Jack looks more promising than anyone I've seen."

Ecstatic, Jack worked as hard as possible, badgering Uncle Brian to play the piano for him so he could dance and sing. He read plays, speaking aloud the lines of every player, trying to adapt his personality to that of the character, even if it meant he sometimes had trouble getting out of the part.

When Lance's play closed and he left Chicago for his home in San Francisco, he asked Jack to come along. "If you want to go where the opportunity lays, Jack," he offered, "come with me to San Francisco.

I have a lot of contacts there that you don't have in Chicago. You can stay with me until you find work."

Besides being a generous guy, Lance really enjoyed the boy. His marvelous wit and ability to attract a room full of people to his side would make him a great addition to the many parties Lance loved to host in his sprawling California ranch home.

A few months later at their home in San Francisco, Lance was planning a get-together after rehearsal for the members of the cast. Among the guests was Bruce Browning, who had been in several movies and was the star of the play. Jack met him at yesterday's rehearsal and had been overwhelmed with happiness when the actor spoke to him, asking him about how he had come to choose show business as his career. To think he singled me out! He thought. He must have liked something about me or he would not have given me so much attention.

He looked up from his script to Lance, who entered the kitchen carrying a tray of stemmed wine glasses he was setting out for the party. "Gosh, Lance. Is there anything I can do to help you get ready? I feel pretty useless sitting here studying my script."

"No, Jack. The bartender is coming soon. He'll be serving tonight and he can finish setting up. I don't want to exhaust myself before the guests arrive."

"Great. I have to admit I'm nervous about this party. I haven't met all the cast yet and hopefully, if the play has a long run, we'll be together a long time."

"No need to be edgy, Jack. Just be yourself and they'll love you."

"Thanks, Lance. I'll just play the hillbilly farm boy from Missouri and have them in stitches in no time."

"Your past does seem to be humorous to some. And you characterize it well. But I wouldn't carry it too far. Like the night you did at "*Chez Paul Bistro François*" on my birthday."

"Yes. I was drunk that night, and more intoxicated with the attention I was getting. I've certainly learned to control how much I drink after that escapade." He grinned mischievously. "There's much about that night I want to forget, but a whole lot more I'll always remember."

"I remember it too" Lance said softly. "It was the highlight of my life."

Because that night was the night that Lance and Jack first made love. And they had been lovers ever since.

It had happened as naturally as if it had been meant to be. On the drive home, Jack had leaned against Lance and was surprised at the feelings evoked when the older man put an arm around his shoulder and began caressing his arm. When they arrived home, Lance simply picked him up with strong arms and carried him to his bedroom.

On the following morning, Jack was engulfed in guilt, and wondered if he ought to move away and go to Confession as soon as possible. He searched his Catechism for an answer. But nowhere in the book could he find a reference to what he had done. It must not be a sin, he finally concluded. Certainly no one was harmed by it. And in a few short days, as the pleasures in Lance's bedroom became more intense, his guilt subsided. What he and Lance were doing was between them. He had grown to love him more deeply because of it. How could that possibly be wrong?

The party, as usual, was a brilliant success, the guests milling and introducing themselves. Laughter and conversation filled the room and everyone seemed to be having a wonderful time.

But when Bruce Browning entered the room, everyone went silent, eying the star with admiration. Jack tingled with anticipation, I hope he notices me, he thought. What am I going to do to get his attention?

He needn't have been concerned. Bruce made his way to Jack's side only minutes after his arrival.

"Hello, Jack. Marvelous to see you again. Are you looking forward to the play?"

"Absolutely. I can't remember when I've been so excited about anything in my life."

"I know. I adore your enthusiasm. I'm hoping it spreads to the cast so the play will be a smashing success."

"Thanks. I just feel so lucky to have the opportunity to do what I love. Life is good right now."

Bruce reached out and touched his arm. "I hear you're very talented, Jack, my boy. Am eager to see you in action."

"Gosh. Thanks for the vote of confidence. I try to do my best."

Bruce moved closer and slipped his arm around Jack's waist. "With your looks, you just have to show up, dear boy. I can tell you'll be a star someday."

"I've got a lot to learn," Jack replied. "I can sing and dance. Just ain't sure how well I can act."

Bruce laughed. "Not much to it. But tell you what I'll do. Why don't you come back with me to my apartment and I'll show you a few things?"

Gosh. He's coming on to me, Jack thought. Much as I'd like to go, I'm not sure how Lance would take it. "I-I can't make it tonight," he answered. "Promised Lance I'd help clean up after the party...Maybe some other time?"

With a knowing pinch to Jack's arm, Bruce replied. "Anytime you can. I'll be waiting."

Later that night, as they gathered the stemware and plates from the party to take to the kitchen, Jack told Lance about Brian's invitation.

"He's hot for you," Lance said, laughing. "What do you plan to do about it?

"Why, nothing," Jack answered. "I...I'm with you. I couldn't possibly betray you."

"Jack, Jack," Lance began, "Sometimes you have to think about yourself. Bruce might be helpful to your career. I've never believed that sex is always about love. I want you to get ahead, to take every opportunity you have and run with it. I won't be hurt if you humor Bruce while he's here."

"Really? I think I would be hurt if you had sex with someone else."

"I probably won't, so don't worry. My days of trading sex for favors are over. But believe me, I've done a lot of it in my day. Just watch for the next chance. There's no doubt he's attracted to you. It won't be long and he'll come on to you again."

During the weeks that followed, Jack spent most of his nights in Bruce's apartment, encouraged by his promises that he would recommend him when he got back to Hollywood, but after the play opened to mixed reviews, Bruce became distant, no longer including him in his parties, nor inviting him to his apartment. Despondent over the closing of the play a week later, Jack returned to Lance and swore allegiance to him alone, believing that his infidelity had contributed to the failure of the production. Frustrated, he reached out to Kate to vent his disappointment.

"It's mail time, Kate. Looks like you got a letter from Jack. That's a pleasant surprise, he hasn't written to you in a long time."

Oh my gosh! Will wonders never cease? Let's see what he has to say." Kate tore open the letter and began to read:

"Dear Little Sister,

You'll always be my "little" sister no matter how tall you get. I hope you know I love you dearly and miss you more than I miss the rest of the family. Except for Mom, of course. But I can't confide in her the way I can with you. Am sure she'd get upset with me if she really knew how I was doing. In truth, for the past few months it hasn't been very well.

I was so disappointed when the show closed. Blame some of the cast members who never should have made the play anyway. I had such a great opportunity, Kate. Working with Bruce Browning was marvelous and he was so encouraging. He said often that I was the most talented member of the troupe. And he ought to know! I suppose I ought to go on, apply for new parts and keep on practicing. But right now, I'm heartbroken. If it weren't for Lance, I couldn't take this.

Kate, Lance is the most marvelous man alive. He has done so much for me and right now he has been so caring and understanding. I can look up to him the way I never could with Dad. Dad was always so downright mean to me, always preferring Mona to the rest of us.

How is the bitch anyway? She's almost through nursing school now, isn't she? Is she coming home after she graduates? If she does, I'll never come back. Perhaps I could sneak into Lowell, stay at Aunt Pearl's, and see you. We could have Mom stop by so I could see her too.

I hope I'm not burdening you with my sorrows. I do have some fun. Lance is still giving his fabulous parties and we go to many more, attend the theater and movies, dine in exquisite restaurants and explore my beautiful city. It's just that my disappointment makes me miss you, and Mom. I feel like a little boy again, wanting to cry on her shoulder.

Let me hear from you soon. All about school and the fantastic basketball team. Give Aunt Pearl my love. Better not tell Mom I wrote though. She will be jealous I didn't write to her. Love, Jack."

Kate put the letter aside on the kitchen table. "What do you think, Auntie? I hope he doesn't go into the pits the way Dad does."

"I don't think so, Kate. Jack has a lot of support from this Lance. He's just suffering one of life's little setbacks. He'll be okay."

Kate sighed and stretched back into her chair. "Do you ever think it's odd—his setup? I just can't imagine anyone putting up with Jack that long. He can be quite a pain. And this guy supporting him all the while. You should hear what Dad had to say about it Sunday."

"Oh. And what was that?"

"He said the whole thing stunk to high heaven. I asked him what he meant, but you know Dad, he pretended he didn't hear me and went off to do something else."

"Perhaps he'll make it clear later. You have to remember that your dad and Jack never did get along well. There are many things there that may never be resolved. It's too bad, but that's the way it is."

"I know Dad thinks that he'll never amount to anything. And you know what? I agree with Dad. Jack is smart. He should go to college, make something of himself. But he won't. I don't feel too sorry for him though. Surely he knows that making it in show business is hard to do. I think he's daydreaming, but he's old enough to make his own choices. It looks like he hasn't had to pay the consequences of his decision yet. In fact, he's living pretty well."

"I think so, Kate. It's not for you to worry about him. Just answer his letter and tell him how well you are doing and let it go."

"You're right, Auntie. Now if I can learn to do the same thing with Mona!"

Chapter 18

1951

It was Saturday night and in the deserted nurses' dorm, Mona was studying for a chemistry test. She could be out with her dorm mates having fun, but she was as obsessed with her exam as the others were partying with boys. They were in the middle of finals, for Pete's sake. And the course work they were carrying was huge. How her roommate, a former classmate at Lowell high, could trade a good grade on a test for the chance to have a blind date with a college boy was beyond her comprehension.

Not that she'd ever had a date. In fact, she rarely had anything to do with boys. They were noisy and uncouth and made her impatient and bored by their emphasis on cars and sports. As if there were nothing else in the world to keep them occupied.

It's all going to be worth it, she reminded herself. In one more year, she would become a nurse. She had spent some time doing practicums on the wards, always with a supervisor overlooking every move. She felt she couldn't wait to be a head nurse. She knew she'd be good at it, not short tempered and bossy as some she'd worked under. She imagined herself moving around the ward like a white-clad angel of mercy. Like Cousin Lily, she would be a comfort to all.

After next week, she would spend a few days at home. She was looking forward to it. She missed her dad terribly, and even though she had been away two years, there were still nights she cried herself to sleep, worrying if he had been sad again or needed her to help him through another bad time. When they studied psychology, a mental disorder called depression was discussed, but Mona figured Dad didn't suffer from any disease, because he had real life reasons to be sad. There had been Grammy and Jack and Kate to break his heart, plus he didn't get much support from Mom. In fact, Mom often made things worse with her critical tongue.

Life just wasn't fair to her dad and she wished she could be back at home helping him through the rough spots that seemed to come up for him far too often.

Following nurses' training, she planned to return to Lowell and work in the hospital there. Then she could live at home, help with the chores now and then and best of all, be there to care for her parents as they grew older. Like Granddad, they would become frail and arthritic. But she would be there to make it easy for them. She could see herself fixing their meals, tucking a blanket around their lap, accompanying them to the doctor.

She wouldn't desert them the way Jack and Kate had done. Jack, so far away in California, and Kate living in town with Aunt Pearl. Unlike them, she would be there for Mom and Dad, stand by them and replace their loneliness with her presence. It wasn't right, to tear the family apart the way Jack and Kate had. She would do the correct thing and stay close.

"I'll be there for them. That they can count on," she said aloud and looked up flushing as her roommate entered the room.

Sally Richardson dropped her purse on her bed and sat down. "You talking to yourself again, Mona? She asked, laughing. "That's what happens when you study too much. You're beginning to show signs of dementia."

"I am not," Mona retorted. "I'm memorizing. It helps me remember when I say things aloud."

"Whatever," Sally answered. "You should have been with me. What a night it was."

Mona sighed. She noticed how disheveled Sally looked. She'd probably been kissing this guy she'd just met; maybe drinking too. "No," she said. "I had enough to do studying. Now, I have to write to my sister."

"So how is Kate?" Sally asked. "Is she going to lead the basketball team to the State Championship again this year?"

"I'm not writing her about that. I just wish she'd go home where she belongs. She's old enough to take some responsibility. It's planting time and Dad needs help."

"Kate's hardly irresponsible. Isn't she an honor student as well?"

"I'm not talking about her grades. It's just that she should be living at home. It's downright selfish of her. I always helped the folks. I think she should too."

"Sorry," Sally answered, "but I've never seen Kate as selfish. She has a great personality. She used to spend time with Bridey at our house and we all loved her. Maybe your folks want her to play basketball more than they need her help. Are you sure this isn't about something else?"

Mona snorted. "Of course not. Don't talk down to me. I know what I want." She stood and glanced around their small quarters wrinkling her nose. "This place is a pigsty, when are you ever going to make your bed?"

"Maybe when you quit being a bitch about it," Sally retorted. She rose and walked to the door. "I'm outta here until you get over this shitty mood."

And good riddance, Mona thought. Sally was nothing but a boy-crazy slut who was driving her half mad with her inane comments about the family. How could she know what it's like in our home? What business of hers is it anyway? Just because her sister Bridey and Kate were best friends didn't make her an expert, the little snot always remarking about how much she admired Nell and Kate. Even thought Jack was a riot. Never mentioned Dad though. It was as if he didn't exist. But that's what our family has done to him, Mona thought, treating him the way they do. It's a darn shame and they all ought to be ashamed of themselves.

She sat down at her desk and began to write.

∽੭

Kate and Pearl were in the kitchen folding clothes when the mailman arrived. Fresh off the line, the sheets had a sweet clean aroma and Kate couldn't help putting them on by one to her face to breathe in the scent.

She loved helping Auntie with the laundry because they usually talked about things important or interesting to her. Today, they'd been discussing how Chuck Teeter had been waiting for her after very class in order to walk her to the next one and how he cheered her on at basketball games. Junior prom was coming up and Kate suspected that Chuck wanted to ask her to go with him.

"If he asks, I wonder if Ma will let me go," Kate said as she stepped to the mailbox to retrieve the mail. Stunned to find a letter from Mona, she tore it open and quickly scanned its contents.

"The sniveling bitch," she shouted, throwing the letter across the room. "The meddling little low-life bastard. If I could just get my hands on her right now I'd wring her neck."

"Whoa!" Pearl interjected. "I thought you weren't going to use language like that anymore. What did she say?"

"Sorry, Auntie. Mona's sticking her nose in my life again and it makes me so mad I could choke her."

"I can see that. What did she say?"

Kate strode across the room and picked up the letter. "Here. Listen to this…she starts out 'Kate,' not even a Dear Kate. So she's insulting me before she ever got started."

"How is that an insult? I bet she was just in a hurry."

"No. You have to understand that this is Mona. It's an insult because there is no way she thinks I'm dear to her or anybody. Let me read it to you and you will see what I mean."

Pearl folded a towel and placed it on a stack on the kitchen table. "Sure. Maybe then I can see what's upset you."

Kate began to read. "Kate. I just want to let you know that I think you are selfish. Mom and Dad are out at the farm working day and night to keep things going while you stay in town with Auntie, who spoils you rotten. It's planting time and after the tournament there won't be any more basketball practice, so I say it's time for you to go home and take the bus to school the way I did and do your part for the family. I expect to hear soon that you have grown up and started to accept some responsibility. Mona."

"So. That's her letter, full of venom and hate and telling me how to live my life. I hate her...my own sister. I absolutely despise her." Kate sat down at the table and burst into tears. "What's wrong, Auntie? Should I go home and help? I dread going out there; it is so depressing with Dad the way he is, rarely talking to me, and Mom always criticizing." She wiped her eyes with the back of her hand and wailed. "Or is it me? I wonder sometimes..." Her voice trailed off and she began to sob.

Pearl pulled her gently from her seat and wrapped her in her arms. "No. It's not all your fault. It's just that it's hard for your family to get along."

"What's wrong with us? Other families aren't like ours. I just don't get it," Kate cried.

"All families have problems, Kate. They usually don't tell anybody. We don't talk much about our problems either."

"I talk about them to Bridey. She seems to know a lot about us without my telling her. Do you think people talk about us...about how weird Mona is? And everyone knows about Grammy and about the time Dad went to bed for weeks after she died."

"You can't let that bother you, Kate. A lot of times we only imagine that people are talking. Usually they're talking about something else."

"But it does bother me. And there's one rumor that I'm almost afraid to tell you about."

Pearl pulled a kerchief from her pocket and wiped Kate's face. "Which one?"

"Bridey says there was a curse put on Grammy by a gypsy woman. That it would be on our family forever. And it's on Mona because of the birthmark...you know, the three sixes. Can that be true? I asked the priest once and he said it was laughable, that people can't put curses on others. But sometimes I wonder if it's true because our family is so weird."

Pearl paused and sat, beckoning Kate to a chair beside her. "I knew you'd hear about it sometime."

"I heard it a long time ago. Jack used to tease me with it. It isn't fair to be a member of this family if that is true. Why couldn't I be your daughter? At least you don't go to bed every time you don't get your way. I mean, if it's a curse, why hasn't it affected you?"

"Who is to say it hasn't?" whispered Pearl. "I've had my share of troubles too; it's just that you were too young to know about them."

Kate stiffened and sat back in her chair. "You?" she asked. "You had problems?"

"Because I'm human," Pearl answered. "I have problems, but mostly with myself. My marriage was unhappy and I suffered for a long time after my divorce, wondering if I had done the right thing."

"Do you think you're cursed? At times I think I might be, especially when I can't control my temper."

"No. I don't believe in the curse and I don't believe you are either. Just because we have family problems doesn't mean we are cursed. What affects me is the gossip. I've had to live with that too."

"But why is it that, much as I try, much as I tell myself it will never happen again, there comes a time I can't control my anger. It's as if a force takes hold of me and makes me kick and scream and fight back."

"But you're better, honey. You haven't lost your temper in a long time."

"Until today," Kate laughed. "Mona always makes me lose it. Auntie, I'm so ashamed of her. She is so weird it's awful."

"Mona can be difficult at times, but we need to remember she is helpful to her dad. Whenever we have a difficult person in our life, it's well to try to see the good in them.

Kate frowned. "I can't find any good in Mona. She thinks she owns Dad. She tries to protect him so nothing upsets him. I think that's weird."

"I used to do the same for Mother," Pearl replied. I think Clint did too, until he got older and then he'd get mad at her. We always thought if we just did something she wouldn't act up. Mona is probably bothered by your dad's melancholy. She's just trying to keep everything smooth so he won't be upset."

"And it doesn't work," Kate said, sighing. "Nothing seems to work. That's why I think it may be a curse."

"It's a curse only if you believe in it," Pearl replied. "Only if you believe it. So long as I choose not to, it won't affect me."

"But enough of that for now." Pearl rose, stood behind Kate, and rubbed her shoulders. "What are you going to do about Mona's letter? Are you going to answer it?"

Clint pulled the car out of the driveway and headed toward town. He was going to pick up Kate after a brief stop at the General Store where his cousin Faye was holding a lay-away for Mona. Faye had taken over running the store when Aunt Lillian retired a couple of years ago. And although she was no longer running the business officially, his aunt still spent a lot of time there. After Alvin died, she said she didn't have enough to do to keep her busy, so did as much as she could to help Faye with the business.

When he entered the store, Clint found Lillian there, helping a customer pick out fabric and a pattern for a new dress. Except for her silver hair, Lillian looked much the same as she did years ago, and, as he noticed, was spry as ever.

She looked up and smiled. "Hello, Clint," she said. "What a pleasant surprise to see you. Will finish up here and I'll be with you in a minute." She slipped the merchandise into a paper bag and slammed the cash register shut. "Now I have some time, come over here where I can see you. Do you realize it's been months?"

"Reckon so," Clint answered. "I been busy getting ready to plant. It's that time of year."

Lillian smiled. "Not since Christmas. The last time I saw you, you were buying a Christmas present for Nell."

"Reckon time gets away from me. You been okay?"

"I've been very well, thank you, but I'm sorry to hear your dad isn't doing so well. What's going on with Tom?"

"His rheumatism's been bad and he's been having heart trouble. His heart will race sometimes and there's nothin' they can do to slow it down. Don't happen all the time, just once in a while. When it does that, it scares him. Mona says it could be serious and cause a stroke. I wonder what Lily would say?"

Lillian frowned. "I'm sure Lily would leave that up to his doctor, Clint. What does he say?"

"Dad's eighty-two years old and doesn't have too many good years left in him, accordin' to Doc. He says he could have a heart attack and go anytime. He has a lot of pain with his rheumatism so most of the time he don't feel good."

Lillian stepped behind the counter and began tidying a stack of blouses. "I'm sorry to hear that, Clint. "And how is Mona? I hope she likes the new sweater Nell put by for her. Do you want to pick it up today?"

"Reckon that's why I'm here," Clint said, grinning. "Mona's good. Only one year to go and she'll be a nurse. I sure miss her, but you gotta let 'em grow up."

"Yes, you do," Lillian replied. "Is she doing well?"

"Extry, Lillian, extry. She likes what she is doing and does her best. Her grades ain't at the top, but they ain't at the bottom either. Best thing is when she comes home. It's all she can talk about."

"She does seem to be motivated. She's been writing Lily every week or so, telling about her experiences."

"Well I'll be damned. She don't write us that often. She's always looked up to Lily though. I reckon she's been a good example for her."

"I'm sure Lily knows that. But I'll tell her anyway. I'm sure she will be glad to hear it. We thought maybe she was lonely, she was writing so frequently. I've been writing her too, now and then, and last week we sent her a batch of homemade cookies."

Clint looked surprised. "That's right nice of you Lillian. I'm sure she appreciates it." He turned quickly and began to squirm. "Reckon I outta pick up that sweater and go get Kate. She'll be lookin' for me."

Lillian arched her brow. "Is Kate coming home?"

"Weekends. We drop her off at Pearl's after Mass on Sunday. Gives her a chance to talk over her week and help Nell out a little."

Lillian wrapped the sweater in tissue paper, put it in a bag and handed it to Clint. "Here," she said. "The balance is three dollars."

Suddenly restless, Clint was glad to go. He reached for his billfold in his back pocket, paid, and left without saying another word.

What we do with Kate and Mona ain't none of her damn business, he thought as he climbed into the car. It's damn odd, Mona turning to her like that without telling me.

Mona lonesome? She ain't said nothin' about it. I can see why she writes to Lily, but can't help wondering what she says. I gotta talk this over with her, make sure she isn't getting pumped for stuff that just as well be kept in the family.

Far as Kate's concerned, there's a lot of people got their nose in that. Wondering why we ain't raising her and Jack, way we did Mona. Reckon they don't know what it's like, seein' Mother in that girl way I did. Nell wasn't gonna get it out of her fighting with her, and this seems to be working as Kate ain't blown up for months. Thank God Mona ain't no problem. She's a damn good kid and I'm damn proud of her. Kate's smart and everything's easy for her. Made her lazy too, that's what.

He turned on the ignition, revved the motor and drove away. It was a balmy spring day, warm enough for him to open the windows and he noticed Pearl's lilac bush was blooming as he came into the drive, the soft scent of its blooms rising into his nostrils. Clint loved spring. Always hopeful, as he planted his crops, that this would be a good year.

His dad was up when he entered the house, and as he stepped into the living room to see him, Clint allowed he looked bad, his face drawn with pain as he sat in the rocking chair, slowly rocking back and forth and twiddling his thumbs. Poor Dad, Clint thought, he ain't got much time for this earth and it don't look like the time he has left will be a good one.

"Howdy, Dad," he said. "How you feelin' today?"

"Poorly, son, poorly. I reckon it's getting time for me to go be with Molly. I ain't much good for this world."

"Dad, that ain't true. You been a big help with Kate."

"She's a fine young girl. Much like Pearl. I reckon she's been pleasant company for me and I enjoy having her around."

"I reckon she's better," Clint responded. "I'm here to pick her up and take her home for a day or two. See if she'll help Nell plant a garden."

"Well, I'm mighty proud of her, Clint. She's smart as a whip and a good basketball player too. Too bad you ain't seen any of her games this year. She's the top scorer on the team."

"With Mona gone, I'm too busy doing chores to get in to a game. Hell, I got better things to do, I reckon, than watch a bunch of girls play basketball."

"How is Mona, Clint? You have to have her stop by and see me when she's home. I ain't seen her in quite a while."

"Mona's doing good. Reckon she'll be home next year and you'll see her often."

"Don't reckon I'll be around next year," Tom answered. "Getting time I go to the Lord."

"Hell. You'll be around a long time," Clint countered. "Wouldn't worry about that."

"Ain't worried, Clint. I'd welcome it. Ain't good livin' this way with all the hurting. There comes a time when you wish it was over. Reckon I'm there now. And it's okay with me. My body's wore out. It's time to put it to rest."

Mercifully, Pearl came into the room, interrupting them. "My goodness," she exclaimed. "You shocked me, Clint. I didn't know you were here."

"Reckon I am, big as life," Clint said, laughing. "Is Kate ready to go? Gotta be getting back to do chores."

Pearl went to the stairs and called Kate, who promptly arrived, carrying her suitcase

Outside, Clint lit a cigarette, turning his back to the breeze to keep the match from going out. "I don't want to smoke in Pearl's house," he said. "I learnt to smoke outside at home too. Your ma says the smoke settles on the windows making them hard to clean."

Kate wrinkled her nose. "Are you going to smoke in the car?" she asked.

"Now don't tell me it's botherin' you," Clint said. "Mona's been after me too. Says smoking can make you sick. Hell, it's the only vice I got. You girls gonna try to make me change my ways. Reckon I'm too damn stubborn," he said, laughing. He dropped the cigarette to the ground and stepped on it with his toe. "C'mon," he said. "Let's head on home so I can get to the chores.

In the car, Kate felt encouraged by her dad's mood and felt she had an opportunity to approach him with the big question. Auntie had suggested she ask him and she figured since he was talking with her, now might be the time. "Dad," she began, "Aunt Pearl said I should talk to you about a letter I got from Mona…"

"You heard from Mona? He asked. "Looks like she's writin' everyone but us these days. What did she have to say?"

"It wasn't a nice letter, Dad. Mona's upset with me."

"What the hell for. She ain't seen you in a couple months."

Kate swallowed hard. This was going to be more difficult than she had planned. "She thinks I ought to go home."

"Why?"

"So...so I can help you. She thinks you have too much to do."

"What in hell." Clint swerved to avoid a car dangerously close to his side of the road. "No," he growled. "I don't need no help. You can come home this summer and help Nell with the garden, but I want you to stay with Pearl."

Kate sighed. "What will I tell Mona?"

"Nothin'. I'll talk to Mona. You pay her no mind. I'll handle her."

Kate could sense he was angry and she wondered if he were angry at her or at Mona. She never could tell with Dad. He'd just clam up and not talk anymore, leaving her confused.

She rolled the window down and felt the warm breeze ruffle her hair. It was a beautiful day, the dogwood blooming in the pasture where a few cows grazed on the new grass. She wasn't going to let Dad spoil it by his pouting. He said she could stay in town with Auntie and that was enough for her. She breathed in deeply of the crisp clean air and closed her eyes. Luck was on her side. Maybe, since Chuck Teeter asked her, she'd ask Mom if she could go to the prom.

Chapter 19

True to his nature of not wanting to inconvenience anyone, Tom Foster died in his sleep on October 15, 1952. As if he had willed it, his huge heart stopped as Pearl slept. A brief sharp pain in his chest had shattered his slumber and he opened his eyes to a soft, warm light permeating the room. Molly was beckoning and he was at peace. With a deep sigh, he gave up his life, drifting back to sleep. This time forever.

He'd been ready to die for months, eager to see Molly again, believing in heaven her sickness was cured. They would spend eternity together he imagined, and, finally, they would be happy.

And on the surface, the family was at peace with it. That is, except Mona, who from the day after he expired was on a witch hunt to find a culprit. Someone was responsible for not caring for him properly and she was going to find out who. From her perch on a chair in Pearl's living room she fired questions.

"What was the doctor doing about his atrial fibrillation?" she asked.

"Goodness. I don't know what that is," Pearl answered. "The doctor never said what was wrong with him. Dad had trouble with his heart. At times it would race and he'd feel faint and have to lie down. Doc attributed it to his age. Said it wasn't uncommon among the elderly."

"What does a small town doctor know? Had you taken him to St. Louis to a heart specialist, he'd be alive today."

"I can't believe this," Mona said. "There have been so many advances in medicine that these small town doctors can't keep up with them. I can't wait until next summer when I'm working at the hospital in Lowell. I want to talk to this Dr. Mason, tell him a thing or two. I can tell I'm needed here. I'll bring them some fresh new approaches to medicine."

"Dad wouldn't have wanted that, he was used to Dr. Mason and a trip to St. Louis would have been too much for him. He suffered so from arthritis, Mona, and got to where he didn't want to go anywhere."

"Humph," Mona sniffed. "It was his life that was at stake. I can't see why Dr. Mason didn't prescribe quinidine. Probably doesn't even know about it."

"Dad was eighty-three years old. That's a long life. He wanted to die and I thought we should respect his wishes."

"Did you consult with Dad? He was his father, too."

"As a matter of fact, I did talk with him often. He didn't offer any suggestions, so the doctor and I just let nature run its course."

Kate rose from her chair and began to pace the room. She had heard enough. "Good grief, Mona. You aren't a doctor. How can you know what was wrong with Granddad? Let him rest in peace. He's dead. Nothing you say is going to bring him back. So stop saying that Aunt Pearl and Dr. Mason weren't taking good care of him."

"There you go again, Kate, causing trouble, never missing a chance to attack me. You have no idea what you are talking about." Mona answered. "So stay out of it."

"Okay girls, that's enough," interrupted Pearl. "This is not a time for arguing. Especially over something that can't be changed. Kate, are you ready for another driving lesson? I need groceries and you can drive me."

Pleased with Auntie's changing the subject, Kate walked quickly to the door. "Good idea," she said.

To everyone's surprise, Clint adjusted to Tom's death well. And when Pearl told him that Tom had left a nice inheritance from the sale of the farm, he was grateful. "I can put a down payment on my farm" he allowed. "And get a reliable car to drive."

Without consulting Nell, he asked Mona to accompany him to the used car lot to look for a replacement for his old one. When she came home next spring, she'd need a decent car to drive until she could afford her own, so he decided to have her help pick it out.

When they arrived home with a big black 1948 Buick Roadmaster, Nell was furious. "That looks like Ira White's car," she cried. "What in God's name are you doing with that?"

"We bought it," answered Clint. "Iry traded it in for a new one last week."

"Holy Mary mother of God! And how do you think we're going to afford that?"

"Dad made a down payment," Mona interjected. "I'll help make the payments when I get home in June. I intend to drive it to work so that's only fair."

"And tell me what I'm going to be driving when you're gone. Nurses work on Sundays too. Are we supposed to take the team and wagon to church?"

"Hell no," said Clint. "I'll take Mona to work and go git her. You'll like drivin' that car, Nell. It has an automatic transmission, Dynaflow they call it, and you don't even have to shift gears."

"I'd like having something smaller that we can pay for ourselves, Clint. We could have spent the money on a lot of things around here and got a smaller car."

"That's enough," Clint answered. "Dad left the money to me, and I'll do what I damn well please with it. How I spend it ain't none of your business."

"It'll be my business when you realize how people are laughing at you for driving around in that thing covered in dust and mud," she retorted. "And when you start moaning and complaining about how the folks in Lowell gossip. They're going to notice this, and they're goin' to have plenty to say. And you'll want me to listen to you. Well,

I won't. If it's not me business now, it's not goin' to be me business then. You can have your darn car if that's what you want, but you'll live to regret it, mark my words." She turned on her heel and stormed back into the house.

Clint turned to Mona. "Reckon she's a bit upset," he said. "Wish I could find a place in the barn to park it, but there ain't enough room. Never thought about that."

"How about we build a garage?" Mona answered. "You can get a pre-fab one from the lumber yard. I'll help you put it up."

"Hell. Never thought about that. Reckon I could, but I hate giving Ben any business. The son-of-a-bitch don't care for me any more'n I care about him. Ever since Iry put him in charge of things, there's hell to pay every time I go there or to the feed store."

"I'll go with you, Dad. He'll be nicer with me there. Why don't we go in tomorrow? I have another day before I go back to school."

"I'll think about it tonight. Just don't say anything to your mother. She's already mad as a hornet."

"She'll get over it, Dad. She always does. I wouldn't worry about it if I were you. Soon as she drives that car, she's going to love it."

A large sheet of finished plywood extended over a wooden frame fashioned Ben's makeshift office desk. Situated in a corner of the showroom, it was high enough for him to wheel his wheelchair up to and work comfortably. From there he could supervise the men as they arranged the pungent, newly sawn boards in neat rows on racks that rose to the ceiling. There, he could greet his customers as they came in, knowing that his presence and friendly persuasion could generate sales like nothing else. Shunning Ira's office as too fancy, he spent his days with his employees and his customers, happy to be present where all the action was, and that way he could also keep informed about what was going on about town.

So before Clint arrived with Mona that morning, he already knew his cousin had bought Ira's used car and was looking for a garage to park it in. How in hell is he gonna pay for that, Ben wondered. Just now paid what he owed on last year's seed bill. I know Tom left him some money, but not that much. Ought to be interesting to hear what he's going to say.

When they walked in, he was ready. Navigating the wheel chair up to them with strong, muscled arms, he greeted them warmly. "Mornin' Clint, Mona, how are you today? Anything we can do for you?"

"Fine," Clint mumbled. "Lookin' for one of them pre-fab garages to put up on the farm."

Feigning innocence, Ben responded. "And what do you plan to use it for? Some of your equipment?"

"Don't matter. I just want to see what you got."

"Well sure. Have some brochures over at my desk. But have to tell you right off, they don't come cheap."

Mona tucked her chin into her chest. "We can pay for it," she interrupted. "Why don't you just show my dad what you've got and then we'll decide whether or not we'll buy it."

"Why yes Ma'am," laughed Ben. "You speakin' for the old man these days?"

Mona looked away, avoiding his eyes. "I don't think that's any of your business," she sniffed. Her voice was thin, wavering. "All we want is to see what you have."

"Okay, okay. Let's move over to my desk and I'll show you."

It didn't take long for Clint and Mona to make a decision. The biggest garage would be the best and house not only the car, but the workbench Clint had in the barn. He could store his tools there and have a better place to work.

"Seven-hundred-fifty dollars?" asked Ben. "And where are you going to get money like that?"

"We can put two-fifty down and pay of the rest in monthly payments," said Mona. "I'll be working at the hospital by fall and we can do it easily."

"While making payments on that big Buick? Are you kidding me? Nurses don't make that much. And with your credit history, Clint, I say it's five-hundred down or no deal. Planting time is coming up and you are going to need seed and fertilizer. How you gonna do that"

Clint clenched his fists and stiffened his back. He was angry now and wasn't going to let the son-of-a-bitch make him lose control. "I'll pay cash for it, damn it. On the day you deliver it. Does that suit you?"

"Hell. Can't argue with that. How about we shake hands and we bring it out Wednesday?"

Clint stuffed his hands into his pockets and walked away. "I'll expect it then," he said. "Bright and early."

Nell's gonna say I told you so, Clint thought, as late that night he pored over his books. He hadn't told her yet he'd bought the garage or that he'd spent all of his inheritance doing it. Seemed like a good idea at the time, but now he wasn't sure. At least, he'd made a down payment on the farm, and now all the profit would be his instead of Iry's. He was glad he did that much for his wife. Thinking back on the transaction with Ben, his face flushed. But he sure as hell wasn't going to admit he'd made a mistake to Nell, or back out of the deal. That would only make the shame worse. He tore up his notes and stood, afraid to go to bed because he knew he wouldn't sleep. "Damn," her muttered. "Sure got myself in a mess this time. When Nell finds out she'll never let me forget it."

Chapter 20

Kate's Diary

January 15, 1954

    Dear Diary,

    It's been some time since I've written. Too bad, because I have so much to say. I'm back in Kirksville starting my second semester of teacher's college and loving every minute. We observed the classroom of a 4th grade teacher this week and she was great. How she kept the attention of a room full of 10 year olds was beyond amazing. Made me wish I could see Aunt Pearl in action. Hopefully, I'll be in Lowell sometime when she is not on break and she'll let me volunteer in her classroom. I imagine she's very good. She's sure had a lot of experience and probably could teach me a lot.

    Christmas break went okay. Spent much of it at home and was nervous about having to room with Mona again, but I didn't lose my temper with her, or Mom, the whole time. Think, as I grow up, I'm becoming immune to their remarks. What they say really can't hurt me unless I let it. And, thanks to Aunt Pearls advice, I have that choice. What a relief! I actually used to think I couldn't control my temper at all, but if I take a deep breath, say a quick prayer, and think of the consequences of a tantrum I can back off.

    Dad even showed some interest in what I am doing in school. Of course, he had to tell me again that I have to get good grades in order to keep my scholarship because they can't afford to send me here. Guess my A average satisfied him. He even said I was doing a great job and to keep it up. Hard to believe he'd say that! He even seemed in a good mood. I think having Mona there has been good for him. Have to admit she's helped him a lot with chores after she gets off work. Funny how Mom won't let her help in the house. Except for cleaning her room, Mona has no house chores at all. Mom won't let her near the kitchen. I don't blame her as I doubt she could cook anything. She never has. Glad Mom and Aunt Pearl taught me to cook. Guess if I ever get married it will come in handy!

Saw Chuck again yesterday. It's fun having him going to school here. Met him in the Quad between classes and we had a coke at Walgreen's. Fun to catch up on his news of Lowell and we made a pact to meet at the same time next week.

Aunt Pearl says Mona is doing well at the hospital, that people stop her on the street to tell her how comforting she is when they or someone in their family has been sick. Said that Ira White's wife was most appreciative of the way she worked with the doctor to revive him the day he died.

And I feel good about that! Maybe she's going to turn out normal after all.

Chapter 21

1955

Mona walked slowly down the marble floor of the ward, peeking into the dim light of each room to make sure her patients were sleeping and no one was in distress. It was 2am and all was quiet. With a sigh of relief, she turned off her flashlight and returned to her desk. She had charting to do and wanted to do it well.

Every week, she had been working two night shifts to relieve the regular nurse as she took her days off. It was her favorite time. First of all, she was alone at the desk with 2 aides to assist her. Without a supervisor, she was in charge, and she did not take the responsibility lightly. Believing in her heart she was the best nurse on staff, she alone made all the decisions. This is what she had dreamed of and she imagined that soon, she'd be directing other nurses on the floor, making them treat the patients more kindly and not allowing them to spend so much time in the nurses' lounge drinking coffee and smoking cigarettes. In the daytime, as doctors called and patients recovered from surgery, critical decisions had to be made. She would be there to make the right ones. But for now, she had to wait. Working the night shift was excellent practice. So far, she hadn't had an emergency, but if she did, she knew she could handle it.

The other reason she loved working nights was that she didn't have to put up with the other nurses. Except for Lily, who was now Supervisor of Nurses, she hated every one of them, how they smelled of perfume and cigarettes, the way they gossiped about the patients. She would not allow that as head nurse. It would stop immediately and the ward would be run efficiently and perfectly. Patient confidentially would be paramount. Lowell was a small town where news spread fast. News of the patients should not be discussed outside the hospital, she thought. And when I'm head nurse, I'll see that it isn't if I have to fire someone.

Down the hall, the light over Mrs. Gibbs room came on and Mona sent an aide scurrying to see what she wanted. Recovering from gallbladder surgery only this morning, she was probably in pain.

Before the aide returned, Mona had already reached in her pocket for the keys to the drug room and gone to check her supplies. Then, filling a syringe with Demerol, she hurried to the patient. No one would suffer long on her watch, of that she was determined.

After reporting to the staff coming on duty at 7:00, she rushed home, changed her clothes and went to the barn to help her dad finish the milking. Clint looked up from his milk stool beside his favorite cow, Old Clara, and grinned.

"Whatcha doin' out here Miss Mona. Don't you need some sleep? Yer ma said you was workin' again tonight and I don't want you going in there tired."

"I'm fine, Dad. I'll just help you finish milking and put out the feed for the cows. I can sleep this afternoon."

"Sure you can," he answered. "But you ain't gonna. You're goin' to bed right now. Around here I'm the general and you're the private. Just gave you an order and you have to obey it."

Mona laughed. "Okay. If that's the way you want it, that's the way it is. I'll get up and help you with night chores if you'll let me. Right now, I'll get some sleep."

"We'll see how that works out when the time comes. You git on now and we'll talk about it over supper."

"Okay, Dad. See you then." Mona turned, left the barn and headed to the house. He's so good to me, she thought. Probably saw how tired I am. I'll get up and help him tonight. He really needs me. It's far too much for him to do alone.

Clint's heart swelled with pride as he watched her leave. It's damn good having her home, he thought. Don't know what I'll do if she ever gets married. She sure don't seem to care much for the boys yet, but that can change the minute she meets someone she likes. I'll just enjoy her while she's here. He rose from his stool, lifted the bucket and went to pour the milk into the strainer on top of a waiting ten gallon can. Finished with the milking, he released the cows from their stanchions and herded them into the corral. Even though it was cold, he wanted to shovel the manure out of the barn before letting them back in to feed. Do that and put the hay in the mangers and he'd be done. Winter on the farm was pretty easy. Without any crops to tend, he had time to replace a link on the broken drive chain of the manure spreader before he went in for dinner and a short nap.

He'd been feeling pretty good lately. Sleeping better since Mona came home. Seemed the girls were doing good. Had been nice seeing Kate, realizing that she hadn't blown up in a long time. Pearl had been good for her and he was grateful. Maybe she wasn't so much like Ma after all. Growed out of it, he reckoned, as he'd hoped she would.

As for Jack, Clint wasn't sure. What they'd heard from him wasn't good. There weren't any more plays, yet he kept saying that he'd tried out for another every time he wrote or called. Each one was gonna be a big one, but something always happened that meant he didn't get the part. Always someone else's fault, according to him. Don't like the way he's livin', that's for damn sure. I don't like that situation at all. It's sorta like Clay and Frank Baker livin' together. I know Frank is takin' care of Clay, but the way they act just ain't right. 'Fraid that's what's goin' on with Jack and that sugar daddy of his. He shook his head. Don't like it, don't like it at all. But there ain't a damn thing I can do about it. If he's a damn queer I don't want to have nothin' to do with him. Just hope he don't come home so I get tested. Just might kick his ass out of here, 'cause there ain't nothing I hate worse.

And Nell seems to have got over her fit about the car and the garage. I ain't, Wish I had the money back, and that car's damn expensive when it needs repairs. She won't say nothin'. Just look at me with that proud look of hers. Last week she ordered more baby chickens for this spring, says she has to sell more eggs if we're gonna buy any seed. Wish I hadn't let Mona talk me into it, but it's too late now. Made my bed and I'm the one's gonna sleep in it I reckon. Can't do anything about it now.

Clint finished pitching hay, hung up his fork and opened the door for the cows to come in. Thought he'd go to the house and have a cup of coffee before he started working on the spreader. If Nell was in a good mood, he'd enjoy the break.

"And the worst job is shoveling shit out of the barn. You have to pick that crap up and throw it out the window into a big pile. Then, when the pile gets big, you fork it into a manure spreader. That's a wagon with a conveyer that moves the shit out of the back and spews it onto the cornfield for fertilizer. You can't begin to imagine how it smells, especially after it sits there a while"

"Really! I can't imagine. How did you do it?" asked a new acquaintance he met at a party. "I'd puke."

"I almost did. It was awful. The smell wasn't so bad in winter when the pile froze, but come spring, when it thawed and you had to spread it— P-U! And with all the farmers doing it at the same time, that's all you could smell. Talk about fresh country air! I've had enough for a lifetime."

Jack was at his best, entertaining a bunch of people he'd just met at a party. Had them all laughing at his tales of the farm and he was feeling on top of the world. After three drinks he was unstoppable, often mimicking Clint's drawl to embellish a story. Anything to keep them captivated. Lately, he'd had to watch how much he was drinking as Lance had remarked that when he was drunk he often repeated himself. Have to be careful, he thought. Otherwise I'll make an ass of myself. Four drinks was his limit. If he spaced them just right he could stay high and not get stupid. But sometimes it wasn't easy. And often, if Lance wasn't there to remind him, he drank too much anyway, always waking the next morning ashamed and wondering if he'd done something he couldn't remember.

That was the worst part, hearing from someone else what he'd done. Drunk, he was often outrageous. Most of the time people thought he was funny, but at times he went too far, insulting people and making a joke of them or indulging in wild sexual orgies doing things he wouldn't have done otherwise. People were beginning to talk about it as Jack vowed over and over to Lance it would never happen again.

Tonight I'll be careful, he told himself. And it was one of the rare evenings that he did. Because Lance wasn't there, he ended up having sex with a guy he'd just met, but it was all in fun and didn't mean much to him either way. The parties he went to often ended up like that. Everyone else was doing it, so why not me? He figured. At least I'm not hurting anybody.

Lately, Jack's life had been a round of parties and night life. Tired of the scene, Lance often stayed home, preferring to entertain in style occasionally and not encourage the wild debauchery of the younger men. Like a parent, he would counsel Jack on the way he was living.

"If you want to work," he admonished, "You're going to have to be a little less carefree and a lot less sarcastic. Granted, a lot of us are entertained by you, but you have to remember that the producer of a play expects you to be at every practice and more. You have to get along with the cast and the way you make fun of others doesn't help. You're getting a reputation and it isn't a good one. No head of casting is going to put you in a play if he thinks you are too irresponsible."

"I don't think it's so bad," Jack answered. "Jimmy Henderson is doing a lot of backbiting. Trying to destroy me. With a wave of his hand, he discounted him. "He's just jealous of me because I'm a better dancer."

"Isn't he the one you locked out of a tryout?"

"It was hilarious. As I was waiting for my turn I went backstage to the bathroom, saw him coming and locked the theater back door. I could hear him pounding on it and yelling, but no one else was back there so he didn't get in."

"And missed his tryout—didn't help you any, Jack. You didn't get a part either. Tell me, how did he find out?'

"I happened to tell a few guys that hate him too. Guess one of them got the word out."

"You were drinking—right?"

"Well yes."

"That's what I've been saying Jack. I love you too much to see you end up like your Uncle Brian."

That remark hurt, Uncle Brian had looked awful last time he saw him, his eyes bleary and his stomach distended. He had begun to walk like an old duck, splaying his feet outward and slapping them down like his web footed counterpart. He had died shortly after their last meeting, drunk and alone.

So later, as Jack sat at breakfast in Lance's bright kitchen he decided to quit drinking. Trying to visualize himself at a party without alcohol, Jack could see himself as a sensible, mature young man. He'd be an example to the others, be a success in his career and all would look up to him. No longer would he be one of the group. He would stand out, like Lance, quiet and self-assured. Tomorrow was a party at one of Lance's friends. It was then he would begin his new way of life. He took a deep breath and quietly remembered the words of the Our Father. With God's help, he knew he could do it. And, when he became famous, would be well worth it.

Chapter 22

May 13, 1976

Kate lifted a plate from a pan of hot sudsy water, dipped it into a rinse and put it in the dish rack to drain. Pearl stood beside her with a towel, wiping the dishes dry and stacking them in a cupboard. They had just finished supper and were looking forward to an evening of catching up. It had been almost a year since Kate had been home so both were eager to hear what the other had done in her absence.

"I'm still not used to retirement," Pearl began. "Didn't know I'd miss the kids so much. I've been volunteering at Sunday school, but it's just not the same. Besides, my hip is bothering me so much I can't do a lot of things I'd like to with them."

"Like sitting on the floor and reading?" laughed Kate. "I do my best work on the floor of the classroom. Seems the kids like to get me down to their size before they'll listen to me."

"I know what you're saying. But sometimes you have to stand at your desk and lead. Order is pretty important and in order to keep discipline you have to have their respect."

"Right on. By the way, speaking of teaching, did I tell you that Ben Hobbs wants me to apply for a position in Lowell?"

"The principal of Lowell Elementary? I know they've had trouble filling positions. Most young graduates don't want to live in a small town."

"I'm going to meet with him tomorrow. See what he has to say. I wouldn't mind being back, and I could help you out on the days your hip is bad. I worry about your being alone."

"No need to worry, dear. I'll be okay. The neighbors help a lot. Especially Dorothy Benton. Think it's so she can keep up with the news just as her mother-in-law did," she laughed. "But I have to admit, I'd like nothing better than having you here. You know you can always stay with me."

"I'll see what happens. Maybe tomorrow I'll know for sure. I really want to do it and I'm ninety-nine percent sure he'll hire me." Kate drained the dishwater and turned the pan upside down on the dish rack. "Let's go sit in the living room," she said. "Would you like me to bring you a cup of tea?"

With the help of her cane, Pearl hobbled into the living room and sat down in her new recliner. The pain was particularly bad today and she thought briefly of the possibility of getting a hip replacement as her doctor had recommended. But she knew that Alice Benton had undergone the surgery a short time before she died. Alice's hip dislocated frequently after the operation and she fell, breaking the other hip. She never recovered.

Pearl feared the outcome of having surgery. Even though she was in a lot of pain, she was still sure footed enough to get around most days and hated the possibility of becoming an invalid, perhaps ending up in the River Valley Nursing Home and losing her independence. Dr. Mason had insisted that her arthritis could incapacitate anyway, but she wasn't ready to take the chance. Leave well enough alone, she thought. I can always change my mind if it gets worse.

The thought of having Kate return heartened her. We've been through a lot together, she recalled, remembering as if it were yesterday the talk they had before Kate broke her engagement to Chuck Teeter.

"I need to see you," Kate said, as she burst through the front door, tears streaming down her face. "I need your advice."

"Not before a hug, dear. Whatever is going on?"

Pearl embraced Kate warmly. "I'm breaking up with Chuck," she'd said. "When we started to plan the wedding, I felt I just couldn't go through with it."

"But why? You were so happy."

"I know. I was happy. I do love him so much, and I know he loves me, but he wants a big family, three or four kids he says. Oh Auntie, I'm so afraid to have a baby. I just can't go through with it, I know."

"I thought you loved kids, Kate. Teaching them and all. I don't get it."

Kate pulled back and lowered her eyes. "It's the curse, Auntie, the curse. I'm afraid all my children will be cursed as we were."

Pearl gasped. "I thought you didn't believe in it anymore," she said. "Don't you know by now it's a matter of faith? That it won't affect you if you don't believe it will."

"But that doesn't stop me from being afraid. So far, I've been blessed. But sometimes I have doubts. And what about my children? What if they believe? What will happen to them?"

"I—I don't know. I never thought of that. Can't you teach them otherwise?"

Kate stopped to blow her nose. "How on earth would I teach that?" she whispered. "When I'm not sure I've learned it myself."

Kate entered the room, teacups in hand, interrupting Pearl's reverie. Years ago Kate had broken her engagement and decided not to marry. Now, she likely would be coming home. Pearl smiled. For that she was grateful. Tomorrow they were going to Clint and Nell's to celebrate Clint's eightieth birthday. After seeing her family, Pearl knew Kate would need her support again. Perhaps now, Pearl thought, they would support each other.

Nell had just finished setting the table when Pearl and Kate came in. A pot roast simmered on the back burner of her new gas stove as a pan of peeled potatoes boiled on a front one. Before she could greet them, Mona was showing off their new home, the old Baker house on Willow Street which they'd bought when they sold the farm.

"This is, of course, the living room," said Mona. "And just off it is a small dining room. Mom's kitchen is over there and there are 3 bedrooms and a bath down the hall. It's just a great little house for us. No stairs for Mom and Dad to climb. I insisted on that. Don't want either of them falling and breaking a hip."

"What are you doing with the extra bedroom?" asked Kate.

"Strange that you should ask," Mona replied. "Jack is coming home for a long visit next month. The guy he lives with died of pneumonia and I don't think he has anywhere to go."

"He's gonna have to get a job if he stays here," interrupted Clint. "I don't want him lying around the house doin' nothin' while Mona goes to work. "Don't think I could put up with him."

Kate stepped across the room and gave him a swift kiss on the cheek. "Happy Birthday, Dad," she said. "How are you feeling today?"

"My legs hurt," he answered. "Doc told me it was circulation and to walk every day, but it hurts more when I do. Mona said I didn't have to if it hurts, so I don't. Get tired sittin' here, but the TV helps entertain me."

"Why does the doctor want you to walk?" Kate asked. "I've read where walking improves circulation."

Mona stared at her, eyes flashing. "I've seen how much pain he has. Dr. doesn't have a clue."

Kate looked down. She knew it was useless to argue with her. "I see," she said and turned to Nell. "C'mon Mom, show me the rest of your new house. I'd like to see where I'm sleeping tonight."

"And I'm glad you're callin' it mine," said Nell as she led Kate down the hall. "Mona seems to think it's hers."

When they reached her and Clint's bedroom, Nell closed the door and began to whisper. "I have to talk to you" she said. "Something has to be done before Mona makes me crazy. She's taking on running our lives and I won't have any part of it for meself. Your dad seems to lap it up like a cat drinking milk though. And you heard what she said. The doctor doesn't know as much as she does, so Dad's care goes wanting and there isn't anything I can do about it."

Kate nodded. "I heard about the walking. Is there anything else?"

"She's making him sick, Kate. Always taking his blood pressure and pulse. And now she's taking to helping him in and out of the bathtub, for heaven's sake. Her own father, seeing him naked like that! She says she doesn't want him to fall. I can't take any more of it. Neither one of them will listen to a word I say."

"Well, since Mona's a nurse, I suppose it doesn't matter." said Kate. "I doubt if there's anything I can say to change it. Mona gets mad if I make a suggestion or criticize. She certainly won't listen to me."

"She won't listen to anybody," answered Nell. "You should see her shave him. Makes me want to throw up. He just leans back in the chair and closes his eyes like a dying old man. As if he couldn't still shave himself. Yesterday I made him lunch and he just pushed it aside and asked Mona to fix him a peanut butter sandwich. It's a wonder she doesn't feed him, she's turned him into such a baby."

"Gosh. That's ridiculous! I'd be upset too. It's not good for Dad to be giving up this way. Did the doctor say there was anything wrong with him?"

"No. He has some hardening of the arteries in his legs. That's why they hurt and he should walk. But Mona thinks she knows better. You heard her."

"I did. Does she try to take care of you too?"

"Now you know better than to ask me that, Kate," said Nell. "I wouldn't let her touch me with a ten foot pole!" I can't wait 'til Jack gets here. Maybe he can put a stop to it."

A dense fog settled on the city overnight, darkening Jack's mood. Recuperating from a bad cold, he was tired and irritable. Since Lance's death a terrible sadness had overwhelmed him and he found it nearly impossible to do anything but stay home and feel sorry for himself. Surprisingly, he had been unable to shed tears. But, God, how he missed Lance! I didn't know it was possible to hurt this much, he thought. Some days I think I can't go on, wishing I were dead as well.

Yet, every morning when he woke, he dragged himself from his bed, pulled a robe over his pajamas, plodded to the kitchen and fixed a breakfast he rarely ate. This morning was no exception. As he sat at the kitchen table sipping coffee, he pushed his filled plate back and tried to think ahead. He was going back to Lowell in a week and wondered how he would ever get ready on time. Many of his personal belongings would have to be given away as he knew he wouldn't need them at home. But where to begin? He sighed deeply. I'm paralyzed, he thought. Don't even have the energy to pack my clothes. I'd ask someone to help, but I'm ashamed to admit how helpless I am. God! I'm just like Dad, lost in a depression. And I can't see any way out of it. I always thought he acted like that on purpose, almost as if he were getting even with someone. Now I wonder. Is it possible that I have it? The family sickness, as Granddad called it. And I can't help myself? He shuddered. "I have to quit thinking this way," he muttered. "I have to pull myself together." He rose and went to his bedroom, thinking that maybe he would begin to go through his clothes, pack some of them. Anything to distract himself from all this thinking!

The fact was, he had to leave a week from today. Lance's sister had inherited the house and she wanted Jack out by the first of the month. Yesterday, they'd met at the lawyer's office to hear the reading of Lance's will. Dated almost a year before Jack met Lance, everything Lance owned, the home, bank accounts, and investments were all in her name now and there was nothing Jack could do to contest it. Shortly before he died, Lance mentioned that he wanted to update his will. That he wanted all that he had to be Jack's. But he was too sick to get it done. "When I get over this," he said, "I'll call my lawyer, I promise." It was too late. He died the next day.

Fortunately for Jack, Lance had almost two thousand dollars in cash in a small box in their bedroom. It was enough to get home. All he needed was to take some time and seek a new direction in his life. I just need a long rest, he thought. Some of Mom's home cooking and plenty of sleep. I will always miss Lance, but I have to move on. For the first time since he'd left home at age 13, Jack was eager to go back.

Chapter 23

Jack's Homecoming

The duty fell on Kate to pick up Jack at the airport in Kansas City. Neither Clint nor Mona would go, and Nell was nervous about driving that far.

In fact, Kate was happy to go, looking forward to the chance to talk with her brother alone on the drive home. She wanted to brief him on the situation there, hoping he would be able to help Mom curb Mona's overbearing attempts to control their life.

As she spotted Jack step into the terminal, however, Kate was shocked at his appearance and couldn't help but show concern. She ran to him and gave him a firm hug. "Jack," she exclaimed. "You've lost weight. You look…"

"Awful," he interrupted. "I think I have a fever, Kate. Feel like shit. The trip back was miserable. I have this awful headache and sore throat."

Kate grinned. "Gosh. Mona will be delighted. She always loves it when someone is sick."

"Oh no! Never thought about that. Well she's not going to nurse me. Think I just have a case of the flu. Will feel better in a few days I'm sure."

"Let's get you home and get you to bed," said Kate. "Let me carry your bag, the car is all the way on the other side of the parking lot. Think you can make it?"

"Sure. Let's get it over with. I'll be glad to get there."

But they had gone only a few yards when he became breathless and asked her to stop. Realizing he wasn't going to walk any further, she found a spot where he could safely wait, left him sitting on his bag, and ran for the car.

They arrived in Lowell two hours later, not having exchanged a word. Jack fell asleep as soon as he got in the car and slept all the way home. She had to shake him awake in order to get him into the house. Maybe it's good that Mona is home today, she thought. Jack is obviously very sick. No doubt about it, she'll know what to do.

And soon as they walked in, Mona rose to the occasion. Brushing Nell aside, she came to Jack's side and ushered him to Clint's recliner. "You have quite a fever," she said. "I can see it in your eyes. Sit here and I'll get a thermometer. Have you taken any aspirin?"

"Haven't taken anything," Jack mumbled. Looking up he saw Nell and smiled weakly. "Sorry, Mom. I can't even give you a decent hug. I sure don't want to give you this."

Nell leaned over, kissed his cheek and squeezed his shoulders. "As if I'd worry about a few germs," she said. "And you'll not be apologizing. It's not like you did it on purpose."

Jack looked around. "Where's Dad?" He asked.

Nell looked down. "He went to bed. Said he was tired and not to wake him."

"He'll be out soon," said Mona, as she came back shaking a thermometer. "Just open your mouth, Jack, and put this under your tongue...my goodness! Open real wide and let me see your cheeks. Be darned if you don't have thrush. Your mouth is covered with it. Has it been sore?"

"What's thrush? I thought that was a bird. And no, I haven't noticed it."

Mona tucked her chin into her neck, folded her arms, looked down on him, and smiled. "It's a fungus babies get," she answered. "Still aren't acting your age, are you?

"Not funny, Mona. Is it because I have this flu?"

"No. But have you taken an antibiotic lately? Penicillin?"

"No. Never have."

"Hmmm. Well maybe you're just run down. What can help is rinsing it with apple cider vinegar. If that doesn't work, maybe Dr. Mason can prescribe something. C'mon now, open up. Let's get that temp."

After a few moments, she removed the thermometer and peered at it. "One-o-three- point- four! No wonder you have a headache! Here, take two aspirin. Mom, get a glass of water. Let's get him into bed. I hope you have his room ready."

"Of course, Mona. But I'm not your nurse's aide. I'll get the water for Jack, but you'll not be ordering me around"

Kate went to the kitchen and came back with the water. "Welcome home, brother," she said, laughing. "Just like old times, isn't it?"

From behind the door of his bedroom Clint listened carefully to the conversation in the living room. He gathered that Jack was sick and would be going to bed shortly and was relieved. Then he could come out and not have to greet him. Didn't know what he was going to do when he saw him but was prolonging it as long as possible. Sure don't want him here, he thought, don't know what I'll do about it. Nell sure as hell is happy about having the boy back so Clint hadn't said anything about how he felt. Knew she wouldn't understand and besides, this was something he didn't want to say out loud. The shame was too great—so damn bad he didn't even want Nell to know. Besides, she wouldn't believe it anyway.

He's a damn queer, he thought. The worst thing he could turn out to be. I'd suspected it for a long time, but after Brian's funeral, I'm damn sure. All that cryin' and huggin' that son-of-a-bitch, Lance. Made me want to puke. Like a couple of girls. Remember a couple of guys like that in the service. They got kicked out fast after a bunch of men beat the shit out of them one night. I've got to get him outta here, that's for damn sure. Just don't know how, especially with him sick. Maybe in a day or so—get him alone when Nell's not here and kick his ass out.

Clint went to the bed to lie down. He could hear them ushering Jack into his room, knowing it would be only a few minutes and he could come out. Damn, he thought. Nell's got a big supper planned. Pearl will be here too. What in hell am I going to do?

Fortunately for Clint, Jack was still in bed when Nell called him to supper. But half-way through his plate of fried chicken, mashed potatoes and gravy, he heard Jack close the bedroom door and head to the bathroom. Without a word, he pushed his plate back, stood, and made his way back to his room. No way the little queer was gonna ruin his meal. He'd starve first.

Chapter 24

January 1976

Back and forth and up and down the living room, Clint paced the night. Mind racing with thoughts of Jack, he hadn't slept well for days, and even though he was dead tired, he didn't want to return to bed nor let go of his obsession. Somehow, it gave him a power he didn't ordinarily have—power to know that he was right and the family wrong. That Nell and Brian had ruined the boy with their pampering and spoiling. All those years he had insisted on disciplining his son and Nell had interfered. Look at him now, he thought. A worthless queer. That's what they got for their hard work. And I can't kick him out because he's sick. Wonder if he's pretending. Even Mona fell for it. Clucks after him like a mother hen. I'm gonna get him outta here if it's the last thing I do. Can't keep living like this. But how the hell can I get him out? If only I could talk to Mona—

His thoughts changed abruptly as Mona walked in. "Dad," she whispered. "What are you doing up? It's three o-clock. Can't you sleep?"

"Hell no" he retorted. "Why do you think I'm out here?"

"Sorry, Dad. But you don't have to stay up this way. I have something that will help you sleep. It's in my uniform pocket. Was prescribed for one of my patients, but she went to sleep without it. Let me give it to you. You need some rest." She pointed to the recliner. "Just sit down and I'll get it for you. I'll make you a cup of hot milk too. That ought to relax you."

247

Clint sighed. No use talking with her now. She's trying to help. Maybe she's right. If I get some sleep I'll feel more like talking to her tomorrow. He sat and waited. She'll be able to help me out on this, 'cause it sure as hell ain't gonna be Nell.

⌒◯

Jack woke with a start, gripped in a dark vise of terror. Drenched with sweat, he'd dreamed he was drowning, that even though she was standing by, Mona could do nothing to help him.

He was back in White Memorial Hospital, the third time since his arrival home in May. This time he'd reacted to a shot of penicillin Dr. Mason had administered in his office for another bout of the flu. Red, watery wheals covered his body and the itching was unbearable. Even though the doctor had given him a cortisone injection two days ago, he had no relief. Benedryl had helped him sleep for a while, but his sleep was fitful, plagued by vivid dreams.

And he was frightened. Terribly frightened. He was going through the same pattern of illness that Lance had in the months before he died. If he had the same thing, he didn't have much time.

In Dr. Mason's office, he had timidly posed the question. "Is it possible to catch something like this from somebody?

Dr. Mason cleared his throat. "You may have caught the flu from someone," he answered. "But I think you're just run down from three bouts of it, one after the other. Your immune system can't keep up with the onslaught. Last time, you had a mild pneumonia. I'm going to give you a shot of penicillin to take care of any secondary infection--see if we can't ward off further trouble."

"But I had a friend who died last year. He had the same thing and in the end pneumonia killed him."

"How old was he?"

"Over seventy, I'm not exactly sure."

"Well yes," the doctor answered. "At that age you might expect something like that, but you're still a young man and in good health otherwise. We'll get you over this in a week or so and you'll be on the mend."

But Jack wasn't consoled. At forty-four he figured he had a lot of life ahead of him. He remembered the good times, the parties, the friends he'd made. He wanted more than anything to get well and return to San Francisco. He'd find work enough to support himself. Perhaps he might meet someone new with whom he could share his life. Maybe now, with Lance gone he'd be more motivated, work harder and be responsible for himself.

Being home had been awful. Even yet, Dad hasn't spoken to me once, he remembered. In fact, I don't think he's even looked at me or acknowledged I'm here. Does he know who I really am? I'm sure he wouldn't like it if he did. Dad's too old fashioned to ever accept me and I don't want Mom to know either. As much as they care about what people think they'd be horrified.

Kate and Aunt Pearl had been great. Am sure they don't suspect a thing. Having Kate back in town had been good for Mom, glad they decided to get along. And Mona? I'm surprised. She's been great taking care of me. Says if I don't get over this she'll take me to the state university at Columbia. They have doctors there who specialize in immune problems. Maybe there I can get some help.

He looked up to see Mona enter the room, carrying her flashlight. "How you doing, Jack?" she asked. "The itch bothering you again? It's time you can have another Benedryl. That might make you feel better."

"Thanks, Sis. Think I will. It helps me sleep too. Do I still have a fever?"

"It was up only a bit last time we checked. I'll bring back a thermometer and we can check it again. Do you still have that headache?"

"No. It seems to have cleared up. Maybe I'm getting over this for good."

"I hope so," laughed Mona. "And after all you've been through you ought to know better than to get another. I'm getting tired of taking care of you."

But before Jack was released from the hospital, his temperature spiked again. He developed a severe cough and it was increasingly difficult to breathe. As he suspected, X-rays revealed pneumonia of an unusual kind. It was exactly what had happened to Lance.

When Kate came to see him the next afternoon, he told her of his fear. "I'm dying, Kate," he gasped. "You can see that can't you? All the antibiotics in the world aren't going to save me from this. Has Mona said as much?" A paroxysm of coughing left him gasping for air.

Kate came to his side and offered him a box of tissues from the bedside table. "Mona thinks you'll be okay," she assured him. "She wants to take you to Columbia but Dr. Mason says you're too sick to travel. He doesn't want to give you more antibiotics right now because of your allergies. I know you've been sick a long time, but don't be discouraged. Surely they'll be able to find something that will help."

Jack shook his head. "Nothing will help me, Kate. I told you I'm going to die. And no wonder. After the way I've lived, maybe I'm paying the price. Or maybe..." His voice trailed off. "Maybe it's the family curse. Maybe it's pre-destined." Tears filled his eyes. "I don't want to die, Kate. I'm scared I'm going to hell. What am I going to do?"

Kate reached for his hand. "Do you want to go to confession?"

Jack shook his head. "No priest will give me absolution," he answered. "I can't go. It's that simple."

Bewildered, Kate tried to console him. "No sin is too great for God to forgive, not even murder."

"It's not that!" he interrupted. "Besides, would the priest understand the curse?

"I asked one about it when I was a little girl. He said it was impossible."

"Do you believe in it? Do you remember Grammie and how she suffered? And Dad? He'd be just like her if it weren't for Mona. Mona with three sixes on her ass." Another fit of coughing interrupted him. "What's in store for her? You seem okay now, but so was I 'til I got this. What happened to this family Kate? Why can't we be like everybody else?"

"Other people have problems too. It's just that no one talks about them."

"Well, they talk about us. How poor we are, how Dad is a shiftless bum, taking days at a time to stay in his room. Just like his mother did."

"None of us kids do that."

"I did after Lance died. I felt like I didn't want to live, even thought about suicide, but now that I'm dying I'm scared to death."

"Oh Jack. I don't think you're dying. Just give it a little time."

"Sorry, Kate, I...I don't have time to give. Would you bring Mom up to see me tonight? His voice trembled. "I'll miss her most." He stopped to catch his breath. "Poor Mom, how could I go off and leave her as I did? Don't think I'll ever get over the guilt."

Concerned that conversation was getting difficult for him, Kate stood, glad of an opportunity to get away. "Of course I will, but I have to go right now. Have some errands to run and supper to prepare. We'll be up at 7:00."

By the time Kate and Nell arrived that evening, Jack could hardly get his breath. An oxygen tank was beside his bed feeding a tube which led to his nostrils. As he lay back against the upraised bed, Nell rushed to his side.

"Jack!" she cried, "What's going on. You look terrible."

"I-I can't breathe," he gasped. "I'm dying, Mom... Please, please forgive me."

She put her head on his shoulder and gripped his hand. "But you've done nothing for me to forgive," she answered. "You've always been good to me."

"I left you here...alone with Dad and Mona. With no one to understand what they put you through." He began to sob as Nell lifted him up and held him tight. An outburst of coughing overcame him as Kate went to find Mona. She was on duty this evening and Kate knew she would know what to do.

Mona rushed in with an aide and went straight to Jack's bed pushing Nell aside. "Call Dr. Mason," she ordered the aide. Now!" Turning to Nell and Kate she shouted. "Leave! You're upsetting him. Can't you see he can't get his breath?"

After ushering Kate and her mother out of the room, she closed the door. Minutes later Dr. Mason dashed in and shortly after came out and embraced Nell. "Nell, your son is very sick. In all my years of practice I've never seen anything like this. His pneumonia has progressed rapidly. I've ordered x-rays to determine how much. We had the lab make a culture of his sputum but the results won't be back until tomorrow. And I'm prescribing another antibiotic that should work. Do you have any questions?"

"Will he be okay?" she asked. "He thinks he's dying. Is he?'

Taken aback by her question, Dr. Mason stammered a reply. "I—I c—can't be sure of anything right now. We are going to do our best to save him, of that you can be assured.

"It's that bad?" asked Kate. "Will we be able to see him soon?"

"Of course, we have a few tests to do, will let you know when we are finished."

Nell fell sobbing into Kate's waiting arms. "My boy. My boy. Holy Mary mother of God what have I done to deserve this?"

Mona came out of the room and directed her remarks to Kate. "Take her to the small waiting room down by the chapel," she said. "She'll upset the patients. They don't have to hear this. I'll come for you when you can come in."

Later, in the semi-darkness of Jack's hospital room, they waited, listening to the wheezing rhythms of his chest become shallower and shallower. And now, the dreaded rattle in his throat. Maybe he is dying, Kate thought. My God this is awful. I'm so glad the priest came and gave him Extreme Unction. Maybe his sin will be forgiven, whatever it was. At least Mom was consoled. I was afraid he'd send the priest away, but he, too, saw that it meant a lot to Mom and remained silent.

Nell sat by his side, one hand on her rosary, the other in his. "Mama, Mama," he had cried out as she entered the room. "I have… have…to tell…you something."

"Shhh, shhh," Nell whispered. "It can wait. Just rest now. I'll wait right here." She leaned over and rested her head on the bed. "Just rest. I'm here."

Jack lay back against the pillows and closed his eyes. The morphine had quieted him and for a moment he dozed, then woke with a start. "Mama" he cried. And with a final gasp closed his eyes for the last time.

Chapter 25

Kate had a secret. A secret she vowed she would carry to her grave. Some things, she thought, are best never disclosed. And even though she considered herself a devout Catholic and believed she was committing a serious sin, she knew in her heart she was doing the right thing. For Nell's sake, Jack was going to have a Requiem Mass. No one needed to know that he died in a state of sin, especially Father Donahue. As an old school priest, and an unabashed critic of Vatican II, he likely would not have allowed it had he been aware. To him, Church law was Church law, no exceptions. To bury a manifest sinner would bring scandal to the Church, something he would not do even for the son of his most devout parishioner.

What he doesn't know won't hurt anyone, Kate thought. We know nothing of Jack's past, but if he died thinking his sins would not be forgiven, it must have been something major. Since no one in Lowell knew what they were, how could there be any scandal? So when the priest asked the family if Jack were still Catholic and regularly receiving the Sacraments, she said nothing. And even when Nell said Jack was very devout, praying the rosary nightly during Lent, she nodded in agreement. Not to have done so would be devastating to Nell who was inconsolable. For Kate to have told the priest about Jack's confession would have only made it worse for her mother, something she would not do.

Since Jack's death yesterday, the family reaction had been unreal. Her own feelings numbed by shock, Kate directed her attention to

Nell, who seemed to be on the brink of a breakdown, the loss of her beloved Jack too much for her to bear. What surprised Kate was her anger, and how vehemently she blamed Clint and Mona for what she considered to be their part in it.

After Kate had quieted her at the hospital and driven her home, they went into the house to tell Clint what had happened. "Dad,' she began, "something has gone terribly wrong with Jack. He suddenly got worse this afternoon....and...and shortly after he died. I...I..."

Clint stood mute for a few seconds, then turned and headed to his bedroom, Nell close behind. "You killed him." She shouted. "You rotten son-of-a bitch, you killed him. Your own son! You broke his heart, Clint, and I'll never forgive you."

Clint slammed the door, shutting her out of the room, saying nothing.

"How could you, Clint Foster, how could you go without speaking to your own son?" She yelled.

Clint still did not respond, and Kate, concerned about Nell, went to her and drew her into her arms. "Just let it go for now, Mom, come let's go to the living room. I'll make you a cup of tea and we can wait and see what Mona says when she gets home."

"Mona! Mona! What can she say that will change anything? Who does she think she is, chasing me out like that?"

"I know Mom, I know. I think she was trying to save his life. She..."

"She was not! She was showing off being a nurse, smarter than I am, she thinks. I know her tricks; she cares only about herself and Clint. Everyone else can go to hell, far as she's concerned." Nell paused briefly and began to sob. "Oh Kate. What am I going to do? Don't think I can live without him. I can't, I can't"

"There, there, Mom. Come. Sit down. Would you like me to pray with you?"

Dutifully, Nell followed her to the living room and sat on a straight back chair. It's going to be a long night, thought Kate; God knows what will happen when Mona gets home.

But when Mona arrived, Nell went into Jack's bedroom without speaking. It seemed to Kate she was getting even with Clint. If he wouldn't speak to her favorite, she wouldn't speak to his. But at least it was quiet. And for that, Kate was grateful. There were arrangements to be made and it didn't look like anyone would be able to make them except herself and Mona.

Kate went to the phone and called Father Donahue to make an appointment to see him early the next morning. And at the meeting, Father questioned them about Jack's faith. "Was he a practicing Catholic?" asked the priest. "He's been here for some time and I've never seen him in church."

"He didn't join us at Mass because he was too sick," Kate offered. "But I can't imagine his not going when he was well."

After that she left the apology to Nell, who related to Father Donahue Jack's insistence that he live with her brother, Brian, and go to Catholic school, and that he was so devout he thought about becoming a priest.

The information Nell was giving the priest had nothing to do with the reality Kate remembered, but it wasn't very important either. The funeral was to be for Nell. Father was to eulogize Jack as Nell saw him and from the sound of things it was going to be moving. To hear Nell, one would think Jack was a saint, a kind, loving, generous man who loved and respected his mother. This is what she wanted her friends to hear. What she had been telling them all along. Her boy could do no wrong and now he was in Heaven, his just reward for a life well lived.

Clint did not attend the wake that night, but on the morning of the funeral he rose early, donned his suit and tie, and asked Mona to drive him to the church. As if everything were normal, he stayed at Nell's side throughout the day and seemed to be supporting her as he should. I'll do what I have to do for Nell, he figured. Nobody can say I didn't stand with her through this, but don't know if I ain't damn glad the boy is gone. His whole life wasted by some crazy idea that he was gonna make it big. Lazy, that's what he was. Livin' off that old queer like some helpless little girl. Just hope no one in Lowell finds out. I ain't sayin' nothing to nobody. It's over now and that's that.

Nell seemed to hold up well during the funeral and graveside service, went to the dinner prepared by the ladies of her circle at the church, but after she arrived home, went to pieces, sobbing and shouting at Clint and Mona to leave her alone. Only Kate or Pearl could console her, both agreeing that to let her express her grief was the best thing to do.

Mona had no patience with her. "She's just feeling sorry for herself," she said. "Wants everyone to see how hard she's taking this. It's time she acted like a grownup and talked with Dad. Dad just didn't understand Jack, that's all. Still mad at him for being such a goof off when he was a kid. Truth is, Jack never grew out of it. Dad's right. Jack was pretty worthless and Mom just won't admit it."

"Not now, please," said Kate. "We can talk about this later. I'll stay here tonight; I can sleep on the sofa. She seems to turn to me right now and I want to be here for her."

Mona sniffed. "Whatever you want. Looks to me like you're making her cry, but what good does it do for me to say anything? Maybe if you'd just ignore her she'd stop."

Disregarding Mona's remark, Kate made her way to Nell, who was lying on Jack's bed wailing like an abandoned child. Shouldn't expect any more from her she thought. Mona was Mona and her behavior was typical. Let her and Dad do what they want. This is one time I'm going to do the same.

From his usual eves-dropping place behind the door of his bedroom, Clint was listening to what was going on. Surprised by Nell's reaction, he was frightened. She'd always been so steady, he thought. Sure, she'd blow up once in a while, but she always came back strong and sure of herself. This time it's her not able to handle something, not me. Wish Mona wouldn't be so hard on her, but Kate seems to be caring for her just fine. He wondered if he should go to her; apologize.

But he couldn't bring himself to do it. It could make her worse and he didn't know if he could take it. She sure did care about her Jack, but I didn't know how much. Can't ever tell her what I know about him as it might kill her. Wonder what she's gonna do now, she's so mad at me. Will she leave? Where would she go? He supposed Pearl and Kate would take her in, but what would he do without her? Mona was good to help, but not like Nell. Nell didn't interfere the way Mona did. Leaves me alone and lets me figger out things for myself. Sure, she scolds, but sometimes that's what pulls me up again. Ain't had a spell of melancholy for a long time. Am I getting over it? I don't know. Just wish I could do something for her now, but I can't. There's just too much wrong with me to try. She might bring it up. Maybe some time when nobody else is here. But right now? No. I'll just wait 'til we're alone. This is something the girls don't need to hear.

Chapter 26

June, 1977

Little by little, day by day, she seized control. With Nell's deepening depression came opportunities to take over. First it was the kitchen. Too many times Mona had come home to find that no supper was being prepared, that Clint's lunch had been scrounged from leftovers in the refrigerator or cans in the pantry, and Nell hadn't eaten at all.

So Mona began to stop at the General Store after work and buy something that was easy to prepare, plus something for tomorrow's lunch. Something that Clint could warm up on the stove when they were ready to eat. At the hospital, she arranged to work only the 7:00 to 3:00 shift, so she could get home in time to feed them both.

Shortly after, it became necessary for her to do the laundry and housecleaning on her days off and now, after the electricity had been shut off because the bill hadn't been paid on time, she was taking over the finances. Family income was her salary, Nell and Clint's Social Security, plus a Veteran's Pension of Clint's. For emergencies, Nell had a savings account with a balance of $11,000. Because of the extra expense of easy to prepare meals from the grocery, Mona was finding that June's income was not going to cover June's expenses. Besides charging expenses to her already overloaded credit card, Mona figured she was going to have to tap her mother's account to cover everything. Nell's savings book in hand, she drove to the bank.

Mona sat at a big desk across from Jay Palmer, the town's new banker.

"You can't withdraw funds on your signature," warned Jay. "This account was set up by your mother. We must have her permission to have access to it, and your mother has denied that to you."

"But she isn't able to do it anymore. I think she has early stage dementia and doesn't know what she's doing."

"Then you have to obtain a court order. What does your dad say about this?"

"He wants me to manage their money. He always left it to Mom and he doesn't want to deal with it. Can he sign for it?"

Not without your mother's permission. When she set up the account she was adamant. Neither you or your dad can withdraw from it."

"Can anyone else?"

"Only Jack, then Kate. And he is deceased. Did he leave a will?"

"No. His death was unexpected. He didn't have time."

"Then it goes to Kate. I'm sorry. But there's nothing I can do. Can you bring your mother with you and come back?"

Mona sighed and stood. "She won't do it. How do I get a court order to declare her incompetent?"

"You'll have to ask a lawyer about that. It's a fairly easy process if the family goes along. Good luck with it, Mona." He rose from his chair and shook her hand. "Come back when it's over and I'll be glad to help."

Kate didn't try to control her rage. "That's not true," she shouted. "Mom is no more incompetent than Dad is. You are not, I said NOT, going to get me to testify against her. She is really taking Jack's death hard, I agree, but she's perfectly aware of where she is and who she is and what is going on. I talked with her yesterday and she seemed fine."

"She hasn't eaten for days," said Mona. "And you can see how she's no longer doing any housework."

"And is that any different from Dad when he's down? He can't do anything either. I don't get it. What do you expect to gain from getting power of attorney?"

"In case she gets sick. Someone has to make medical decisions for her."

"That and her savings account. If you need money why not ask me for it?"

"You said once you didn't make much money. I thought…"

"You do not have the right to do my thinking for me Mona Foster. Or Mom's. What does Dad have to say about this?"

"He didn't say anything. When I asked him if he'd talk with the judge, he said he would. He's pretty worried about her."

"I want to talk to Dad too. Because if you two try this, I'm going to stand up for Mom in court. I don't even believe this, Mona. It's the most outrageous thing you've tried to do. So, you can forget the whole idea, because I'm going to fight you all the way."

"Okay then. You be responsible for what happens to her. She won't talk to me anyway. I want her to have a checkup with Dr. Mason but she won't go."

"Maybe she feels just fine. Why go to the doctor when she doesn't need to."

"Because," Mona sniffed. "Yesterday she told Dad she had a stomach ache. I wouldn't be surprised if she has an ulcer. All this stewing over Jack is making her sick."

Kate sighed. "I think she'll tell us when she's sick, Mona. I'll stop by and see her this afternoon and expect she'll be just fine."

Kate pulled into the gravel driveway and surveyed the yard. It sure needs attention, she noticed. The grass needs mowing and there are tall weeds in the flower beds. I'll come back tomorrow morning and take care of it. Luckily I'm off for the summer and it's the one thing Mona might let me do to help. She stepped out of the car and made her way to the house hoping Dad was taking his nap so she could talk with Mom alone.

She walked through the cluttered living room, noting that the breakfast dishes were still piled by the sink. Gosh. Mom must have stayed in her room all day, she thought. If she knew her house looked like this she'd be out here cleaning it.

The instant she saw her, Kate knew that her mother was seriously ill. Curled up on her side, facing the door, her face was flushed and drawn with pain.

"Mom!" she cried and rushed to her. "What's wrong?"

Nell moaned and did not answer.

"My God! You're burning with fever. Let me get you to the doctor fast. Do you want me to call Mona to go with us?"

"No—no—not Mona. You take me. Oh, Kate. It hurts so bad. Right here." She motioned toward her stomach.

"I'm calling Dr. Mason first. I think you should go to the hospital. Just a minute. I'll see what he says."

Later, in the hospital waiting room, Kate waited for news of her mother's emergency appendectomy, reliving the previous hours to see if she could have done things differently. Dr. Mason had insisted on her calling an ambulance and met her at the emergency room. As soon as he examined Mom, he'd started barking orders for a lab technician, stat, and directed the nurse on duty to start intravenous saline and antibiotics and to prep her for surgery while he got ready to operate.

"I'm sure it's a ruptured appendix," he told her. "How long has this been going on?"

"I'm not sure. She told Dad yesterday that she had a stomach ache. That's all I know."

"She's likely got peritonitis, an infection of the abdominal cavity," he said. "Kate, right now I'm trying to save her life. I hope we're not too late. You wait here and I'll talk to you after surgery. Where's your Dad? Didn't he come with you?"

"No. He was too upset. I'll send Mona to get him when she gets off duty."

"Good. I think he should be here in case…in case things don't go well. Kate, I have to go now. I want to be ready when they wheel her into the operating room"

Kate waited in stunned silence. This can't be, she thought. So soon after Jack died and now this! What will Mona say? Probably say I should have called her first. How am I going to tell her that Mom didn't want me to? As for Dad, I asked him to come with me. Maybe Mona will get him. I'm not sure he will come with me. I wonder why. Is he afraid? God, I'm so confused, help me get through this. Don't let her die, please God, please.

Mona walked in, interrupting her prayer. "What's going on?" she sneered. "They told me upstairs that you brought Mom in and she's going to surgery. How could you admit her and not let me know?"

"I was beside myself with worry," Kate answered. "Everything happened so fast I...I didn't have time."

"What did doctor say? I wonder why he didn't contact me. I could have scrubbed for surgery and see what is going on."

"Dr. Mason was in such a hurry he probably didn't even think of it. He thinks it's her appendix," she answered. "That it's probably ruptured"

"Did he order labs? Or put her on an antibiotic? She could have peritonitis for all I know."

Kate fought to maintain her calm. "I'm sure the doctor knows what to do, Mona. We'll just have to wait until he's finished. There's nothing else we can do." She clenched her teeth. I'll be damned if I'll tell her anything else, she thought. Mona should have checked on her yesterday. Maybe it wouldn't have got this bad.

Abruptly she changed the subject. "Could you go get Dad? Doctor says he should be here. He didn't want to come with me, maybe you can persuade him."

"You should have made him come," snarled Mona. "He's probably just scared."

"I can't know why he didn't," answered Kate. "He didn't say. Perhaps he'll tell you."

"I'll go get him after I talk to the doctor. I want to know what he's going to do about her aftercare."

Kate sighed. There wasn't much sense in responding to her, she thought. She only cares about her role in this, nothing more. Everything that happens, she makes about herself.

As soon as he got to her room, Clint took Nell's hand and sat at her side, there to remain until she passed early the next morning. "It's okay. It's okay. It's okay," he said, reciting his sad litany of forgiveness as he so often had before. Whatever she had done, he knew he deserved. Much as he tried, he couldn't be the man she expected him to be. It wasn't her fault for missing Jack the way she did. As for his not speaking to Jack, he was at fault. I just couldn't do it. I couldn't tell her what I knew. An old memory, long shrouded in denial, flashed through his consciousness. *In the dark attic with Ben.* No. No. It never happened. Thought I'd forgot about that. Again he concentrated on Nell. "It's okay," he murmured. "It's okay."

In Nell's hospital room, Kate and Mona waited for Clint to return. Nell was laid out on the bed, covered in a crisp white sheet. The funeral director would be there soon to pick up her body and prepare it for burial.

"She was in septic shock," said Mona. "I sensed it the minute I saw her. And her labs confirmed it. Her white blood count was elevated, her respirations rapid, and her heart rate was 100 per minute. At the end, her organs shut down. If she'd only said something when the pain began, but she was so stubborn…"

"Stop!" exclaimed Kate. "She's dead, Mona. Look at her laying there, dead. No need to diagnose her now. I don't want to hear any more." She stepped to Mona's side, towering over her. "It was our mother, for God's sake. It's not about you."

"You're crazy," said Mona. "You just don't want to know why she died."

"That's right! I don't. I have a funeral to prepare for. Would you look after Dad? Just get him home. If anyone's in shock it's him. He's in the restroom, crying. Can't you see that?"

"Of course I can. I don't need you to tell me what to do."

"Then do it, damn it. And leave me alone." With that, Kate stormed from the room, slamming the door behind her. She had much to do and no time to deal with Mona. I'll leave her with Dad while I go get Aunt Pearl, she thought. He needs them right now. I can't do anything for him. They can comfort him while I get things done.

In the men's restroom, Clint leaned over the sink and splashed cold water on his face. He had to pull himself up and out of this crying spell before he went back to face the girls. If only I'd had more time I'd been able to make it up to her, he figured. But she's gone. Gone. There's nothin' I can do. We fought plenty of times and we always made up. Until this time. Her hangin' on to the idea that I kilt Jack. All because I couldn't tell her the truth. That would'a kilt her too. He remembered her singing in the kitchen or at the clothesline, her bright blue eyes, her dark hair, now turning gray. She was too good for me, I know. Didn't deserve my melancholy, my attention to everything but her. I didn't even call the priest. She died without the sacraments, all because I forgot to call the priest. No wonder she couldn't forgive me. It was too much for a woman to take. I've kilt her, he sobbed. It's all my fault and now she's dead.

Mona opened the door and stepped into the men's room. "C'mon Dad," she demanded. "It's time to go home

Chapter 27

March 1978

A fleeting ray of sunshine sliced through the morning fog, turn-ing a frost encrusted elm into a dazzling display of diamonds. On her morning run, Kate paused to rejoice in its beauty. Sun! She thought. Finally! After weeks of gloom, the sun is shining! Maybe we'll have spring after all. With a smile, she resumed her jog toward home. Today's duties were beckoning and she had to get back. It would be another busy day, but with the sun overhead, a much more pleasant one.

Today was Saturday, for most teachers a day off, but for Kate, a day to tend to her family. After Nell's death, both Mona and Clint had dropped into a dark pit of depression. And although Mona managed to get to work most days, she became unwilling or unable to tend to the housekeeping, leaving it for Kate who managed to do what she could on weekends. Just at a time when Auntie needed her more, Kate felt a strong sense of responsibility for her Dad. Years of inactivity had made him weak, and an inadequate diet had left him thin and frail. At eighty-two, he thought he didn't have much time left, and vacillated between days of desperately trying to prolong his life with doctors and drugs, and days of surrendering to the fact that his life was waning and a welcome death was not far away.

Kate was sure it was Mona's influence that affected him. The slight-est twinge of pain set them both in a panic, certain that the fateful curtain was about to be dropped. After a few days of doctor visits and tests, both relaxed when no problem was found, leaving Clint alone with his thoughts and, perhaps, to accept the reality that at his age, death was approaching.

After she arrived home, Kate woke Auntie, quickly made her bed, helped her dress, and hurried to the kitchen to prepare their breakfast. "Sit down, Auntie," she said. "What are you drinking? Orange juice or tomato?"

Pearl smiled. "I'll take the coffee please, and the tomato juice on the side."

"Sorry, I didn't bring your coffee." Kate poured two cups of the steaming brew from the percolator and set them on the table. "I'm rushing this morning. Have to go tend to Dad. Do you want to go with me? You can talk with Dad while I clean the house."

"No. Not today. I have a good book and look forward to reading it. I have my walker to get around, and the hip is better today, so I'll be fine."

"Call if you need anything. After I'm done there, I'll go to the new supermarket in Harperville. Since Lily sold the General Store it's become nothing but a hold-up. I'll have to get groceries for Dad and us. Would you like to join me then?"

"I'll see how I feel. Do you need money?"

"No. I'm using the money Mom left me. Figure that's what it's for...helping Dad. I do get the house payment and utilities payments from Mona, although at times she doesn't have enough to cover it. I don't understand. She makes a good salary."

"She spends a lot on those magazine subscriptions for one thing and her quick stops at the General Store for another. Outside of that, I don't know."

"She bought that new Buick. I suppose she has some pretty hefty payments on that."

"For sure. But I suppose our worrying ourselves over it doesn't do much good. Unless she tells us, we'll probably never know."

Kate stood and began to clear the breakfast dishes from the table, thinking. "She also bought a dishwasher and a new washer and dryer," she said. "It's all adding up now. Especially if she's paying a lot of interest. Mona never uses common sense when it comes to money."

"That's too bad," said Pearl. "I hope she puts some by for retirement. It comes up faster than you'd think."

Kate glanced up at the kitchen clock as she put away the last dish. "Gosh," she said. "I better get going if I'm going to get back by noon. Need anything before I go?"

"I'm fine, honey. Tell Clint and Mona hello for me. Can't help but worry about Clint, he didn't look good the last time I saw him."

Kate picked up her purse and car keys and headed to the door. "I'll be back soon," she said. "Will call and let you know how Dad is doing first chance I get."

Clint sat at the dining room table, sipping cold coffee and waiting for Kate. Sure hope she's coming, he thought. Want her to make me some fresh coffee. This stuff is from yesterday and thick as molasses. Think Mona made it yesterday and warmed it up this morning.

He pushed the cup away and looked around the room. Dirty dishes were piled in the sink and unwashed pans still rested on the stove. Mona sure ain't doing much around here, he thought. At least she went to work today. Reckon if it weren't for Kate, nothin' would get done. The girl's like her Ma, wants everything clean and neat. He sat and stared for a moment, lost in thought. Reckon I miss Nell more'n I ever thought I would. Just wish she'd gone out without us disagreeing. I shoulda done more. I shoulda thanked her for doing such a good job. Reckon I was too damn proud. Never was good enough for her. Now she's gone, there ain't a damn thing I can do about it. He looked up as he heard Kate's car in the driveway. Good, he thought. She's here now. Gonna be good to see her.

Kate breezed in through the front door, deposited her purse and jacket on the living room couch and gave Clint a quick kiss on the cheek. "Morning Dad," she said. "How are you doing today?"

"Ain't too good," he answered. "The rheumatiz is bothering me again."

"Sorry about that Dad. Hey. This coffee looks bad; want me to make a new pot?"

"Was hoping you'd ask that." Clint managed a small grin. "Reckon this pot's more like mud than coffee."

Kate rinsed the percolator, added fresh water, put ground coffee into the strainer and plugged it in. "This will take a few minutes," she said. "I'll go get the sheets off your bed and the towels out of the bathroom and start a load of wash. I'll be back when the coffee's done and have a cup with you."

"Sounds good to me," he answered. "Reckon I'll be waitin' for you right here."

Later, as they sat at the table, Kate tried to quiz Clint for information about his well-being. "How have you been this week?" she asked. "At least you're up and at 'em this morning. I hardly got to see you last week."

"Awful tired. Even though I been in bed, I ain't slept all that much."

"Any reason why?"

"Reckon the rheumatiz has a lot to do with it. But I been worried about Mona a lot. She ain't been herself after your Ma died. I didn't think it would affect her this bad. And she ain't got it too good at work right now."

Kate arched her brow. "Oh. What's going on at work?"

"Ever since Lily retired they've given her three or four new bosses, one after the other. Each one worse than the last."

"I understand Mary Pauley is her supervisor now. What's the matter with her?"

Clint raised his voice. "Hell. She's 10 years younger 'n Mona. They outta know that ain't gonna work."

"But I understand she has a degree. She got her training at the university, Dad. Her training took four years and Mona had three."

"Mona said book learning ain't nothin' like experience. Guess Pauley lords it over the other nurses pretty good. Mona's finding it hard to keep her mouth shut."

"I suppose she does." Noticing that Clint was getting angry, Kate changed the subject. "But let's talk about you. What does the doctor say?"

"He thinks I'm doing okay. Reckon if he lived in this old body he'd change his tune."

"But your heart and lungs are good. Right? All that seems to be wrong is your arthritis and circulatory problems in your legs?"

"That's what he says. But Mona said my circulation problems could cause a heart attack someday. That ain't good."

"Are you doing anything about it?"

"Not much I can do. Just get used to it I guess." He managed a slight grin.

Kate stood, smiling back. "Guess we have to get used to a lot of things, don't we Dad?" She paused and brushed his hair back from his forehead. "Like you turning into a long-haired hippie if you don't get a haircut. Want me to take you to the barber this week?"

"Let's see what Mona has in mind."

"Okay, Dad. Gotta get busy now. I'll talk to Mona when I drop off the groceries this afternoon. She can let me know then."

During visiting hours the ward was quiet, leaving Mona time to finish her charting before the next shift came on. This morning there had been a brief meeting with Mary Pauley, the Director of Nurses, and Mona was still fuming over its content. Mary had said that the drug inventory didn't represent actual prescription orders by the doctors, that some narcotics usages had been unaccounted for, and that she felt certain that one of the nurses must either be giving patients extra dosages to quiet them or using them themselves. Infractions which would lead to immediate dismissal if she found the culprit. This meeting, she told them, should serve as a warning to any guilty party. All nurses would now be required to take inventory of the drugs on hand at the beginning of the shift and again when the shift was over.

This new order would require Mona to stay at least half an hour after her shift had ended. Some more of her nonsense, Mona figured. She was getting sick of it. Last week it had been housekeeping, the week before patient relations, whatever that meant. Every week she comes up with something and throughout the meeting stares at me as if I'm the one she's blaming. Bitch! I did take a few phenobarbital to give Dad occasionally so he could get some sleep. He needs that when he goes days without sleeping and Doctor won't give him anything. Says he'll fall and hurt himself. Guess I better be careful. It was easier when I worked nights, because some of the patients it was prescribed for would go to sleep without it.

She closed the last patient's file, stood, and arched her back, then straightened it. Visiting hours were over and visitors were milling in the corridors, leaving a friend or family member in the safety of the hospital room as they headed home. Another hour, she would be finished with her shift. Then to take a nap, and get up and have supper with Dad. Another long evening stretched before her and she hoped there would be something good on TV that she could watch to fill in the time. She was always so tired lately. Need to have a check-up she thought. Something must be seriously wrong.

Chapter 28

April, 1978

The shrill call of the alarm roused Mona from a deep, drugged slumber. Fighting the impulse to turn over and go back to sleep, she sat briefly on the side of the bed remembering last night and the conversation she had with Dad before he went to his room.

"Wonder if Kate's comin' back Saturday," he said. "Will you be working?"

"Yes, I'm on day shift this weekend. Have tomorrow off to get rested up for it."

"Yeah. Your schedule makes it hard for you. Sure helps havin' Kate come over and help with the housework. Nice to have the place cleaned up for a change."

As if she had just been slapped, Mona reacted quickly. "It wasn't that bad. Kate's just got her nose into our business again. She has to see what's going on"

"No, no, no," Clint responded. "It ain't that. She's a fine girl, that Kate. Just like Pearl, always ready to help."

"Well, that's new," Mona snapped. "I thought you believed she was just like Grammie."

"I did once. She used to have that terrible temper, but she got over that. Sendin' her to live with Pearl was the best thing I ever did. I look forward to her comin' over. Reckon I don't know what I'd do without her, she's been such a help."

"Hmmph." Mona turned away, speechless, and began to straighten the room.

Clint stood, stretched, and made his way to his bedroom. "Gotta get myself to bed," he said. "Didn't sleep much this afternoon and I'm tired. You gonna go to bed now?

"Yes," Mona snapped. "Soon as I get the dishes put away. Goodnight Dad."

"Goodnight, Mona. Reckon I'll see you around noon tomorra. You planning to sleep late?"

Pretending she hadn't heard his question, Mona headed for the dining room table and began to pick up the dishes.

He's comparing me to Kate, she thought. Damn her. Coming over here and brown-nosing, trying to take over. I'll show her, the bitch. She ran hot water into the sink, added detergent and left the dishes to soak overnight. She doesn't know what it's like, being on your feet all day. Most times I'm too tired to do anything but go to bed when I get off. All she does is sit at a desk. Gets every weekend and summers off too.

After clearing the table, Mona went to her room, slipped into her pajamas, and tried to sleep. Over and over, she relived Dad's remarks. What did he mean he can't do without her? Doesn't he even notice all I do? Things are going to change around here. It's good I'm starting the night shift after the first of May. I'll be rid of Mary Pauley and I'll have time to do the housework here.

After tossing for the better part of an hour, she remembered she had a sleeping pill she'd saved that one of the patients didn't need. It won't hurt if I take it, she thought. Have a lot to get done tomorrow and need some sleep.

In a fog upon rising, she stumbled to the kitchen and made a big pot of coffee. She was going to need it if she was going to get every-thing done she planned to do.

⌒⊙

When Kate arrived at the house the morning of April 15, she was pleasantly surprised. Everything was immaculate, the refrigerator and pantry filled with fresh food, and Dad up and dressed for the day. What's got into Mona? She wondered. It's about time she did something around here. Must be feeling guilty. Or maybe she feels better because the weather is so nice. Dad seems better too. Good thing, because I have a lot of other things to do today. Guess I'll visit with Dad a while and go home and get started.

But Clint had other plans. "Wonder if you'd do a favor for me, Kate. Since Mona cleaned up in here yesterday, I reckon you might have time to take me for a drive."

"Why sure Dad. Depends on where you want to go. Think we can be back by noon?"

"Oh yeah. I'd kinda like to go out to the old farm where I lived as a boy. Know where that is?

Kate paused. "I think so. I remember going there to see Grammie and Granddad."

"It's just a few miles west of town. Not far from our farm. You'll remember it when we get there."

"I'm sure. Shall we head out now? You look like you're ready to go."

Kate backed the car out of the driveway and headed toward the main road. "Nice day to go out there, Dad. It's supposed to get to 70 degrees today. Bet it makes the farmers happy."

"I reckon," he answered. "Time to plow the fields and get ready for plantin."

"Do you miss the farm, Dad?"

"Reckon I don't miss the work. But times I miss the old place. Got lots of memories, some of 'em good, most of 'em bad. It was hard growing up with Ma. Never knew what to expect of her. Now I'm gettin' old, I'd like to sort them memories out. Make a little sense out of 'em."

Kate nodded. "Know what you mean, Dad. Some of the things I believed as a kid changed a lot when I grew up. I used to daydream a lot, couldn't separate fact from fiction."

"Reckon I still can't." Clint paused for a moment, looked briefly out the window and went on. "There's an old oak tree out in the field, right next to the road. I used to go out there when things got too big for me. I'd go there to sort 'em out. Reckon I think about that tree a lot. Just like to see if it's still there."

Kate spotted the tree ahead on the left. A dark spidery silhouette against the bright sky. She pointed. "Is that it over there?"

"Damned it ain't. Can we stop a while?"

"Sure. I'll pull over." Kate parked the car on the narrow shoulder and opened the door. "Want me to help you get over there?"

"Just help me get through the fence. I can make it from there."

Kate lifted the top row of barbed wire so he could get through. "Any scratches?" she asked, laughing.

"Nope. Guess I'll go over there and sit a spell. There's a big rock there and it makes a fine stool." He looked back at Kate. "Reckon I'll be okay here awhile if it's all right with you."

Sensing that he wanted to be left alone, Kate answered. "Sure, Dad. I'll walk down to that tree that's blooming down the road. Maybe I can get some blossoms for Aunt Pearl."

It ain't the same, Clint thought as he looked up at the tree. Hell, it's just getting old, like me. A few limbs were dead now, ready to snap free with the next strong wind. And even though many of the branches were sprouting new leaves, all around him lay evidence that many had also fallen to the ground since the last time he was here.

He sat on the rock, trying to understand why he didn't felt safe here now and wondered if he might outlive the tree. If at the end of his life he would be deprived of the comfort he had always known here. Where then, would he turn?

No longer would it be to Mona. Her melancholy last winter had reminded him of Ma. That surprised him. She'd always been such a help to him before. Still was, when it came to his health. Reckon she's a good nurse, but I wish she'd mix a little more. Don't think she has any friends where Kate's always doing something with some of them teachers. Mona's a loner like me. Ain't good. Ain't good at all. At least I had Red as a kid, and Brian 'til he took up drinking. I always been close to Pearl too. Wiping tears from his cheek, he stood and looked to the car to see if Kate were there. I'm too old and tired to be here he thought. Too many things coming to me I don't know how to handle. He started toward the car, stopped and looked back at the tree. It's all about death in this place now, he thought. Reckon it's time both of us go.

Chapter 29

Summer 1979

When Clint awakened that morning, it was with a looming sense of dread. He slept poorly, thinking of Nell. Between that and the sounds of a thunderstorm, he tossed and turned the better part of the night. Had nearly given up and asked Mona for one of the sleeping pills she'd brought home from the hospital. But he resisted, knowing they'd make him groggy the next day when he wanted to be wide awake. Kate was coming to get him and take him to see Pearl and he was looking forward to spending the day with them both.

Slowly, he slid his feet out of the bed and tried to sit up when a swift, powerful force grabbed his chest and began to squeeze his breath. My heart! He realized. I'm having a heart attack! I need to wake Mona. His torso fell back on the bed, his legs still over the side. "Mona. Mona," he cried. "Come quick."

Luckily, Mona was awake, having finished the night shift at 7:00. She ran into the bedroom, lifted Clint's legs to the bed and propped pillows beneath his head. Only then did she pick up the phone and call the ambulance. "Get here stat," she ordered. "He needs to get to the hospital immediately."

He remembered all of it as a hazy dream. From a comfortable place above he watched it unfold. Cold metal objects being placed on his chest, his back arching with a terrible shock, a mask over his face, blue uniforms filled with kind young men consoling him, holding him down. Then he saw a warm bright light at the end of a spiraling tunnel. He wanted to stay there, but a siren called him back. Mona was talking. He recalls a room, glaring lights; Dr. Mason was there, shouting. He saw white clad nurses hurry, attaching tubes, writing on charts, following the doctor's commands. Again, the pain of the electrodes, over and over, finally bringing him back to the table wide awake.

From afar, Dr. Mason's voice was speaking. "You've had a heart attack, Clint, but you're going to be okay. I'm going to admit you to the hospital for a few days for treatment and observation. You'll have Mona here to take care of you."

Mona smiled. "Dad," she began, "you scared us for a while there."

"Scairt me too," Clint said. "Reckon I'd just as soon it never happens again."

Mona went with the aide to Clint's hospital room. As she hung up his clothes, she thought about what he might need to keep him comfortable here. First of all, knowing how much Dad hated the open back hospital gown, she would bring pajamas and he would need slippers and a robe for when he got up. Maybe she should also bring some socks. Dad always wears socks to bed, she remembered. His feet get cold without them. She pulled back his blanket and saw that he was still wearing them. "Feet warm enough, Dad?" she asked.

"Hell no," he answered. "Could you bring me them wool slippers?"

When she learned from a neighbor that Clint had been taken in an ambulance, Kate rushed home to get Aunt Pearl and headed for the hospital. She suspected Mona hadn't called in order to punish her for not calling the day Mom died. That would be just like her, she thought. Mona's been darn protective about Dad lately. Ever since the day she decided to start keeping house, Mona has shut me out. Acts like she doesn't even want Auntie to visit him. Geez. I hope Dad's okay. That's the last thing this family needs—another funeral. Not sure I can take it. She glanced at Auntie and saw she was wiping tears. "We'll be there soon," she said. "I'm worried too."

Later, in Dad's hospital room, she felt relieved to find him propped up in the bed and eating lunch. When she reached his bedside, he reached out and held her hand. "I've gotta ask a favor of you, Kate" he began. "I want you to talk to Mona."

"Sure, Dad. What about?"

"I want you to tell her not to put me through that again"

"Put you through what?"

Clint looked across the room to Pearl and shook his head. "It was awful. Them sireens and them damn shocks they gave me. Don't let her do that. Will you tell her?"

"I will. But you should tell her too. And tell Doctor Mason. It would be good if he knew too."

Clint dropped her hand and turned away. "Don't do no good, me talking to her, Kate. She won't listen. She's a nurse. Reckon she'll do what she's been taught. Will you tell her?"

"I said I would, Dad. Trust me, I will. And if you want me to tell Dr. Mason, I'll do that too. You just rest and get well. I'll take care of it."

"Okay," he answered. He looked again at Pearl who sat in a chair by the wall. "C'mon over here, Pearl," he said. "How's the hip doin'?"

Seeing that Dad was getting tired, Kate and Pearl left after a few minutes, just missing Mona who arrived shortly after. She had stopped at the nurses' station and checked his chart and seeing that his blood pressure was still low, hurried to his room to check it again. "Still low, Dad," she said. She picked up the bag of his belongings, and began to put them in a dresser drawer. "Hey," she said. "I want to change your socks. I noticed that the bottoms of the ones you have on are dirty. Bet you were walking around without your slippers, weren't you?"

"Reckon so," Clint answered. "Don't always take time to put 'em on."

Mona slipped the right sock off and gasped. "My God, Dad," she said. "Your foot is black. How long has it been this way and why on earth didn't you tell me?"

"Hell, I don't know. Guess I thought it was because I'm gettin' old. It don't hurt me any. What's wrong with it?"

"It's gangrenous," she answered. "That's what it is." She turned the sock inside out and gasped again. "Tissue is sloughing off in your sock. Oh my God, Dad. This is serious. We might have to amputate your foot, that's how serious it is. I'm going to call Doctor right now. See if he'll come have a look at it."

"How in hell could I get gangrene? I ain't hurt it or nothing."

"It's because of poor circulation," she said. "The blood doesn't get to the extremity and the tissue dies. It doesn't have anything to do with trauma."

"Well I'll be damned. I sure don't want you cuttin' off my foot."

"We have to. This could get infected or continue to grow. It's life threatening, Dad. There's no other choice."

"When's Doc comin'?"

"Soon as I get hold of him, I hope. I'll go down to the nurses' station and call him now."

An hour later Mona sat fuming at the nurses' station, waiting for Dr. Mason to return her call. It had already been an hour and she was getting impatient. "He's with a patient right now," his receptionist had said. "He will return your call later." This is an emergency, she thought. Who does he think he is, treating a patient this way?"

As if she intended to calm Mona's thoughts, the head nurse on duty reported her findings. "I just checked your Dad's vitals and he seems to be okay. His blood pressure is low. His temp and pulse are normal. So no need to be alarmed until Doctor gets here. Are you on duty tonight?"

"Yes," Mona snapped. "I need to get some sleep. He should be on an antibiotic now. Where the hell is Mason? His office said he'd call back."

"Why don't you go home and take a nap? I'll tell his doctor what's going on when he calls, and if he's going to do anything soon, I'll call you."

"I can't sleep 'til I know what's going on. Think I'll just wait here."

"As you wish. I expect he'll come by after five o'clock when he's done seeing patients."

"It's only one-thirty," Mona said. "That's too long. I'm going call him again. See if I can get his attention."

When she finally got through to him after screaming at his receptionist, she found Dr. Mason in a foul mood. "So you think he's gangrenous," he said. "How are his vitals?"

"He's stable right now, but we have to get antibiotics going, right now. If we don't take care of this immediately, he's going to get septic. I think you should see him right away."

Dr. Mason, more than a little upset with Mona's claim to be part of Clint's treatment, responded angrily. "I can't see him now. I have a waiting room full of patients to see. Are you on duty?"

"No. I come on at eleven o'clock tonight. Why."

"Let me talk with the charge nurse. She's responsible for carrying out orders, not you."

Mona took a deep breath, composed herself and replied. "Well if that's the way you want it, Doctor, I'll turn the phone over to her. But there's no reason you can't give me the order."

"Put her on, now. I have work to do, and the longer you hold me up, the longer it's going to be before I get there."

In her iciest tone, Mona retorted. "Well. Okay here she is." She handed the phone to her cohort and stormed toward Clint's room.

Dr. Mason didn't arrive until five-thirty and Mona was livid. "Dad's going to need surgery right away," she announced as he entered the room.

Ignoring her, the doctor went to Clint's side and lifted the sheet covering his feet. "So you're having a problem with your foot, Clint. Let me look and see what's going on."

"Sure, Doc." Clint answered. "It don't hurt me any, but it's sure an ugly son-of-a-bitch."

"How long has it been this way?"

"I dunno. Noticed it three or four days ago on the toes, I reckon. But it seems to have spread a little."

"It must have. Looks like you've got a gangrenous foot here Clint. What's happening is that you're not getting enough blood to the foot. The blood carries oxygen to the tissue of the foot and when the tissue doesn't get oxygen, it dies."

Clint looked to the foot of the bed at Mona. "Mona says you'll have to amputate my foot. I don't want that Doc. Is she right?"

"Not if I can help it," the doctor began."

"What?" Mona shouted. "He could get an infection in there."

Trying to control himself, Dr. Mason answered. "I put him on an intra-venous antibiotic, Mona. Please allow me to continue."

"What are you gonna do, Doc?" asked Clint.

"I'm ordering labs to check the tissue. I'm going cut that dead tissue out and then we'll know how extensive it is. Sometimes that's all we need to do."

"But what if it is extensive?" Mona said. "Why not take care of it all when you have him in surgery?

"Because I won't put your Dad under general anesthesia, Mona. His heart's been damaged too much to take that chance. I'll use a local anesthetic to debride the tissue and we'll wait and see what happens." He grasped Clint's arm. "That okay with you, Clint?"

"Sure. When are you gonna work on me?"

"In about an hour. We'll have the nurse get you ready and they'll take you up to surgery so we can get going. Shouldn't take too long. You'll be awake through the whole thing, so if you have any questions you can ask them there."

"Thanks, Doc. Reckon I'll see you in a while."

"Yessir." And with a salute, Dr. Mason turned and left the rooms with Mona close behind.

"I'll scrub and help you," she offered.

Dr. Mason turned to face her and raised his voice. "I won't do any procedure with a family member in the surgery suite, and that's final. If you want this done tonight, you better accept that Mona." He turned on his heel and walked toward the nurses' station, leaving her speechless.

∼◦

Kate and Pearl were just finishing dinner when Mona called with the latest news of Dad. "He's in surgery now," she reported. "No need for you to come up tonight. I'll be working the eleven p.m. shift and can call you if anything happens. He's really tired and is going to need some rest."

"I'm sure." Kate replied. "But Mona there's something I want to talk with you about. Could I come over before you go to work? Or are you going to be sleeping?"

"I'm only going to be home a few minutes. Have to get a clean uniform and brush my teeth and get back here as soon as I can. I don't want Dad left alone."

"How can you work when you've been up all day?" Kate asked. "Can't you get someone to come in for you?"

"I'll be fine," Mona replied. "I've done it before."

"I'm not sure that's a good idea. What if you went to sleep on duty?"

"I won't. But how I go to work is none of your business," Mona answered. "Goodbye."

Mona slammed the phone into the receiver and clenched her teeth. Don't need her telling me what to do, she thought. She doesn't know I have some Dexedrine handy for times like this. Doctor Carter will prescribe about anything I need. He understands what it's like to work the night shift. How darn hard it is to stay awake sometimes and how hard it is to get to sleep after. I pick my prescription up in Harperville when I go over to get the groceries. Just as soon the little drug store here doesn't know what I'm taking. They'd probably spill it to someone. Damn this little town. Everyone in it would know all about it in a few days.

An aide knocked on the door and called out to her. "Your Dad just got back from surgery," she said. "Doctor Mason says you can see him now."

Mona rose from her chair and hurried to his side.

⌒〇

The telephone call had interrupted their dinner, taking away Kate's appetite. She pushed her plate away and turned to Pearl

"Oh, dear," Kate moaned. "I really wanted to tell her about Dad's wishes not to be resuscitated again. I hope he's okay tonight."

"Clint needs to speak for himself, Kate. He can't be relying on you to speak for him," said Pearl.

"I suppose…but with Mona it's just so hard…"

"Yes, and your dad created the problem. He depended on Mona for everything and now he can't even tell her what he wants."

"I suppose so. But poor Dad, he was begging me. I told him I'd talk with her and I couldn't reach her today. Same thing with Dr. Mason. He didn't return my call either. But that's my fault. I told his receptionist it wasn't an emergency."

"Why not try to get some sleep tonight and talk to them tomorrow morning. Trust God that he'll be okay 'til then."

Kate smiled. "You're right, as usual, Aunt Pearl." She rose from her chair and began to clear the table. "I'll clean up here and you go see if you can find something fun to watch on TV."

The next morning, Kate showed up at the hospital at seven a.m., hoping to catch Mona before she went home. Parked next to Mona's car, she waited, trying to figure out just how she was going to say what she had to say.

Gosh. She looks awful, Kate thought as she saw Mona approach. Hope she goes home and gets some sleep. But I'm going to tell her now, no matter what shape she's in. I have to get to her before something happens to Dad.

She opened the car door and got out, greeting Mona with a question. "How's Dad?" she asked. "Did he rest okay last night?"

"He's weak. Doctor says he removed quite a bit of tissue. I didn't see how much. The area is bandaged and I can't remove the bandages to look, so guess I'll have to take his word for it. Now it's wait and see."

"Suppose that's good news for now. Could I see him?"

"Sure. They'll let you in. Are you going to spend the day with him?"

"Why?" Kate asked. "Surely the hospital will let us know if he needs us. Why don't you go home and get some sleep?"

Mona lifted her chin. "I want one of us to be there," she said.

Figuring she'd ask the charge nurse what to do, Kate decided to allay Mona's concerns. "I can run home and get some things, set things up for Aunt Pearl and come right back," she said.

"Okay." Mona replied. She unlocked her car and began to get in.

"Wait a minute," Kate said. "I want to tell you something Dad asked me to do for him."

Mona got into the car and sat behind the wheel, leaving the door open. "What?" she asked.

"I guess he just hated being resuscitated," Kate began. "He asked me to tell you not to do that to him again."

Mona laughed. "He was just scared," she said. "He didn't understand what was going on."

"I don't think so. Why don't you ask him? He was almost begging me not to let you do it to him again."

"I'll talk to him tonight," she said. "I'll explain to him what happened and maybe that will make him feel better." She put the key in the ignition, started the car, and reached for the door handle.

"But..." Kate began as Mona closed the door and began to move the car forward. "But that's no..."

With a wave of her hand, Mona drove away.

In the following days, Clint lay in his hospital bed, praying to die. Somethin' I ain't skeered of, he thought. What skeers me most is what they might do to me here. Reckon my foot don't look too good and Doc's contemplatin' what to do with that. An ever worsening pain centered near his heart, but I'm not telling anyone, he decided. Doc and

Mona are picking up sounds in them stethoscopes. And the tests show my heart's worse'n it was. Hell. Leave me alone to die, he thought. If I could just go home everything would be okay.

It was visiting hour, and Kate was bringing Pearl in to see him. He'd asked her to, hoping he'd get a chance to visit with her alone. And shortly after they walked in, he was relieved to know that Kate had an errand to run and would come back for her aunt later.

"Bring your chair up to the bed so we can talk, Pearl. Reckon it'll be good to talk while the girls are away."

"Where's Mona?"

"She went home for a while."

"I see she's brought a cot in so she can sleep here. She sure is determined to take good care of you."

Clint pulled the blanket up to his chin and lowered his voice. "Too good, Pearl. Too good."

"Have you told her that, Clint?" asked Pearl.

"Hell no. You can't tell Mona nothing. She means good, but…"

"But she won't stop unless you come down hard on her Clint. Surely you're old enough to do that now," said Pearl, smiling.

"I reckon. But she don't listen to nobody."

"Just like her father?" asked Pearl.

Clint managed a weak grin. "Reckon they's been plenty of times when I should of."

Pearl laughed. "Didn't get you anywhere, did it?"

Clint shook his head. "Lord knows I'd a' done it differently if I knew what I know now but it's too late. Times I think I'm just like Mother, spend too much time thinkin' about things I can't do nothing about."

"I can do that too," Pearl said. "But if I get busy with something I can pretty much let it go."

"Ever think about that curse?"

"Once in a while. But I just can't believe it's more than a superstition of Aunt Lillian's. I've had hard times, it's usually because I'm doing something wrong."

"Reckon it's on me, more'n on you. My life ain't been a good one, Pearl. I'm just looking forward to gettin' it over with."

"I don't know Clint. You have had it rough. But you've come through it."

"To this here?" He spread his arms as if demonstrating his reality.

"We'll all die, Clint. And I think most of us wonder why we lived at times. Wonder if it was all worth it."

"I reckon. One thing I did right was send Kate to you. I want to thank you for all you done. She's a fine young woman. And you deserve the credit."

"Kate's a joy to me, Clint. I love her like a daughter." She reached across the bed and took Clint's hand. "I should be thanking you, Clint."

An aide came in interrupting their conversation. "Time to take your walk, Mr. Foster. Would you step out of the room for a few minutes, Ma'am. I have to help him to the bathroom first and we'll be ready to go."

When Kate returned to pick up her aunt, she was stunned by her dad's appearance. Hooked to an IV and with an oxygen tube in his nose, he seemed thin and vulnerable against the white of the pillows. Tears formed in her eyes as she hugged him goodbye. "I love you, Dad," she whispered. "Be back tomorrow."

The gangrene was spreading as the flesh on Clint's lower leg blackened, as dead now as he wished to be. Mona was beside herself. Thank God, Mason is on vacation, she thought. But there's no way I'm going to allow his partner, Dr. Mike Fallon to see him. The arrogant little bastard had yelled at her about one of his patients and she wasn't about to let him take care of Dad. Instead, without consulting anyone, even Clint, she called Dr. Carter and asked him to take over.

She introduced him to Clint in the hospital room. "Dr. Carter, this is my dad, Clint Foster. Dad, this is Dr. James Carter. He's seen your chart and is going to be taking care of you while Dr. Mason is away."

Clint looked surprised. "Doc told me I'd be seeing Dr. Mike."

"You don't want him, Dad. He's a quack. I've seen enough of his stuff to write a book. He's a rotten Doctor, Dad. I don't think you want him near you."

"Oh." Clint looked to Dr. Carter. "What are you going to do?"

"First of all, we're going to get you into surgery and clean up that leg."

"Ain't gonna cut it off are you?"

"Well, I hope not. We'll do what we have to. We're going to sedate you to still your anxiety. Then, we'll give you a spinal block so you won't feel anything. You'll be fine, Clint." He turned to Mona. "We'll have them prep him for surgery and see him up there. Are you going to scrub too?

Mona was beside herself with anticipation. "Of course. I want to be with him much as I can." She put her hand on Clint's shoulder. "We'll see you upstairs, Dad. Don't you worry. I'll be right there."

Clint woke in his hospital room with searing pain in his right leg. He lifted it in order to move it and was amazed at how light it seemed. He looked down, seeing for the first time the stump ending just above the knee, all that remained of the leg he'd had just hours ago. "No, Mona, no!" he cried. With tears streaming down his face, he reached for Kate's hand as she stood at his bedside. "I told them not to do it," he said. "I said not to cut it off."

The family waiting room was cozy and comfortable, a pleasant place with stuffed sofas and chairs lining the walls. But Kate wasn't about comfort when she entered with Mona. She had something to say to her and it wasn't going to be nice.

"We didn't have any choice," said Mona as she tried to fend off Kate's wrath. "It would have killed him if we hadn't. Ask Doctor Carter."

"To hell with Doctor Carter," retorted Kate. "How you could be a part of this is more than I understand. Dad asked you not to do it, Mona. Don't his wishes account for anything?"

"He doesn't understand, that's all. He has no idea of what it would be like if the leg got infected."

"So he might die. Isn't he dying anyway, Mona? Why prolong his suffering?"

"You don't understand either. I'm a nurse and I know what I'm talking about. He would really suffer then. You can't see that, Kate. I can."

Kate moved menacingly toward her sister. "I see him suffering more now, Mona. He didn't have any pain 'til you did this. Get out of my sight, Mona. I can't stand to look at you, I'm so damn mad."

Mona rose to her tallest, put her chin in the air and moved away. "I won't be threatened," she said, defiantly. And with that she left the room.

No doubt existed that Clint was depressed. After surgery he began to push his meal trays away and refused to eat anything. Any attempt to cheer him was fruitless. He hardly spoke and if he did it was only to Kate, Pearl and the nurse or aide when they asked him if he was having pain. He refused to speak to Mona, who went on as if nothing had happened, reporting on his vitals and encouraging him to eat and drink. His chest hurt more each day and twice he'd had episodes of a feeling of cramping. But he didn't report it. The pain killer they had prescribed for his leg pain helped somewhat. Overall, he just wanted to die. His fear was that Mona wouldn't let him.

After the third day of his fasting, Mona and Dr. Carter agreed that something must be done. A feeding tube was inserted through his nose and into his stomach so he could receive nutrients in a liquid form. "Just until you feel strong enough to eat," said Dr. Carter. "Then we can take it out."

Too weak to object, Clint allowed the doctor, with Mona's assistance to put the tube in. But he wasn't too weak to be angry with Mona. He was just too weak to confront her. Feeling more and more helpless with each indignity, he suffered in silence, all the time hoping that Kate would rescue him. But Kate couldn't know the depth of his feeling. Unvoiced, it stayed within, adding layer and layer of weight upon his heart.

Later that day, the pain in his chest became so unbearable that he told the nurse when she came in to check on him. "It's…it's hurtin' real bad," he said. He motioned to his chest. "Right in here."

The nurse listened to his heart with her stethoscope and patted his shoulder. "There's lots of noise in there that we better have your doctor check. In the meantime, I'll call him and see if he'll up your pain meds a little. Make you feel more comfortable."

"Thanks," he mumbled. "Maybe that'll help."

When Mona returned to the hospital that afternoon and found out that her dad was suffering a lot of pain, she was furious. "Why didn't you call me?" she asked. "I leave for a couple hours to go home and do laundry and all hell breaks out around here. There's no excuse and you know it."

"I wasn't on duty 'til three," replied the charge nurse. "So don't blame me. Your dad is more comfortable now, although he's still in a lot of pain. Keeps pointing to his abdomen. I don't get what that is about."

"When's Carter coming in?"

"After he's done in his office. Around five I suppose."

Mona turned her back on her and headed down the hall to Clint's room. Luckily she'd brought her stethoscope. She'd have to check him herself.

Suppose it's pericarditis, she thought, as she tapped his abdomen. Sounds like it too. But the pain in his abdomen confused her. "Where does it hurt, Dad?" She asked.

With a large sweeping motion, Clint indicated that the pain was in his chest and belly. Mona tapped his abdomen. "Here?" she asked.

Clint nodded.

Other than in his torso, Mona couldn't find any other areas that were hurting him. This is a hard one, she thought. Wish Carter would hurry up. I'm thinking maybe it's his stomach, an ulcer or something. Tomorrow is the day the radiologist comes from Harperville to do fluoroscopes and read the week's films. Maybe Dr. Carter should order an x-ray of his stomach. If there's a problem there, we can medicate it and make him feel better. She folded her scope, put it in her pocket and went to her cot on the other side of the room. Good thing she wasn't working tonight. She'd be staying here with Dad to make sure he didn't have to wait for anything.

⤳⟡

X-ray was always busy on Thursday. That was the day that Lowell doctors referred their patients for studies that required the radiologist to be present. Fluoroscopy was one of those studies. For a fluoroscope study of the stomach, the patient was required to drink chalky liquid called barium, in order for the doctor to watch, in action, the workings of the stomach as it emptied its contents into the small intestine. Before moving Clint from a stretcher onto the x-ray table, though, the technician couldn't help but see how weak and breathless he was and thought the doctor should check him before they started the procedure.

Too weak to respond to the doctor's questions, Clint could do little but point to his chest and abdomen. He wanted desperately to be away from here, back in his hospital room.

"This man is too sick to go through this," said the radiologist. "Get Carter on the phone for me. I'd like to know what good a GI series is going to do when the patient is almost dead. This patient has an inflammation of his heart, pericarditis. That's what's causing his abdominal pain. It's rare, but it happens. Take him back to his room. I won't put him through this."

Mona was there when they wheeled Clint's stretcher back to his room. "What did they find out?" She asked.

"Doctor refused to do the study. Says your dad is too sick." With a single, swift motion, the technician and his orderly lifted Clint, along with the sheet that had been placed under him, onto his bed and left the room.

Turning to her dad, Mona reached for his hand to take his pulse. Clint pushed her hand away and with all the effort he could muster,

291

began to speak. "Leave me alone," he gasped. "I want...want...to be left alone." Mona raised his bed so he could better catch his breath. "Don't do no more." He paused, gasping for air. "I want to die, Mona. Just let me die."

Without replying, Mona stood, stunned into silence. After all I've done for him, she thought. All my life, I've done all I could just to make him happy. And failed. He'll be gone soon, I know. What can I do now?

Suddenly, she brightened. She had an idea. She was working tonight, the timing was perfect.

She reached out and touched his arm. "I'm sorry, Dad," she whispered. "I'll make it up to you, I promise."

Luckily, tonight the ward was quiet, and when the aide on duty mentioned to her that she was sleepy, Mona sent her to the nurses' lounge to take a nap. "I'll come get you if I need to," she offered. "Have a little rest and don't worry. I'll take care of everything."

It was four a.m., time to get to the task she had given herself. After opening the drug room with the keys she had in her pocket, she looked around. First the morphine tablets, she decided, measuring out the correct dosage into a cup. Next, the sleeping pills, five should do. She closed her eyes and said a silent prayer. God help me to get him to take them, she thought. She paused for a moment, and then thought of something. The applesauce, of course. She would put them in applesauce so they would be easy to swallow. She went to refrigerator where the perishable drugs were kept and got a cup. Then, took a deep breath, exhaled, and headed to Clint's room, ready to do her duty.

She had to wake him to begin to feed him the meds. "Dr. Carter, ordered an oral pain med for you, Dad. I know it's hard for you to swallow, so I put it in applesauce to make it easier."

Groggy from his last shot of Demerol, Clint didn't notice the morphine tabs, it was with the sleeping pills that he balked. "That's a lot of pills, ain't it?" He asked. "What the hell's it for?"

"Mostly, for your pain. But we gotta treat the infection too. And we are all out of the two-hundred milligrams he ordered. I'm giving you four fifties instead."

Clint opened his mouth. "Okay," he said. "Let's get her over with."

Mona went back to check on him an hour later, to find him still alive, his respirations shallow and his pulse weak and slowing. Nothing must hurt him, she thought, I doubt if he can feel anything now. She returned to the drug room and drew three hundred units of insulin into a large syringe.

In her skilled hands, the rest was easy.

Chapter 30

Mona's reaction

Mona didn't try to go back to work until three months after Clint's funeral. Instead, she spent her time at home, sleeping or staring into space. Never shedding a tear. As if she felt nothing.

Concerned, Kate finally persuaded her to talk with her nursing supervisor. Maybe she could start out working part time, Kate thought. Anything to get her out of the house. Funds were running low and Kate needed Mona's salary to pay the monthly bills. "It will be good for you," Kate said. "I know you miss Dad terribly, but you have to go on."

When Mona finally called, Mary Pauley, her supervisor, wasn't sure how to respond. The large quantity of drugs missing on the day of Clint's death had to be explained. Because Clint's death, Mona hadn't been able to make a report to the next shift, so the drugs hadn't been accounted for until that shift left at three pm. Mary sensed that Mona had given the drugs to her dad, but she couldn't be sure that someone on the day shift wasn't responsible for taking them either. Unfortunately, there had been no autopsy, Dr. Carter and the family thought it wasn't necessary.

When Mary expressed her concerns to the hospital administrator, she asked to call for a police investigation. But he didn't want the scandal that was likely to ensue. "Even if she did take them," he told Mary, "it wasn't very important. Clint was her dad and she was being merciful. Living with the guilt is enough punishment. For now, I think we should let it go."

With those parameters in mind, Mary opened the door to her office and invited Mona in. "Good morning, Mona, come on in. What can I do for you today?"

"I thought I told you on the telephone," Mona answered. "I'm ready to go back to work."

"I'm glad you're feeling better. We've found an excellent replacement to work your shift. I'm not sure we can work you in."

Mona stiffened. "I've worked here for years. My dad died, for Pete's sake. You can't replace me for taking a short leave."

Mary went to a bookshelf and began to straighten the books. This isn't going to be easy, she thought. She's already angry. I wonder how she'll react.

"Mona," she began, "it's not just that. It's the drug situation. You know what I'm talking about, don't you?

Mona looked around Mary's pleasant office, reached out and pinched a petal off the bouquet of flowers that sat on her desk. "These are nice," she said. "Who gave them to you?"

Taken aback by Mona's non-response, Mary asked her question in a different way. "Did you take the drugs, Mona? I want an answer."

Mona slumped in her chair and began to hum a popular tune. "Do you know that song?" she asked. "They play it on the radio a lot."

Obviously this woman is seriously mentally ill, thought Mary. Either that or she's manipulating me. "Look, Mona," she began. "I don't think you're ready to come back to work. Your dad's death was hard on you. Would you like to talk with somebody?"

Picking at the imaginary lint on her skirt, Mona answered. "I like to talk to people. Trouble is they won't listen." She laughed. "Are you listening to me, Mary?"

"I am," Mary responded. "Before you can come back to work I want you to see somebody. Doctor Bob Garrett is a psychiatrist. His practice is in Harperville and you'll have to drive there. I think he can help you get over the grief for your dad."

Mona drew in her chin, pursed her lips and began to twist her thumb. "A psychiatrist, huh. You must think I'm crazy."

Mary stood and placed the tips of her fingers on the desktop. "I think you need help," she answered. "Did you drive yourself here, Mona?"

"Yes. You want me to go?"

"There's nothing more we can discuss. I think you should."

Mona stood and picked up her purse from the chair next to her. "Well, if that's the way you feel about it," she answered, and left.

That night, she slashed her wrists.

She'd found a new double-edge razor in Clint's room, removed the safety cardboard surrounding the blades and calmly cut, first her right wrist and then the left. She was surprised how little it hurt, and as she stood over the sink watching the blood dribble down the drain, she wondered what would happen next.

Disappointed in how small the blood flow was, she began to rub her wounds, trying to stimulate the bleeding. But the cut wasn't deep enough, so she finally gave up, wrapped towels around her wrists and went to the telephone to call Kate. She managed a wry smile. Maybe she'll take me to the hospital. That would really set Mary Pauley off. Ought to show her what she did to me, the bitch.

Kate was grading papers when Mona called. "You what?" she exclaimed when Mona told her what she had done. "How bad is it? Shall I take you to the hospital?"

"I don't care." She answered. "Maybe you ought to come over."

Kate dropped everything and went to Aunt Pearl's room to tell her she was leaving for Mona's. "Go ahead and get some sleep," she said. "I should be back soon."

By the time Kate made it to Mona's, the bleeding had stopped. The cuts weren't deep enough to do much damage, and by then, Mona decided she had enough.

"Do you want to go to the emergency room?" Kate asked as she looked at the wounds. "Maybe you should get some stitches so it'll heal."

"If I go there, everyone will know," Mona answered. "What do you think I should do?"

"Why don't I call Dr. Carter? See what he says."

"I wouldn't take her to the hospital here if she's doing okay," Dr. Carter said. "For confidentiality you ought to take her to Harperville. Dr. Garrett has a small psychiatric treatment ward in the hospital there. I'll call him and see if he's got room."

"Could I wait 'til tomorrow? She seems okay right now. I have to make arrangements to be gone all day."

"Will she be alone?"

"No. I'll take her home with me. You can call me there after you talk with Dr. Garrett."

"Good. And let her have two of those sleeping pills I've prescribed. That ought to give her a good night's sleep and you can get some yourself."

When the metal door of the psychiatric ward clanged shut behind her, Mona had a brief moment of panic. Knowing that she couldn't leave here was frightening enough, but her fear of the other patients was far worse. She wondered what they'd be like; she'd seen enough of mental patients when she'd done her practicum in school. A lot of them were violent at times, tranquilized into zombies at other times. I don't belong here, she thought. There's no way I will associate with them. Ever.

During her pre-treatment interview she refused to answer any questions, sitting wordless throughout and staring at her feet. If he's a psychiatrist, he ought to be able to figure out why I'm here, she figured. Pompous little jack-ass. Probably took his residency in psych because he was crazy himself. Half these guys are. She noticed the gaudy tie he was wearing and smiled smugly to herself. His way of getting attention, she thought. With his long hair and moustache he looked like a dressed up hippy. Ridiculous.

She was surprised when he admitted her. All the while thinking that he didn't have enough information to make a diagnosis. For observation, he said, and told her it would take less time when she started to co-operate.

On the fourth day, she finally broke her vow of silence and spoke up in the stupid therapy group they made her sit through.

Joe was complaining for the second time this morning and said, "My dad used to beat me and my Mom. He left us when I was ten and never contacted us again, I still have a feeling of abandonment. I hate him, I really do. I don't care if I ever see him again." Joe, a patient in the group, had said the same thing yesterday and the day before and Mona was sick of his whining.

"You're not supposed to hate your parents," she interrupted. "And you shouldn't be talking about them behind their backs."

"Why do you say that, Mona?" asked the therapist who facilitated the group.

"Because it's true," she answered. "He should stop being a baby. What good is it doing me to listen to him say the same thing all the time?"

"Do you have something else you want to talk about?"

Mona glared at the leader and refused to answer. The fat bitch. Who does she think she is, talking down to me like that? Mona folded her arms and drew them tight to her chest. Let them whine, she thought. See if it does them any good.

Later that day, when her roommate was out playing cards with the other patients, Mona moved a chair up to the tall dresser in her room, pulled herself to the top, and jumped off, breaking her ankle. Now I can get out of here, she figured. They'll put me downstairs in the orthopedic ward. After that, I can go home.

For the two days she spent on the orthopedic ward, Mona was a model patient, thanking the staff often for all they were doing for her. She learned from her orthopedist that her fractures were nasty. Both leg bones, the tibia and fibula, were broken as were several of the small bones in her ankle. Surgery was required to return them to their original configuration, after which a plaster cast was put in place to hold them in position while the fractures healed.

The episode seemed to enliven her and when it came time for her to return to the psych ward, she refused to go. "I'm all right now," she told Kate. "I can walk okay with crutches. Think I can take care of myself if you'll get groceries for me."

Uncomfortable with Mona's decision, Kate checked with Dr. Garrett to see what he recommended.

"We can't force her to stay," he said. "She can make up her own mind. We can commit someone only for ninety-six hours. Anything more than that requires a court order. Frankly, I'm not sure she's as ill as she pretends. Your sister is one helluva manipulator. My guess is that she'll hurt herself again, but I doubt that she's really suicidal. I think it's just a play for attention."

"How should I handle that?

"Don't over react. Tell her you know what she's doing and act like you're not upset. I think she wants to be noticed. Just don't give her the wrong kind."

Mona stayed in the guest room at Aunt Pearl's for a week after discharge from the hospital. After that, she insisted on going home. Because her left leg was the broken one, she could drive the car and thought she could make it on her own. Inwardly, she glowed over all the attention she received when going out. People noticed her cast and wanted to know what happened. She even fabricated a tale to tell them. "I got on the dresser to straighten a picture," she'd say. "And fell off." Telling it so often, she finally believed it.

Two weeks later, Kate got another bizarre call. "I took a shower with my cast," Mona told her. "I forgot to put plastic over it. Now the cast is falling apart. Can you take me to Dr. Carter and have him re-cast it?"

"I know you did this on purpose," said Kate as she drove Mona to the doctor's office. "Do you have a good reason why?"

Mona lowered her chin, hunched her shoulders and seemed to pull into herself. "The cast was hurting me. I had to have some relief."

"No." countered Kate. "You're bored at home and want to get some attention."

"You can't know what happened," said Mona. "You weren't even there."

"Do you want to go back to the mental hospital, Mona? 'Cause that's where you're going if you don't cut this out."

"I don't like to be threatened," cried Mona. "Just stop it."

"It's not a threat," Kate said. "It's a fact. Next time you'll go to the state hospital 'cause you can't afford anything else. We'll see how you like it there."

"We're here," Mona said as they drove up to the doctor's office. "I can go in by myself."

In March of nineteen-eighty-three Mona began to complain of heavy menstrual flow and extreme pain with her periods. At forty-plus years of age, Mona figured she was going through menopause, but wasn't satisfied with her doctor's diagnosis. "I'm pretty sure I have endometriosis," she told Dr. Carter. "The pain is awful and there's nothing that will stop it. Get so sick, I vomit."

"Do you want a hysterectomy, Mona?" asked the doctor. "You'll go into immediate menopause if you have one."

Mona tucked her chin into her neck and answered in her meekest tone. "I want to get rid of the pain, she said. "I want to get rid of the pain."

⌒◯

"And what, for heaven's sake is endometriosis?" asked Kate. "I didn't know you were having a problem." She had stopped by Mona's after work to bring her a prescription.

"It's about the lining of the uterus." Mona replied. "Every month it sloughs off the cells that line the uterus when we have our period. But in endometriosis, the cells attach to the uterus' exterior, and even to the membranes of the abdomen. It causes painful cramping, sometimes between periods."

"And Dr. Carter is going to do a hysterectomy?"

"He has to. There's no other way to get over it."

"Amazing," said Kate. How are you going to pay for it?"

"I've applied for Medicaid. Since I'm disabled, I should get it."

"But what about the house? Can you get help from a program if you still own the house?"

"The house is in Mom and Dad's name. I suppose it belongs to both of us, as they didn't have a will. I told them the house was yours. They'll never know otherwise."

"I don't think that's honest. What if you get caught?"

"I won't. No one has to tell them."

Kate shook her head and prepared to leave. "Okay, she said. "Whatever you say. Just don't involve me."

Next year, it was Mona's gallbladder. Convinced she had stones, she asked her doctor for a referral for x-rays. In order to make the gallbladder visible on the x-ray, she was required to take tablets containing iodine several hours before the procedure. For this exam, Mona knew what to do to make sure the surgery was done. She didn't take the tablets, and showed up on time for x-rays the next morning.

"Non-functioning gallbladder," read the radiologists report, which was enough to encourage Mona to ask Dr. Carter to remove it.

This time, even Dr. Carter was furious. "There's nothing wrong with her," he told Kate as he gave her his post-surgical report. "She faked her menstrual problems in order to get a hysterectomy and didn't take the contrast tablets the night before her gall-bladder x-ray. Her gall bladder is healthy and I didn't remove it."

"Have you talked with her about this?" asked Kate.

"No. She's still recovering from the surgery. This is the second and last time I do surgery on that woman. She needs a psychiatrist," he said. "Not me."

It was Christmas, 1982. And as Mona backed her car out of the driveway she couldn't help but feel the spirit of the season. A light snow had fallen the night before, turning the town into a winter wonderland. With a back seat loaded with presents and a day with her family before her, she was in a generous mood. She had spent all week shopping and wrapping, with the intent of making Kate and Auntie happy, getting them off her back.

It had been hell lately, with Kate checking up on her all the time. She usually stopped by each morning on her way to work, opened the door with her key and walked in as if she owned the place. Often Mona would pretend to be asleep and would lie in her bed seething with resentment as Kate stood over her, watching to see if she were still alive. Once she held her breath, and put a panic into her sister, who reached out and shook her shoulder, causing her to breathe again. There were also times when she'd breathe irregularly, alternating one deep breath with several short, shallow ones. Knowing each time she'd succeeded in making Kate anxious. I'll see if I can make her late for work, she thought. The bitch.

It never worked though. If Kate became too concerned, she'd wake her to make sure everything was okay.

Then, every weekday afternoon at precisely four-o-clock, Kate would stop by again, pretending to see if Mona wanted her to do anything, get groceries, a prescription, whatever. She never stayed long. She had to get home and check on Aunt Pearl, who was becoming increasingly incapacitated.

Just for fun, sometimes Mona would try to make her stay. "I'm lonely." She would say. "Sit down and I'll make some coffee." Watching carefully to see when Kate was getting anxious, she'd make small talk, following Kate as she edged to the door, laughing inwardly at her discomfort.

Now, laden with gifts, she walked through the front door and into the living room. A large Christmas tree stood in the corner. Kate had decorated it well, incorporating the handiwork of her students into a whimsical display.

Noticing only four wrapped presents under the tree, Mona felt a smug sense of satisfaction, that among the three of them, she was the most generous. And I'm supposed to be the crazy one, she thought. Well, I'll show them. She piled her gifts under the tree and went to greet Aunt Pearl who was steering her wheel chair into the room.

"I'm not sure you should kiss me today," said Pearl. "I don't feel well."

Shifting into nurse mode, Mona became solicitous. "What's going on?" She asked.

"Just a case of the flu, I think. My throat's a little sore and I have a headache."

Mona put her hand on Pearl's forehead. "You've got a fever," she said. Do you have a thermometer?"

"Upstairs, in the medicine cabinet."

"I'll get it," Mona offered. "If you have any aspirin, I'll bring you two of those."

"Already took some a few minutes ago," said Pearl.

Mona ran up the stairs and returned with the thermometer. "Open wide," she said laughing. "Be sure and get it under your tongue."

A few minutes later, Mona pulled out the thermometer with professional efficiency. "Oh, oh," she clucked, "it's one-oh-oh point eight. Do you want me to help you get back in bed?"

"No." Pearl answered. "Kate has freshly baked cinnamon rolls and coffee waiting for us in the kitchen. "I don't get a breakfast like that every day. Let's go enjoy it, and then we can open our gifts."

With the help of aspirin every four hours, Pearl was able to stay up all day. But after an early dinner she became extremely tired and asked Kate to help her get to bed. As Kate tucked her in, Mona joined them in the bedroom, insisting on taking her aunt's temperature again.

"One-oh-two point four," she announced. "Don't you think we should call Dr. Mason?"

"No-no-no," said Pearl. "Let him enjoy his family. It's Christmas. Think it's just the flu anyway. There's nothing he can do about that."

"You just get some rest, Auntie," said Kate. "Call me if you need me. I'll be right here."

Pearl turned on her side and smiled weakly at Kate and Mona. "Feels good to be in bed," she said. "Just need some sleep and I'll be all right."

Mona was talkative as they cleaned up the dishes. "It's dangerous for old people to have the flu. They're susceptible to pneumonia. Did she have a flu shot?"

"She wouldn't." Kate put the last dish away and hung up the dish-towel. "She was afraid the shot would give her the flu"

"Some people do get a little sick with them, but nothing like she is now. You get her to the doctor tomorrow, and see if he'll put her on an antibiotic as a preventative."

"Don't worry. I will. Just glad we have Christmas break this week so I can take care of her."

"Maybe you'll get it."

"I had a shot. You never know what you'll catch from kids." She laughed. "I used to get everything they did, but now I have some immunity. Haven't caught anything in two years, and, knock on wood, won't this year either." She rapped her knuckles on the wooden door frame as they made their way to the living room. "Let's sit in here where it's comfortable. Would you like more coffee?"

"I'm okay," said Mona as she sat on the couch. "It's nice in here. Maybe we can just talk."

"Good." Kate said, ensconcing herself in Auntie's recliner. "What've you been doing that I don't know about?"

"Nothing." She answered. "Just watching TV. Do you watch the "Nightly News" on NBC?"

"Sometimes, why?"

"They've been talking a lot about AIDS, you know, that fatal disease that homosexual men get."

Kate leaned back and raised the footrest to elevate her feet. "I've heard about it. There was an article in Sunday's paper. All about AIDS."

Mona lifted her chin. "That's what killed Jack," she said. "I'm pretty sure he had AIDS."

Kate bolted upright in her chair. "Do you mean he was a queer?"

"Just think about it. He lived with that rich man who supported him all those years, never, ever, had a girlfriend and then he got sick like that. He kept insisting that the man he lived with died of the same thing."

"I don't know. I just never thought about it that way. You never dated either. Does that mean you're a lesbian?"

"Hmmf," Mona scoffed. "Of course not. I'm not living with any-one. You know what I'm talking about. You just don't want to admit it."

"I did think it was a little strange. His supporting Jack and everything."

"Jack had all the symptoms before he died, the fungus in his mouth, the wasting, and finally that strange pneumonia. I just hope none of us caught it from him. It's pretty contagious, you know."

"I thought it was just in homosexual men."

"No. They think it transfers in all bodily fluids. I handled the emesis basin that he'd cough stuff up in."

Kate paused for a moment, remembering Jack's comment about his unforgiveable sin. She looked up at Mona. "It's all beginning to make sense to me now," she said. "Have you talked to the doctor about it?"

"I don't want him to think Jack was a queer. I'm just glad Dad isn't around to hear this. Can't imagine what he'd do."

"Or Mom. It'd break her heart."

Before Mona could respond, Kate heard Auntie call out for her. Concerned, she rose from the chair and ran up the stairs.

Pearl died of pneumonia a week later in her own bed, with Kate at her side. Just the way she wanted. She did agree to see Dr. Mason the day after Christmas. She would not go to the hospital as he suggested. "Kate will take care of me," she told him. "I'll take the antibiotic and stay in my own room."

Like Jack had done, Pearl reacted to the antibiotic with a terrible allergy and the pneumonia worsened as Kate had feared. "Don't tell Mona how sick I am," she begged Kate. "I know she's a good nurse, but she's too much for me right now. I want you here, and that's all."

Kate never left for more than a few minutes, sleeping in the cozy chair in the corner by the window. Every four hours, giving her the antihistamine Carter had prescribed and waited, wishing Pearl'd go to the hospital, but admiring her courage for staying home. *This is what she wants, and this is what I will do, wait with her 'til the sickness is over.* "And however that happens," said Aunt Pearl, "is in God's hands, not mine." In silence, Kate prayed to agree.

The funeral was well attended. Many of the former students of Pearl extolled her virtues and the effect she'd had on their life. Kate and Mona stood in a receiving line, thanking them for their caring enough to gather here to honor her life.

But Mona didn't like it. All this attention to Aunt Pearl and none for Dad. That's the way this town is, she thought. Callus *and* uncaring. Pearl brownnosed her way through life and Dad wouldn't. A real man, he was, solid and strong yet no one appreciated him. She began to defend him to those who came to her offering condolences. "Clint Foster was her brother," she'd say. "My dad. He had a rough life, but things were always easy for Aunt Pearl." Or, "My dad was her brother. He was nice too."

When Kate began to notice the odd looks Mona was getting, she made an announcement. "Come over to the house everybody. The ladies' of the church have prepared a lunch for you. I hope I will see you there."

"What was that about?" hissed Kate as they drove to the house. "Mona, some of these people never even knew Dad. Don't you know they came to honor Auntie?"

Mona pulled into herself and drew in her chin. "They didn't appreciate him," she said. "It's not fair."

"Fair has nothing to do with it," said Kate. "This is not about Dad; it's about Auntie."

Mona fidgeted in her seat and looked out the window. "Take me home," she said. "I'm tired."

Glad to oblige, Kate turned around and drove Mona to her house. "I'll call you tomorrow," she said. And drove away.

Having put away all the extra food, and tidying the kitchen, the last of Auntie's church members left the house at eight p.m. Exhausted, Kate kicked back in Pearl's recliner and fell asleep, only to be awakened an hour later by the shrill ring of the phone. "It's Mona," said a weak voice. "I took a whole bottle of sleeping pills. They'll have to pump my stomach."

Kate hung up the phone and sprang into action. First, she dialed the ambulance and arranged to meet them at Mona's. Next, she grabbed her coat and purse out of the front closet and hurried to the car. Damn her, she thought as she turned the key in the ignition. She'd have to do this tonight. It's to the nut house for you this time, sister. I've had enough.

After pumping Mona's stomach, Dr. Carter agreed to help Kate commit her to the state mental hospital in Fulton. They'd transfer her by ambulance tomorrow as Kate was afraid of to drive her there for fear that she might harm herself.

And Mona seemed resigned to it. At least superficially. In turmoil internally, she berated herself for going too far. The state mental hospital of all places. Why on earth did I call Kate? Knowing she would be put in restraints if she acted out, she cooperated fully; even answering most of the questions asked her in the admitting interview.

"Why did you take the pills? Asked the doctor.
"I wanted to die." she answered
"And why did you call for help"
"I was afraid."
"Will you try to kill yourself again?"
Mona's answer was honest and direct. "I don't know," she said. "Probably."

Because she was on suicide watch, Mona's every action was observed carefully by the staff and her sessions with her psychiatrist went well. She behaved appropriately and in a few days was put in the therapy group with all the others that were able to be there.

But the therapy group was more than Mona could bear. She'd sit with her legs crossed; arms clutched tightly to her chest and watch the others make damn fools of themselves telling family secrets. No way would she say anything about her family. She'd told the psychiatrist about all the recent deaths and pretended to be in mourning, brushing away an occasional tear to illustrate her point.

One woman, Loretta, particularly offended her. An overweight, peroxide blonde, Loretta talked about episodes that should never have been shared, saying that her father had abused her sexually, that she became promiscuous in her teens, and later became an alcoholic to bury her pain. As if none of it was her own fault, thought Mona. And ignored her at mealtime and recreation, turning from her as if she had a contagious disease.

After about a week of listening to her in group, Mona had heard enough. Interrupting Loretta's story about running off with an escaped convict, she finally expressed herself. Pulling herself up in the chair, she looked down her nose and in her sternest voice said, "You're nothing but a whore. Loretta, and I'm sick of hearing about it."

Loretta lunged at her, knocking her off the chair. Quickly, two orderlies came to Mona's rescue and took the guilty party to her room as Mona stood triumphantly, relishing her victory.

When Kate visited her the following week, Mona was in a much different mood. Angry and resentful, she'd been admonished for talking down to Loretta and told she was at fault *for telling her the truth. Now Kate's coming to visit and I have to put up with her. Who does she think she is?* Mona thought. Acting superior to me because she put me in here. I wish she'd just stay away. Probably went in and told the doctor everything about us. I'm sick of all their talking behind my back.

Aware of Mona's hostile attitude, Kate made careful comments so as not to upset her further. "How are you feeling?" she asked.

Mona glared at her. "How do you think anyone feels in the nut house, Kate? Are you glad you finally got to put me here?"

"Look, Mona," she began. "You have to remember you tried to kill yourself. I think you know that I simply wanted to see you get the help you need."

"Bullshit. Don't you know there's nothing that can help me?"

"That's not true, Mona. Of course there is."

With a nervous laugh, Mona responded. "What if I'm cursed?" she asked. "What then?"

"Oh that again," said Kate. "Surely as a nurse you don't believe in that old tale."

"It's real. And don't try to talk me out of it."

"C'mon, Mona. This conversation is getting us nowhere. Let's change the subject."

"What if I don't want to? Listen to me for once, Kate. I want you to hear what I have to say."

Kate looked at her shoes.

"Look at me Kate," said Mona. "Look at me now. Here." She extended her arms in a sweeping gesture. "In this hell hole of a place. And tell me you don't believe in the curse."

Stunned, Kat looked around the room.

"Now. Look at me, Kate. And tell me what you see," hissed Mona. "It's right before your eyes." She stood, raised her arms and pointed the thumbs of her clenched fists to herself. "Here is the curse, Kate," she cried, "It's me!"

Chapter 31

January 30, 1985
Dear Diary,

We buried Mona yesterday. My dear friend Bridey Richardson Murphy and I. After a funeral mass, we drove behind the hearse to the graveyard, said a few prayers over the casket with Father Donahue, and went out to lunch.

Her cause of death is listed as the result of an accident, but her psychiatrist told me otherwise. She was strangled by another patient in an attack from behind in the patient recreation room. The doctor said that Mona had antagonized the woman in group, that this woman had developed a bitter resentment of Mona. Apologizing for the neglect of the staff to protect Mona, he wondered if I might ask the hospital for restitution for my loss.

Of course, I won't. I know how abrasive Mona could be. This time it seems she offended the wrong person. Most of all, I want all this behind me. To finally get on with my own life, bury myself in working with children, and forget the past as much as I possibly can. More than anything else, I love being with kids. Especially the ones who are neglected or abused. Am toying with the idea of taking in a foster child and plan to look into that soon.

Have thought often of Mona's parting remarks the last time I saw her, wondering how long and how much she had believed in the curse. Certainly, it affected her. Just as it has affected all of us as we've watched it's manifestation in the life of each other. Whether or not it's real doesn't seem to matter. What's real is the faith that fuels the myth. Whatever it is, it destroyed this family. No one can doubt the power of that kind of evil. An evil it seems, that only death can destroy.

So this, my grandmother's legacy, is now left to me. What happens from here on remains in the hands of a merciful God. Like Auntie, only my faith in Him will protect me.

The End

About the Author

P eggy Lins is retired and lives in Oro Valley, Arizona with her husband, Del. Mother to four children and grandmother to five, she
has written many short stories for their enjoyment. "A Cruel Legacy"
is her first novel.

16099850R00196

Made in the USA
San Bernardino, CA
18 October 2014